Undoing Democracy

Undoing Democracy

The Politics of Electoral Caudillismo

Edited by David Close and Kalowatie Deonandan

LEXINGTON BOOKS
Lanham • Boulder • New York • Toronto • Oxford

LEXINGTON BOOKS

Published in the United States of America
by Lexington Books
An imprint of The Rowman & Littlefield Publishing Group, Inc.
4501 Forbes Boulevard, Suite 200, Lanham, Maryland 20706

PO Box 317
Oxford
OX2 9RU, UK

British Library Cataloguing in Publication Information Available

Library of Congress Cataloging-in-Publication Data

Close, David, 1945–
  Undoing democracy : the politics of electoral caudillismo / David Close and Kalowatie
Deonandan.
    p. cm.
  Includes bibliographical references and index.
  ISBN 0-7391-0808-5 (cloth : alk. paper)
  1. Nicaragua—Politics and government—1990– 2. Alemán Lacayo, Arnoldo, 1946– 3.
Political corruption—Nicaragua—History. 4. Political parties—Nicaragua—History. 5.
Democracy—Nicaragua—History. I. Deonandan, Kalowatie, 1958– II. Title.
F1528.C583 2004
972.8505'4—dc22   2004003197

Printed in the United States of America

♾™ The paper used in this publication meets the minimum requirements of American
National Standard for Information Sciences—Permanence of Paper for Printed Library
Materials, ANSI/NISO Z39.48–1992.

Contents

Preface and Acknowledgments

Nicaragua has never had an easy time of it. The first four decades of its existence as a nation were marked by a series of civil wars. Although a thirty-year hiatus of stable government then followed, by the end of the nineteenth century Nicaragua had again embarked on the road to conflict and chaos. When calm was restored in the 1930s it was the work of the Somoza family dictatorship that would rule and pillage for forty-two years. Then in 1979 the Sandinista Revolution offered what many hoped would be Nicaragua's way out. Eleven years of revolutionary government did bring great changes and significant benefits to the country, but in the end the system could not be sustained. However, the Sandinistas did hand over power peacefully in 1990 to a more conservative and orthodox democracy, presided over by Violeta Chamorro. Thus, while hopes for the revolution had been scotched, it still appeared that Nicaragua was at last on the road to sound, humane government. However, Nicaraguans, at least those making up the nation's political elite, seemed determined to throw away their chance to build a democracy.

A troubled election in 1996 produced a troubling government. The new president, Arnoldo Alemán Lacayo, was a Liberal whose roots ran back to the days when Somoza family, Liberals too, ran Nicaragua as their personal domain. He was a relative newcomer to politics, entering the electoral fray for the first time in 1990 when he merged as mayor of Managua, the capital city. Known as a doer with little patience for legal restraints and something of an eye for the main chance, Alemán easily defeated the Sandinista candidate, ex-president Daniel Ortega, and became Nicaragua's chief executive in January 1997. Over the next five years, the president, along with his family and friends, made free use of public funds for private enrichment. More disturbingly, toward the end of his term Alemán set to work with Ortega to remake the country's political order so that it would forever let political strongmen operate without regard to accountability or transparency. Alemán's plans, however, were put paid to by his own former vice president, Enrique Bolaños, who succeeded his erstwhile boss as president in 2001. Vowing to clean up corruption, after only two years in office Bolaños saw Alemán convicted of pilfering and laundering state funds to the tune of $100 million and sentenced to twenty years in prison.

With a record like this Nicaragua ought to have been a prime candidate for analyses of democratic transitions. However, the country's timing was off. In the early 1980s, when the first wave of Latin American transitions was under way, Nicaragua was undergoing a much less dramatic shift toward a liberalized radical democracy under the Sandinistas. Then in 1990, when the Sandinistas turned the reins of government over to Chamorro, communism was falling in Europe, again pushing the Central American state to the back of the line as a research interest. Even the attempt to roll back democratic progress that began after the election of Arnoldo Alemán generated little interest until details of the by then ex-president's corruption began to surface in 2002. In fact, aside from a strong flurry of interest during the Sandinista years, Nicaragua has done well to merit a footnote in most scholarly studies of Latin America, let alone the Third World as a whole.

This book does not attempt to redress all that balance. Its objective is to investigate the administration of Arnoldo Alemán, which is both timelier and more modest. We chose this goal for two reasons. First, since the Sandinistas left office in 1990, news from Nicaragua usually comes with hurricanes, tidal waves, earthquakes, or volcanic eruptions. We believe that the political history of the country in this period has been improperly neglected, which leads to our second reason. Political science is known for creating short-term "cottage industries" built around the analysis of some momentarily topical question. From the late 1980s through the middle 1990s studies of democratization filled that role. How countries left behind their authoritarian pasts and came to embrace a democratic future, democratic transitions, was the first phase of the project. It was quickly succeeded by the analysis of democratic consolidation, the study of how democracy becomes embedded as the intuitive political preference of a nation. It is our contention that Nicaragua's experience with the Alemán administration raises important issues for the study of democracy.

It is conventional to criticize the democratization literature for being Pollyannaish and predicting a quick and detour-free path from whatever kind of authoritarianism to consolidated, constitutional democracy. We believe that a more telling criticism is that political science has not sought to analyze the deviations from the ideal in a systematic way. Without significant steps in that direction we shall not be able to understand why and how different countries arrive at different definitions of just what constitutes an acceptable form of democracy. Nor will it be possible to see what these imperfect democracies do well and to think of how that might be preserved. Worst of all, without a solid descriptive and theoretical base, analysts and practitioners will be less able to reform systems to make them more democratic. This book is offered as a step in what we believe is the right direction.

The eight authors who have contributed chapters to this collection all have long experience in and significant commitments to Nicaragua; two in fact are Nicaraguans. Admittedly, this may cloud our vision and make us more critical of those whose actions we believe are harming the country. Nevertheless, none of us can imagine having a long history in a country without developing significant bonds with the place and its people. Yet this interest in Nicaragua's well being is compatible with scholarly objectivity. If we do not examine reality as rigorously as we can and report on it as fully and objectively as we can, our product will be faulty and may actually harm the causes that we find important.

Finally, we should explain why a book about an administration that passed into the history books in January 2002 is only seeing the light of day in 2004. We first of all confess to the usual debilities of academic authors and will offer no excuses for those. However, by delaying the completion of this work we have been able to include much more material about the investigation, trial, and conviction of former president Alemán on various corruption-related charges. The successful anticorruption campaign of President Bolaños is both an important event in Nicaragua's history and a hopeful sign for its future.

Acknowledgments

Bringing a book from being a vague idea to a finished product demands a lot of work by a lot of people whose names never appear on a cover or in a table of contents. We want to take this occasion to thank some of those people. First among them is Peggy-Ann Parsons who put our somewhat unruly text into recognizable, camera-ready format. And we want to acknowledge the encouragement and assistance offered by the acquisitions and editorial staff at Lexington Books, with special thank-yous to Jason Hallman and Rebekka Brooks.

David Close wishes to recognize a number of individuals. In Managua, and in alphabetical order, Judy Butler, Carlos Fernando Chamorro, Luis Humberto Guzmán, and Maria Elena Martínez have all offered advice and support over many years. In St. John's, Sherrill Pike did her usual extraordinary job of proofreading and translating academic prose into something more like English. The Memorial University of Newfoundland contributed to this book by granting a half-sabbatical in winter 2002 that facilitated clewing up the final bits of research. And the Department of Political Science was, as usual, tolerant of the many pages of photocopying that comes with publishing a book.

Kalowatie Deonandan wishes to thank Leigh-Anna Gates and Maria Laura Basualdo for their research support, and Diane Favreau for her assistance in the battles with computer technology. She extends her appreciation too to the Department of Political Studies at the University of Saskatchewan, along with the University's Publication Fund, for their monetary contributions which was critical in getting the manuscript ready for publication. Finally, and with much enthusiasm, she acknowledgs the invaluable support and encouragement given by Raj Srinivasan throughout the process.

Chapter 1

Undoing Democracy in Nicaragua

David Close

In 2001, at the end of the administration of President Arnoldo Alemán, Nicaragua was a less democratic country than it had been at the start of his term in 1996. The system of checks and balances had been undermined. Citizens had fewer electoral choices. Key state institutions had lost their independence and been turned into fiefdoms for partisan patronage. Freedom of the press was under attack. And most people were still desperately poor.

Nicaragua did not become less democratic due to the machinations of faceless external forces, internal warfare, or a military takeover. Rather, it was a series of conscious, overt actions taken by the government and supported in most respects by the largest opposition party that let this happen. The country's political class, at least the part of it represented in Alemán's Constitutional Liberal Party (PLC) and the Sandinistas (FSLN) of Daniel Ortega that wins over 90 percent of the national vote, decided to loosen the bonds of democracy to reduce accountability, competition, and the role of nonpartisan institutions in Nicaragua.

The successful efforts of the Alemán administration to halt and reverse Nicaragua's first steps toward a working system of checks and balances will probably influence his country's public life long after his government's most newsworthy scandals have been forgotten. Examining how this was done offers us the chance to study a successful attempt at undoing democracy. Note, however, that democracy has not been destroyed. There was no coup or anti-democratic revolution, but there was a concerted and successful effort to restrict democracy's impact on the operations of government.

There are several premises that all the contributions to this study share. Constitutional democracy[1] defined by the rule of law, enforceable personal freedoms, functioning accountability structures, and the apparatus of representative government working to facilitate citizen participation is weaker in Nicaragua at the end of the Alemán administration (2001) than it was at the beginning (1996), for three reasons:

1. Conscious decisions of the Liberal government, supported at critical points by the Sandinista opposition in the form of a bipartisan, Liberal-Sandinista Pact to secure key constitutional amendments and legal reforms, produced this weakening.
2. The specific targets of these efforts were the 1995 amendments to Nicaragua's constitution that brought the country its first inkling of functioning checks and balances and were a critical step toward consolidating democracy.
3. As a result, the executive has slipped its short-lived constitutional bonds and Nicaragua's democratic prospects are gloomy.

This introductory chapter is divided into four parts. The first section defines two central concepts, "undoing democracy" and "electoral caudillismo." It is followed by a summary history of Nicaraguan democracy. Next is a historical overview of the Alemán administration. The chapter concludes with a synopsis of the articles and their arguments.

Concepts

What It Means to Undo Democracy

Since 1974 political science has devoted substantial time and energy to analyzing how countries build democracy. The first steps away from authoritarian rule were studied as democratic transitions. As new democracies evolved analysts began speaking of democratic consolidation. Before long, however, it became apparent that the road to democracy was not smooth, straight, or guaranteed actually to arrive at democracy. Political science then turned to democracy's imperfect subspecies, among them low-intensity democracies[2] and delegative democracies.[3] Undoing democracy is the work of making a democracy more imperfect. It is undertaken by a government to remove some of the impediments that democracy places in the way of easy administration. That is, democratic governments undo democracy to allow themselves to govern with fewer restraints and less accountability.

It may seem odd that a government that came to power through a democratic election should want to restrict democracy. A moment's reflection suggests otherwise, however. Governing is hard work, because a state is a very big and enormously complex enterprise. Democracy complicates the task greatly by demanding, on the one hand, transparency and accountability from those in power and insisting, on the other, that citizens be encouraged to participate in governing, and not just by voting in periodic elections. Even worse, there is no job security, as the governors can lose their positions after a few years in office if the citizens vote them out.

In poor countries, where there are fewer golden parachutes for former politicians, the temptation to hold on to office may be especially great. This is partly the result of a shortage of economic opportunities. Thus, politicians may not only be tempted to retain power by any reasonable means, but they can also come to see government as the best source of future riches. This makes corruption a rational route to financial security, allowing material interests to supercede democratic principles.

A government whose commitment to democratic values was never strong will have yet greater incentives to undo democracy. If an administration's purpose in seeking office was to enrich its members and friends or punish its opponents, the openness demanded by democratic government will seem intolerable. Such a government will have to overcome the obstacles that constitutional democratic rule sets in place specifically to discourage improper behavior. If it is lucky, the government can simply ignore the constraints, but it may feel compelled to attenuate their effects or remove them.

If one essential characteristic of undoing democracy is that it is a conscious act of an elected government, an equally important feature is that it does not destroy democracy. Elections remain the only legitimate way to take power, although the rules governing elections may restrict choices or bestow distinct advantages on selected competitors. Political opposition is still legal and open, but opposition parties and groups may find it more difficult to make any headway against the administration. Courts and parliaments continue to function and independent administrative agencies remain in place, yet none of them will have much success if its views run contrary to the administration's. So democracy still exists but it no longer has the same effect or brings the same benefits that it once did. Nevertheless, democracy retains sufficient strength and vitality that a future government could restore it to its previous state without using extraordinary means. This at least is what Nicaragua's experience indicates.

We can think of what has happened as democracy decomposing into its component parts. Democratic decomposition becomes, then, the inverse of democratic consolidation, just as political decay was the inverse of political development.[4] Whereas consolidation institutionalizes democratic rules and processes, decomposition returns them to the status of instruments to be kept or discarded depending on their usefulness to the powerful. Decomposition may be a brief detour or it can mark a more durable change of course, but in either case it moves a polity further from the norms of constitutional democracy. Finally, although in the present case democratic decomposition is the result of conscious actions taken by domestic political elites, the process could equally well be the consequence of external pressures or even the unintentional product of policy choices gone wrong.

Although the rest of the book lays out numerous concrete instances of how democracy has been weakened or evaded in contemporary Nicaragua, it will be useful to sketch a couple of examples here. There are two forms that the assault on Nicaraguan democracy has taken. One is the work of the government alone while the other is a bipartisan effort. The latter is more important, because it indicates that the most important elements of the country's political elite agreed that the democratic status quo of 1996 was unacceptable.

Actions attributable to the president include demanding that all judges resign so that Mr. Alemán could appoint new ones; repeated clashes with journalists; threatening and then jailing Nicaraguan's comptroller general; frequent resort to bureaucratic harassment of political opponents; gerrymandering electoral districts to disqualify electoral opponents, and egregious corruption. However disagreeable twenty-first century democrats may find these actions, they are no more than variations on themes developed over many years by caudillos and other strongman, boss-style, politicians, even in historic consolidated democracies. Unless a country offers no alternative governing formulas, the effects of these governments are remediable.

More troubling is the precedent set by an arrangement struck between Alemán's Liberals and Ortega's Sandinistas to pass a number of key reforms. This bipartisan deal, known as the Pact, changed the electoral law to give the two dominant parties a huge advantage over a much reduced field of competitors and permitted the adoption of constitutional amendments that eviscerated the institutions intended to assure accountability.[5] Its apparent objectives were to institutionalize what we call electoral caudillismo, divide important government positions between the Liberals and Sandinistas, and create a political duopoly in which the Liberals and Sandinistas controlled entry to Nicaragua's political market. The net result of these changes was to leave Nicaraguans a government of highly partisan men instead of one guided by the rule of law.

Having the weight of the country's political elite behind extensive political reforms that undid prior democratic progress suggests that Nicaragua's governors neither set much store by formal institutions nor held the constitution in high regard. The objective that the Liberals shared with their Sandinista foes was to design a political system that produced fewer competitors for power and gave the victor freer rein to enjoy the spoils. The outcome is essentially the same as what O'Donnell labeled delegative democracy,[6] save that Nicaraguans did not need a great crisis as pretext to shed the restraints of strict constitutional rule. We shall consider further the implications of this bipartisan support for what is effectively electoral caudillismo in the concluding chapter.

Electoral Caudillismo

Caudillismo, government by a single—usually charismatic—leader, driven by personal ambitions and with little interest in building any institutions besides his own perpetuation in power, is the Latin American version of strongman or boss politics.[7] As practiced historically in Latin America, the caudillo has relied heavily on coercion as a governing instrument. In this regard, the caudillo resembles closely the Big Man dictator common in late-twentieth-century sub-Saharan Africa, and indeed dictators the world over. The coming of constitutional democracy should make caudillismo impossible by establishing competitive, free elections as the only acceptable route to power. To a substantial extent, this has happened. However, there are other forms of personal rule that can function within a formally democratic framework.

Although the political boss is often thought of as a product of late-nineteenth- and early-twentieth-century U.S. history, the phenomenon is more widely known. Wherever clientelistic ties are the glue holding the political system together and the drive for patronage is the principal motive behind partisan electoral competition, political bossism can flourish. All that is needed is a strong leader, almost always a man, able to dominate a party, win votes, raise lots of money for elections, and distribute favors, funds, and jobs where they best contribute to keeping the boss and the party in power. Where the boss's powers of appointment include judges, members of regulatory boards, and the auditors who supposedly monitor government operations, the term "elected dictator" fits perfectly.

Bosses need a culture attuned to clientelistic politics to flourish because citizens there will expect politicians to deliver roads and jobs to their supporters instead of pursuing more inclusive versions of the public good. They need parties innocent of policy objectives beyond winning office and handing out benefits, since those parties judge success almost exclusively in terms of electoral victory and what is required to assure it. Bosses differ from traditional caudillos in relying far less on force to govern, preferring instead to use other forms of influence. Granting or withholding government jobs and contracts can usually generate sufficient pressure to assure compliance with a boss's wishes. Where it does not, nonviolent forms of government intimidation—inspections, license reviews, court cases, or tax audits—can be applied.

Boss politics are also patrimonial politics. In patrimonial political systems, the ruler treats public property as his or her personal possessions.[8] This assures the boss has unfettered access to the money needed to retain power. Thus boss politics breed corruption and demand very weak accountability structures that let dishonest bosses escape punishment.

Reform politics is the boss's worst enemy, but to work reformism needs a society without a large population dependent on government-controlled handouts. That means a society that is well educated and in which access to basic services such as health and housing, not to mention jobs, are within easy reach of the vast majority of citizens. When these conditions start to become the norm, as they did one hundred years ago in North America, bossism becomes expendable. Bossism's costs to society at large so far outweigh its benefits to individuals that the system is no longer sustainable.

However, where the above conditions are absent bossism is not only possible, but may be the easiest way to conduct democratic (i.e., electoral) politics.

Thus, in countries with a history of caudillismo bossism can be a natural adaptation to democracy, unless the political scene is dominated by parties with strong programmatic orientations. Bossism lets established elites retain control over the political process and define politics as a way for favored individuals and groups to get special benefits. It is democratic in that anyone who supports the boss qualifies for favors and because the boss and his party can only get power through fundamentally open elections; hence the label electoral caudillismo. However, the system is undemocratic because it limits citizen participation to elections, entrenches elite interests, and excludes the consideration of serious reform from the political agenda. Clearly an improvement over historic caudillismo, electoral caudillismo still falls far short of twenty-first-century democratic norms.

Nicaragua is a natural place to find the boss-style politics of electoral caudillismo. In the last century it knew little but caudillo politics. Including just the Zelaya and Somoza epochs accounts for fifty-two years. Bringing in the second half of the Sandinista period, when Daniel Ortega was emerging as the FSLN's strongman, adds six more. And since the twenty-five years of chronic unrest that first brought and then accompanied the U.S. occupation from 1909 to 1934 should probably be set aside because of their singularity, we might be able to put the first five years of the revolutionary government (1979-1984) and President Violeta Chamorro's six years (1990-1996) down as Nicaragua's twentieth-century experience with noncaudillo politics. With this background, it would be easy for the politically ambitious to conclude that successful leaders are caudillos.

The above suggests that Nicaragua's transition to a modern constitutional democracy with strong, independent institutions and a relative equilibrium among the branches of government was always uncertain. Nevertheless, as the next section shows, the last half of the Chamorro administration witnessed a radical break with earlier political patterns and practices. Nicaraguan politics could have moved beyond electoral caudillismo, but its political leaders decided otherwise.

Democracy in Nicaragua

Nicaragua's political history offers far more instances of authoritarian rule than of democracy. Indeed, it lacks even a substantial history of predemocratic, constitutional oligarchy, the political system that became the foundation for democracy in Europe. Nicaragua's political past is so studded with civil wars, dictators, and foreign interference that a meaningful democratic history should start only in 1979, with the Sandinista revolution.[9] Starting a country's democratic history with a revolutionary government demands an explanation, because revolutionary regimes do not observe the tenets of constitutional democracy. Constitutional democratic rule subjects the state to the rule of law, legally guarantees and enforces personal freedoms, builds working accountability structures, and maintains an apparatus of representative government that facilitates citizen participation. Revolutionary systems, however, seek the redistribution of power, privilege, and wealth to secure a society that is more egalitarian in spirit and equal in fact. They have less interest in structures and are suspicious of restraints on their powers.

Like other revolutionaries, the Sandinistas emphasized democratic results. Thus, education, health care, land reform, and programs to redistribute income were essential parts of their program. These were the social bases for a radical democracy, the tools that ordinary people, the majority, needed to make good their claims to a fulfilling life.

However, the FSLN did not ignore the forms of constitutional democracy. Although the government established immediately following the Sandinistas' triumph of July 19, 1979, was geared to producing rapid and radical change, it did not take long for signs of a new approach to appear. Beginning in 1983, with the adoption of a political parties' law that recognized the possibility that an opponent could win power, the revolutionaries built an interesting set of institutional bases for what they hoped would be a long-lived regime. By the time elections were held, November 1984, the Sandinistas had scrapped much of the initial revolutionary state machinery and replaced it with the conventional structures of representative democracy. The new constitution, adopted in 1987, continued this trend, although the text enshrined revolutionary values and gave exceptional powers to the executive.

Through their willingness to reconfigure the machinery of government to keep power, the Sandinistas steadily moved Nicaragua toward the forms of constitutional rule. By the end of its term, February 1990, the FSLN showed that it had also learned the norms of constitutional democracy by recognizing electoral defeat. This marked the first time in the country's history that an administration had surrendered power peacefully to its opponents. Thus expectations were high that President-elect Violeta Chamorro would build on this base and extend the bounds of Nicaragua's newfound democracy.

These hopes were only partly fulfilled. The electoral alliance that Chamorro led to a resounding victory, capturing 54 percent of the vote to the Sandinistas' 41 percent, the UNO (National Oppositional Alliance), was a fourteen-party grab bag of anti-Sandinistas of all stripes, from Communists to Conservatives. The unwieldy group never became a fully fledged governing coalition, let alone a unified party, and eventually turned against the woman who had led the ticket to power. As a result, the Chamorro administration's six-year term was marked by continual conflict between the president and the National Assembly, producing perhaps the weakest executive in the nation's history.

Although the Sandinistas had recognized electoral defeat, their adjustment to the realities of constitutional opposition produced its own challenges to the new administration. Faced with having to leave office two months after losing power, the FSLN convened a lame-duck session of the National Assembly and began passing legislation that the party hoped would protect the legacy of the revolution. Foremost among the measures adopted were three bills to regularize the titles of property the revolutionary state had expropriated and redistributed. As many high-ranking Sandinista officials found themselves owners of expensive properties thanks to the legislation, the whole process was dubbed "la piñata," or swag bag. The FSLN's former reputation for probity was damaged beyond repair.

Once actually out of office, the Sandinistas assumed the role of principal opposition party. In doing so, they did not abandon their past but rather incorporated a significant extraparliamentary dimension to their oppositional activities. This is not unusual in consolidated democracies where mass parties conventionally use their large popular bases to stage demonstrations against government measures they oppose, but it created extra problems for the Chamorro administration.

Assessing the record of the Chamorro administration reveals a complex balance of both strengthening and weakening democracy. The debit side of the ledger begins with her administration's neoliberal economic policy. Cutting inflation, actually hyperinflation here, means inducing recession by cutting government expenditures, raising interest rates to the point that firms no longer borrow to expand, and depressing demand by lower wages and higher unemployment. Add to this the strictures that come with Structural Adjustment Programs (SAP), which aim to restructure economic policies to conform to free-market standards, and the social policy base constructed by the Sandinistas could not survive. In fairness, however, it is unlikely that a Sandinista administration could have resisted pressures to adapt to the new economic reality; indeed the FSLN had tried stabilization in 1989, even without pressure from international financial institutions (IFI) like the World Bank and International Monetary Fund (IMF).

More specifically politically, this administration reopened the doors to business and the establishment generally. Where the FSLN claimed to listen to the logic of the majority, both the Chamorro administration and the UNO-controlled legislature were more heedful of the elite's logic. This did not disenfranchise the popular classes but it did make their access to power more problematic. It should be noted, however, that this shift to the right appeared radical only because it followed a decade's revolutionary rule. Where democratic rule was the long-standing norm, the Chamorro government would have been no more than a normal corrective swing of the ideological pendulum.

The last entry on the negative side comes from President Chamorro's reluctance to yield any of her vast executive powers or even have them overseen by the National Assembly. In mid-1993 Nicaragua verged on becoming a failed state, one where the central authority could not preserve order. Out of that experience grew a movement to change the country's constitution. Because the system that gave rise to disorder was built on the strongly executive-centered 1987 Sandinista document, the proposed amendments focused on creating a better equilibrated balance of powers through a functioning set of checks and balances. President Chamorro, her cabinet, and counselors, and eventually Daniel Ortega and the Sandinistas, opposed these changes.

Two examples give a sense of the executive's position under the 1987 constitution.[10] First, the president had effectively unlimited decree power, including the power to levy taxes. From this arose the second example: the claim made by President Chamorro in 1994 that the executive and the executive alone had the constitutional right to deal with fiscal matters. Throughout the last quarter of 1994 a multiparty alliance, led by the Assembly's president, Luis Humberto Guzman, a Social Christian, worked out a package of sixty-five amendments, one of whose principal aims was to bring the president's powers back toward the norm among Latin American democracies.

Naturally, the president resisted these changes, and when the Assembly would not repudiate its amendments institutional deadlock followed. From February to July 1995, Nicaragua's legislature accepted a different constitution from the one the president followed. Recourse to the courts was impossible, both because each side had its own view of how the nation's courts should be set up and because the dispute meant that there was no way to replace Supreme Court magistrates whose terms had expired, leaving the Court without a quorum. Eventually, mediation by an international Group of Friends was required to sort the matter out and have the new checks and balances constitution accepted by all.

Some of President Chamorro's actions plainly strengthened democracy, however. During her six years in office there was arguably greater tolerance of dissenting views and constitutional opposition than at any time in Nicaragua's past. Further, as befits a president whose family's newspaper had been censored by both the Somoza and Sandinista regimes, freedom of the press and information was respected as never before. Finally, although the government faced repeated crises, it did not impose martial law or systematically use force to repress protest. An important lesson of Chamorro's term is that a president, even one facing a hostile legislature, can govern and maintain a modicum of stability without departing from constitutional legality.

As President Chamorro's administration entered its last year, 1996, there were signs that Nicaragua was inching toward a new democratic balance. It was possible then to hope that the rule of law would become the norm in Nicaragua and that the transformative zeal of the revolutionary era could be rediscovered and made to work through constitutional channels. Unfortunately, the approach of national elections drew the country's political class back to its old ways, where parties and their leaders preferred to trust their own resources rather than legal frameworks. Thus the important legal changes wrought by the constitutional amendments of 1995 did not become part of Nicaragua's political culture. Although the country was far more democratic in 1996 than it had been in 1979, both legally and substantively, it was about to see its progress drastically slowed.

The Alemán System

The political system Arnoldo Alemán inherited on taking office had six key traits:

1. The constitution had a flexible amending formula and had been the focus of contention since 1990.
2. Although the legislature had grown stronger relative to the executive, it had limited policy-making capacity, because it had little research assistance; this also inhibited its oversight functions.
3. The country was extremely polarized, reflecting political divisions carried forward from the revolutionary period.
4. Party politics reflected this polarization, continuing the break into Sandinista and anti-Sandinista camps evident in 1990. Alemán's PLC emerged as the uncontested anti-Sandinista leaders. Though many parties existed, an artifact of the electoral law, the principal protagonists divided over 90 percent of the vote in 1990 and 1996.
5. Basic state institutions—courts, civil service, and regulatory agencies—were weak and administrative capacity slight.
6. Politics were leader-centered and highly conflictive.

Clearly, Nicaragua was far from being a consolidated democracy or even having a stable political climate. Continuing progress toward a solid constitutional democracy was certainly possible, but by no means guaranteed. Both the FSLN and Liberal presidential candidates were caudillos and neither group had ever shown much enthusiasm for creating strong state institutions, independent of partisan control.

With Arnoldo Alemán's election as Nicaragua's chief executive, the movement away from constitutionalism gathered momentum. The new president had built his reputation by being the "can do" mayor of Managua. He built traffic circles (one with illuminated fountains), paved streets—putting up signs to let drivers know where the national government became responsible for the bad roads that followed—and generally played civic booster. Alemán also showed a cavalier attitude toward the niceties of accounting and the finer points of the law, which often brought him into conflict with some of his councilors.

Alemán had also been one of the figures involved in the revitalization of the Liberal Constitutionalist Party (PLC), a dissident splinter of the old Somoza Liberal party that had survived the Sandinista period only to find itself teetering on the verge of irrelevance. By 1994, when elections in the autonomous regions of the Atlantic Coast were held, however, the PLC had emerged as a leading anti-Sandinista political force. In the polarized political culture that characterizes contemporary Nicaragua, heading the PLC became tantamount to leading everyone whose political preference was "anybody but the Sandinistas." In 1996, this turned out to be 51 percent of the voters. Making an energetic, strongman politician like Arnoldo Alemán the leader of the PLC helped assure the party's success, as many Nicaraguans still favored colorful caudillos to gray technocrats, and opened the way to boss-dominated, machine politics, reminiscent of early-twentieth-century North America.

Since the rest of the book sets out the details of how President Alemán's system operated, we will only outline the highlights here. Nicaraguan politics remained polarized and partisan, as Liberals and Sandinistas clashed over many issues. Politics also continued to have a strong extraparliamentary, direct action component: students, health care workers, the owners and drivers of buses, and coffee growers all found that only highly confrontational and conflictive protest politics got the government's attention. And corruption, which had lingered just beneath the surface since 1990, came roaring back to assume a position in national life it had not held since the Somozas ruled.

But the capstone was the Pact. Pacts are so familiar to Nicaraguans that the word takes on a special meaning. It is a deal between the government, elected or not, and its most important opponents to allot "quotas of power." That is, the two biggest political players in the country share the spoils: government jobs, electoral offices, protection for their followers. Naturally, the governors get the lion's share, but the officially designated opponents do pretty well. Pacts between the Somozas and a band of tame Conservatives split the returns, electoral and otherwise, two to one. The deal maintained the dictator's unquestioned power but gave his opponents enough of a stake in his system to keep them quiet.

The Pact struck between Arnoldo Alemán's Liberals and Daniel Ortega's Sandinistas was different in significant ways from those of a half century before. There would be no guarantees of seats or positions, and elections were understood to be competitive and without foreseeable results. Yet it was still about quotas of power, because this Pact cemented support for a package of constitutional changes and amendments to other laws that protect the interests of the two leaders and their parties.

Instruments to assure oversight and control of the executive, brought in with 1995 constitutional amendments, were weakened and put under partisan control, with the PLC and FSLN naming a majority and minority, respectively, of members of the comptroller's office, Supreme Court, and Supreme Electoral Council. Government financial activities would be audited by partisan appointees, partisan appointees would staff the final court of appeal, and electoral disputes would be settled by appointees of the two biggest parties. To assure that the PLC and FSLN remained the biggest parties, the electoral law was revised to make the formation of new parties extremely difficult. And to guarantee that the leaders would keep control of their parties with minimal difficulty, the ex-president, who cannot succeed himself, now gets an automatic set in the National Assembly, where he is joined by the runner-up in the latest presidential election. Thus Messrs. Alemán and Ortega had public positions, salaries provided by the taxpayers, and parliamentary immunity from prosecution. The two leaders, both caudillos in style and substance, remain in the public eye, able to control their machines directly.

The Pact presents us with the spectacle of the overwhelming part of a nation's political elite, for the PLC and FSLN capture 90 percent of the vote in national elections, deciding to undo democracy by removing the tools that let citizens control their rulers. Nicaraguans are not deprived of their right to select their governors, but they are offered fewer choices. Citizens still have recourse to functioning courts and electoral authorities, but they cannot be sure that partisan justice will not be dispensed. And taxpayers still have a public auditor to monitor the accounts of the administration, but they may suspect that loyalty to party counts for more than probity among those who are appointed controllers.

Democracy still exists in Nicaragua, but it will not thrive unless the system built by the Pact fails to work. It is a decomposed democracy, one which has all the elements required but which does not assemble them into a working whole.

On Balance

Nicaraguan democracy has not followed what Thomas Carothers,[11] one of the leading critics of contemporary thinking about democracy promotion and consolidation, has called the transition paradigm. This model, which has guided theory and practice for two decades now, assumes that the construction of a democratic polity follows set steps; that history, tradition, and level of material development do not effect democratization; that elections are ipso facto proof of democracy; and that there is no backsliding. Thus, once a country has moved away from its authoritarian past, a status that is both all-encompassing and ill-defined, it boards the democracy express, bound for glory as a consolidated democratic political system. There is no place in this paradigm for democratic decomposition.

There are almost as many ways to fall outside the transition paradigm as there are third wave democracies (states that began experimenting with constitutional democracy after 1974). Nicaragua brings to the table a constitutional system designed to be compatible with weak institutions, a very strong and unaccountable executive, and a two-party politics that is so strongly legally entrenched as to constitute an effective duopoly. Further, by automatically awarding outgoing presidents, who cannot succeed themselves, a seat in the legislature, Nicaraguan politics lets a political strongman retain power without the bother of fighting an election. Finally, the big changes in Nicaragua's political framework have been a collaborative venture, backed by parties that won over

98 percent of the vote in the 2001 presidential election. This indicates that the system crafted between 1996 and 2001 has the backing of most of the country's political class.

Determined efforts by Nicaragua's president, the Liberal Arnoldo Alemán, abetted at critical junctures by Sandinista leader Daniel Ortega, moved the country further from what both political science and democracy promoters consider a consolidated democracy. Electoral choice is constrained; political institutions are weaker; checks and balances are undermined; and executive accountability debilitated. All of this was done without a crisis to justify suspending democratic practice. The purpose of this book is to describe how this happened, analyze why it happened, and explain how and why this experience might repeat itself in some other country.

The Book and Its Contents

Studies of democratic construction and consolidation naturally emphasize political institutions. However, we take a broader view of politics. Our objective is to show how the various parts of the work of undoing democracy comes together and how the result affects a broad range of democratic practices and possibilities in Nicaragua. To this end we present chapters treating political institutions, civil society, and political economy.

As the defining event of the Alemán administration was the Liberal-Sandinista Pact, the book opens with Katherine Hoyt's study of the Pact's dynamics. However, the next two chapters address the administration's political style and its relations with citizens. Kalowatie Deonandan's chapter evaluates the effects of five years of undoing democracy on political pluralism in Nicaragua, reviewing the cases of labor, the media, and civil society. Karen Kampwirth's study of Alemán's use of populism demonstrates how that government was able to paint itself as the people's representative while it relentlessly chipped away at Nicaraguans' basic freedoms. Taken together, these three chapters provide an excellent introduction to the logic and dynamics of undoing democracy.

Two chapters that analyze specific policy areas and actors follow. Andrés Pérez-Baltodano looks at the disturbing links joining church and state in late-twentieth-century Nicaragua. Particularly striking is its defense of the Alemán administration's record of misfeasance and malfeasance. As the Catholic Church began to fix its sights on the media since the new Bolaños administration came to power, the chapter provides important background for understanding how church-state relations during the Alemán years still affect the shape of Nicaraguan politics.

Elvira Cuadra's study examines how the Alemán administration dealt with the problem of rural violence. She finds that Alemán's government automatically classified any instance of political violence, even conflictive protest, as criminal behavior, hence outside the bounds of politics. Adding this dismissal of confrontational politics to the administration's closing of conventional political channels leads her to conclude that the government's objective is a quiescent, depoliticized citizenry.

Nicaragua's political economy is the theme of the next two chapters. David R. Dye and David Close give an overview of the Alemán administration's economic policy. More importantly, they present a detailed sketch of the corruption in which that government was steeped. This permits us to ask what part a government's desire to turn public goods into private gains plays in weakening democratic institutions.

Salvador Marti Puig's chapter has a narrower focus: the international economic relations of the Alemán government. He gives special attention to the administration's dealings with the IMF in pursuit of Nicaragua's admission to the HIPC (Heavily Indebted Poor Countries) Initiative. Here, as in the contributions by Deonandan and Kampwirth, we must consider if the neoliberal model of democratic governance contributes to the concentration of power in the executive, hence encouraging some form of electoral caudillismo.

As originally conceived, the study was to be limited to the Alemán administration. However, although he had been Arnoldo Alemán's vice president, Enrique Bolaños set Nicaraguan politics spinning during his first months as president. With no forewarning, the newly elected chief executive began an anticorruption campaign that quickly put several key members of the Alemán government behind bars and turned a very uncomfortable spotlight on the ex-president, himself. Although we cannot see this part of the story through to its conclusion, we felt obliged to sketch its beginnings. David Close's chapter on the current scene reviews Bolaños's first year in office, a year which saw the arrest and indictment of Arnoldo Alemán on corruption charges. The chapter also offers a preliminary assessment of their effects on Nicaraguan democracy.

Kalowatie Deonandan draws the several chapters together in the conclusion. However, she also addresses a question that underlies every contribution to this book: the perils to democracy of an extremely powerful and essentially unaccountable executive.

Notes

1. We emphasize constitutional democracy, as opposed to substantive democracy, for two reasons. One, constitutional democracy is what is actually available in the first years of the twenty-first century. Two, in the historic constitutional democratic world, citizens have been able to use legal-political democracy to secure the elements of social-economic-cultural democracy.

2. Barry Gill, Joel Rocamora, and Richard Wilson, eds., *Low Intensity Democracy* (London: Pluto Press, 1993).

3. Guillermo O'Donnell, "Delegative Democracy", *Journal of Democracy* 5, no. 1 (1994): 55-69.

4. Samuel Huntington, *Political Order in Changing Societies* (Cambridge, MA: MIT Press, 1991).

5. A November 2002 Supreme Court ruling declared parts of the electoral law reforms unconstitutional. Lourdes Arróliga, "CSJ: luz verde a pluripartidismo," *Confidencial* 317 (November 24-30, 2002).

6. O'Donnell, "Delegative Democracy."

7. I use the masculine pronoun to describe caudillos because all Latin American caudillos have been men.

8. Originally applied to ancient and medieval systems of personal rule by Max Weber, analysts of contemporary African politics use the concept to explain the political systems evolving under Big Men, African caudillos, such as Zaire's Mobutu (Robert Jackson and Carl Rosberg, *Personal Rule in Black Africa* [Berkeley: University of California Press, 1982]; Jean-Francois Bayart, *The State in Africa: The Politics of the Belly* (London: Longman, 1993), 60-86; Naomi Chazan, Peter Lewis, Robert Mortimer, Donald Rothchild, and Stephen John Stedman, *Politics and Society in Contemporary Africa* (Boulder, CO; Lynne Rienner, 1999), 168-76; Alex Thomson, *An Introduction to African Politics* (London; New York: Routledge, 2000, 107-17). There is also an extensive literature on the links between patrimonial politics and corruption: Robin Theobald, *Corruption, Development and Underdevelopment* (London: Macmillan, 1990) and "So What Really Is the Problem with Corruption?" *Third World Quarterly* 20, no. 3 (1999): 491-502; Arvind K. Jain, ed., *Economics of Corruption* (Boston: Kluwer T, 1999); Alan Doig and Stephanie McIvor, "Corruption and Its Control in the Developmental Context: An Analysis and Selective Review of the Literature," *Third World Quarterly* 20, no. 3 (1999): 657-67; Susan Rose-Ackerman, *Corruption and Government: Causes, Consequences, and Reform* (Cambridge: Cambridge University Press, 1999); Joseph Tulchin and Ralph H. Espach, *Combatting Corruption in Latin America* (Washington, DC: Woodrow Wilson Center Press, 2000); Gerald E. Caiden, O. P. Dwivedi, and Joseph Jabbra, eds., *Where Corruption Lives* (Bloomfield, CT: Kumarian Press, 2001).

9. For those who wish to investigate Nicaraguan politics between 1979 and 1996 the following are good places to start: George Black, *The Triumph of the People* (London: Zed, 1981); John Booth, *The End and the Beginning* (Boulder, CO: Westview Press, 1985); Thomas Walker, ed., *Nicaragua in Revolution* (Boulder, CO: Westview Press, 1982), ed., *Nicaragua: The First Five Years* (New York: Praeger Press,1985), ed., *Revolution and Counterrevolution in Nicaragua* (Boulder, CO: Westview Press, 1991), and ed., *Nicaragua Without Illusions* (Wilmington, DE: Scholarly Resources, 1997); David Nolan, *The FSLN: The Ideology of the Sandinistas and the Nicaraguan Revolution* (Coral Gables, FL: University of Miami Press, 1984); David Close, *Nicaragua: Politics, Economics and Society* (London: Frances Pinter, 1988), and *Nicaragua: The Chamorro Years* (Boulder, CO: Lynne Rienner Publishers, 1999); Roger Miranda and William Ratliff, *The Civil War in Nicaragua* (New Brunswick, NJ: Transaction Publishers, 1993); Harry Vanden and Gary Prevost, *Democracy and Socialism in Sandinista Nicaragua* (Boulder, CO: Lynne Rienner Publishers, 1993); Katherine Hoyt, *The Many Faces of*

Sandinista Democracy (Athens: Ohio University Press, 1997). This constitutes only a sampling of an extensive literature.

10. D. Close, *Nicaragua: The Chamorro Years*, 153.

11. Thomas Carothers, "The End of the Transition Paradigm," *Journal of Democracy* 13, no. 1 (January 2002): 5-21.

Chapter 2

Parties and Pacts in Contemporary Nicaragua[1]

Katherine Hoyt

Democracy has several definitions. Some observers restrict it to the institutional forms of electoral democracy while others feel that it must include participatory aspects between elections such as a role for citizens in decision making on important public issues. I belong to the latter group and find the developments in Nicaragua, where elections are held regularly and the outward forms of democracy are maintained but where accountability has been restricted and participation constrained, to be distressing.

Democracy has only a tenuous foothold in Nicaragua. Its history has not been promising. Traditionally, the party in power changed only when the opposition leader put together an army and overthrew the government. The strong influence of the United States in Nicaragua has not helped matters. The U.S. military occupied the country for twenty years during the last century and controlled many aspects of its government and economy. The United States "oversaw" elections in the 1920s and was able to convince Liberal general Jose María Moncada to lay down his arms by promising him the presidency in 1928 before the election was held.

After suffering for forty-five years under the dictatorship of one family, the Somozas, Nicaragua experienced a true social revolution beginning in 1979. The country achieved what some analysts argued was the most democratic distribution of land in Latin America. In 1984, the Sandinistas held what most observers (but not the Reagan administration) classified as free and fair elections and, by early 1987, the country had approved a democratic constitution. But as late-twentieth-century revolutionaries, the Sandinistas held a unique combination of democratic and vanguard principles. They believed that they represented the general will of the people and could submit themselves to free elections and win them fairly, even while fighting a war against U.S.-financed counterrevolution-

17

aries. In 1990, the Sandinista government held elections again and, much to its surprise, lost.

The FSLN turned over political power to a tenuous coalition that had been cobbled together by the United States and was led by Violeta Barrios de Chamorro. Many Nicaraguans seemed to feel that Mrs. Chamorro, who had held together a family divided by the conflicts between supporters and opponents of the revolution, could heal some of the wounds of the whole nation. While her government engaged in none of the vengeance hoped for by anti-Sandinistas, she subjected the country to the harsh structural adjustment ministrations of the IMF and World Bank. These policies included abandoning the food subsidies and expanded health and education services the Sandinistas had instituted as well as switching agricultural priorities from state farms, cooperatives, and small farmers to big private growers. Her aides and high officials were also accused of corruption.

One of the fourteen parties of Chamorro's National Opposition Coalition (UNO) was the Constitutional Liberal Party of Arnoldo Alemán. Alemán was elected to the coveted post of mayor of the nations' capital and largest city, Managua. From that base, he was able to enlarge his party's influence and his own power base. In 1996, he was elected president of Nicaragua, defeating his principal electoral opponent, Daniel Ortega, running again at the head of the Sandinista ticket.

This chapter will examine how two leaders, Arnoldo Alemán and Daniel Ortega, respectively of the Constitutional Liberal Party (PLC) and the Sandinista Party, now the two major political forces in the country, returned Nicaragua to the old days of caudillismo by means of a political pact. In brief, the Pact divided government positions between the supporters of the two leaders and guaranteed to Alemán and Ortega immunity from legal prosecution. With this agreement, Nicaraguan democracy suffered a severe setback as the Pact undermined the efficacy of the nation's fledgling democratic institutions and processes. While this chapter represents an analysis of the Pact, it also pays particular attention to the role of the FSLN and its leader in bringing about the deal, and (in so doing), contributing to the undoing of Nicaraguan democracy.

We will examine the events leading up to the Pact and its negotiation. As well, the contents of the Pact will be discussed, including the constitutional amendments and changes to the electoral law which were pushed through the National Assembly to expand the membership of the Supreme Court, of the Office of the Comptroller General of the Republic, and the Supreme Electoral Council, among other measures. Opposition from within the two major parties and from outside the parties among civic leaders and citizens in general (which was unable to prevent the various aspects of the "Pact" from being put in place) will occupy our attention next. We will then turn to examining the Pact's impact upon the country's institutions and upon municipal elections in 2000 and general elections in 2001.

We will see that many believe that while the hopes for an effective democracy that were raised with the revolution and the subsequent emergence of electoral democracy have not been dashed, they were put into serious question by the return of the old caudillismo and a political pact that echoed those of an earlier era in Nicaraguan history when the old Conservatives and Liberals pacted to protect their interests and divide the spoils of the nation.

Arnoldo Alemán and the Constitutional Liberal Party

Arnoldo Alemán comes from a Liberal family, with both long attachments to Somoza politics and strong antipathy toward Nicaragua's historic, Conservative elites. When asked about his involvement in the leadership of the Somoza youth organization, he stated merely that he had never served in the Somoza government or in the Sandinista government.[2]

The Constitutional Liberal Party (PLC) broke away from the Somozas' Nationalist Liberal Party in the 1960s. In the 1970s, it proposed a dialogue between the government and the opposition, including the Sandinistas, and allied with the centrist parties of the Democratic Liberation Union (UDEL) led by Pedro Joaquin Chamorro. During the Sandinista era, the PLC was a member of the Coordinadora, a right-wing alliance of parties that opposed the revolutionary government. After 1983, exiled Somocistas, who had no party because the Somoza era Nationalist Liberal Party (PLN) had disintegrated, began to join the PLC, which gradually became the PLN's successor.[3] In 1989, the PLC joined thirteen other parties in the National Opposition Union (UNO), which swept the 1990 elections. The PLC's important achievement was the election of Arnoldo Alemán as mayor of Managua on the UNO ticket.

During his tenure as mayor, Alemán built fountains and traffic circles, paved streets, and painted over Sandinista murals on government buildings. In 1991, he attempted to organize his own private police force which he called "municipal inspectors." This proposed force was likened to the AMROCS, a paramilitary shock force of the Somoza era. When Daniel Ortega said that the FSLN would call up ten members of the Sandinista militias for every member of Alemán's force, the project died.[4]

Alemán used the resources from the mayor's office to expand the PLC as a national organization loyal to him. Where the PLC's original support came from that sector of the bourgeoisie that was most damaged by the Sandinista government (as opposed to those who knew how to coexist with the revolution), the party built a nationwide, organized grassroots base, not unlike the Sandinistas', based on the country's poor. The PLC's vote-getting ability was put to the test in 1994 in the elections on the Atlantic Coast and the party came out on top.[5]

The Constitutional Liberal Party is not an ideological party in the sense that there are debates among its members about political philosophy and policy. But the party is a member of the Liberal International and Alemán has claimed the

inheritance of the Liberal Party of Nicaragua, which brought about liberal economic reforms, public schools, and the separation of church and state in the
1890s. In one particular area, however, the PLC has strayed from Liberal ideology by allying itself with Cardinal Miguel Obando y Bravo and the hierarchy of
the Catholic Church. Marcos Membreño explains why:

> First, because of his weakness. He does not have military power, or
> police power, but in its stead he has put his faith in spiritual power....
> (Second), Cardinal Obando is furiously anti-Sandinista.... In addi-
> tion, Alemán knows that in allying with Obando he is able to achieve
> an element of ideological cohesion within his cabinet.... And it is
> known that the circle of power ... closest to him is composed of
> highly conservative Catholics, and some of them are Opus Dei.[6]

It has also been noted that, where the Somozas gave women the vote, government jobs, and encouraged their political activism as professionals and workers, Alemán has taken a much more traditional stance on women's issues. He
joined the Conservatives and even the FSLN in praising their role as mothers.[7]
Under the Alemán presidency, for example, the Nicaraguan Women's Institute
was absorbed into the Ministry of the Family.

Membreño notes that Alemán has had to attempt to reconcile the interests of
the small urban and rural property owners who voted for him with those of Somocista capital and Cuban capital in Miami who financed his campaign. Somocistas expected to be able to return to Nicaragua and retrieve properties expropriated by the revolutionary government. But much of the large-scale, state-
owned property was already privatized and had passed into the hands of the old
oligarchy. And, with the Sandinistas holding a substantial number of seats in the
National Assembly and Sandinista sympathies still very much alive in the army
and police, the return to Somocistas of properties that had been given out under
agrarian reform and urban land reform was not possible.[8]

At about the time of Alemán's inauguration in January, five Liberal Party
members wrote a strictly confidential strategy document entitled "PLC Strategy
2000" which laid out the steps they felt the PLC must take to remain in power
"until 2016." The document states "The Liberal Alliance is fragile. Our first goal
must be Liberal reunification under a single banner taking the PLC as the center
... This unification will be realized sooner and more effectively if ... the Liberal
family comes together as in 1855, 1893, and 1946, around an authentic caudillo
of quality, [who] in this case is Dr. Arnoldo Alemán Lacayo." The strategy paper goes on to say that a major goal must be to legitimize and welcome back into
the party the Liberals who have been attacked by the Sandinistas since 1979,
noting that "their economic means, friends, and influence would be of great assistance."[9]

The document also states that the historic parallels must be reestablished
and that the Sandinista Party cannot be allowed to usurp the place that the Con-

servatives traditionally held in Nicaragua, allowing Liberals to govern with the consent of at least a wing of the Conservative Party. Meanwhile, it emphasizes that "the most important objective is to effectively recover properties" from the Sandinistas, with the strategy of not attacking agrarian reform frontally, but rather gaining the return of mansions and large properties, especially any in the hands of the "nine comandantes." Second, the links between the FSLN and its bases of support must be broken by social programs benefiting the poor and by cutting off the financial oxygen of the presumably pro-Sandinista nongovernmental organizations.[10] The document turned out to be prophetic in some areas and emphatically wrong in others. The Alliance really was fragile. In fact, even before the inauguration, the small Nationalist Liberal Party (PLN) had already left, saying that Alemán had violated a promise to make the PLN leader Enrique Sanchez Herdocia head of the National Assembly.[11]

In 1998, Eliseo Nuñez, then Liberal house leader in the National Assembly, left the Alliance, accusing Alemán of wanting to dissolve the Alliance and strengthen the PLC. He stated that the president had asked all Cabinet ministers and National Assembly deputies to renounce party membership in other Liberal parties and join the PLC. The president was also accused of favoring exiles from Miami and of concentrating control of patronage in his own hands. Nuñez added that Alemán kept his closest associates off balance by frequent cabinet shuffles.[12]

The Alemán government did not inaugurate any programs for the poor that might have broken the link between the FSLN and its base; it did, however, regularly attack the nongovernmental organizations and their work. But what needs explanation is the pact he forged with the Sandinistas, one not unlike the pacts the Somozas struck with the Conservatives.

Conservative deputy Jose Cuadra notes that, from January of 1997 to June of 1998, President Alemán did not need a pact with the FSLN. With forty-two Liberal deputies in the National Assembly (out of ninety-three) and twelve reliable votes from other parties, he had an assured majority that was a mere two votes short of the number required to amend the Constitution. But halfway through 1998, eight deputies, led by Eliseo Nuñez left the Liberal fold. Although four eventually returned (Nuñez included), several of the twelve allies began to waver. Cuadra suggests that Alemán wanted to change the Constitution so that he could be reelected and for that he needed the support of the FSLN.[13]

Conventional wisdom in Nicaragua maintains that President Alemán needed a pact with the Sandinistas in order to amend the Constitution to protect himself from prosecution for corruption. His accumulation of personal wealth as mayor of Managua and later as president has been especially noteworthy because of the rapid drop in living standards for most Nicaraguans.[14]

Comptroller General Agustin Jarquín was himself the source of many of the charges of corruption against the president and his administration. The authority of the Comptroller General of the Republic (CGR) was greatly enhanced by amendments to the Nicaraguan Constitution in 1995 and by Jarquín's appointment as comptroller in 1996. Jarquín obtained financing from international donors to give his office the capability to audit all the government's accounts, including the autonomous agencies and the state-owned banks.[15] In 1998, he uncovered corruption and illegal activities at Channel 6, the state-run television station, and the Central Bank. He fined the Managua mayor's office (the mayor was a Liberal) and the Ministry of Finance and uncovered problems in the state-owned electric company and basic grains distributor.

President Alemán countered by accusing Jarquín of arrogating power, being too slow in investigating corruption in the previous Chamorro government, and receiving funds from outgoing Chamorro administration officials. Alemán said that there had been "irregularities" in the comptroller's review of the electric company, the telephone company, the Social Security Institute, and the Customs Agency. Dissident Liberal Eliseo Nuñez, however, said that the president was only seeking to cover up the corruption in his own government.[16]

After FSLN deputy Victor Hugo Tinoco formally accused Alemán of acquiring property by irregular means, the CGR began an investigation. It took the president's own report of his properties and wealth when he took office as mayor of Managua in 1990 and compared it to the one he made upon assuming the presidency in early 1997.[17] In February of 1999, Alemán, upon hearing that the assessment process could lead to a formal audit of his recently acquired properties, threatened the comptroller, telling him, "If you want to play hardball, we'll play hardball."[18] The CGR released its report that same month. It revealed that the president's wealth had increased from the US$26,118 that he reported in 1990 to over three hundred thousand dollars in 1995 and close to one million dollars in January 1997. According to the report, the president had continued to acquire properties, bank accounts, and stock, and was using government funds and workers to make improvements on his properties, including roads, wells, and fencing.[19]

But the president did not take the matter lying down. He refused to meet with the comptroller to discuss the charges. Instead, he alleged that Jarquín had signed large and "possibly illegal" contracts with journalists and others to investigate the government and to promote the work of the comptroller's office. In the most serious case, Danilo Lacayo, a well-known Managua TV host, was hired under a false name to investigate corruption.[20]

On August 30, the CGR annulled the privatization of 51 percent of the stock of the government-owned Nicaraguan Bank of Industry and Commerce (BANIC). The comptroller demonstrated serious irregularities throughout the process of capitalization and privatization of the bank. A large majority of those implicated were members of President Alemán's closest circle. BANIC granted large, irregular loans to cronies of the president and to the corporation that had been buying land for the presidential family. Outgoing BANIC directors illegally approved over 20 million córdobas (about $1.5m) in bonds, compensation pay, and salary overdrafts for themselves during the capitalization process. Officials rejected the charges and foreign bankers in control of the bank said that they would sue the comptroller![21] In the flurry of bank failures that hit Nicaragua in 1998, BANIC also went under.

On November 8, 1999, Jarquín, Lacayo, and former advisor of the comptroller, Nestor Abaunza, were arrested and charged with fraud against the state for hiring Lacayo to do undercover investigation of corruption. In an interview from jail, Jarquín addressed the question of whether Nicaragua was faced with a dictatorship. He described the degradation of Nicaragua's democracy as not yet producing a breakdown, but rather creating "a real threat" of such a breakdown:

> The present government was elected democratically; it is a civil government, but clearly we can see that it is not headed in the correct direction. For example, when a system is set up in the government agencies to collect "voluntary quotas"—in quotation marks—for the party in power, this is an aberration that is totally in opposition to democracy.... When we see the intervention of the Executive in the National Assembly, in the court system, we are seeing negative signs that could lead to a dictatorship. When there is excessive protection of officials, based on immunity, and officials do not take seriously their responsibility to adequately manage public funds, then we are generating a situation that could end up as a dictatorship. We are faced with the fact that there has, indeed and lamentably, been a regression in the country.[22]

Ambassadors from donor countries visited Jarquín in prison and noted their concern. Businesspeople and economists were worried about the affair's impact on investment and international aid. Farmers, protesting a denial of credit to small farmers at the Inter-American Development Bank, waved signs saying "Si hay para robar, también hay para sembrar!" (If there is money to steal, there is also money to plant!) and "Con Jarquín hasta el fin!" (With Jarquín to the end!). The government loosened up somewhat, allowing previously suspended audits to move forward in the Ministry of the Treasury, the Internal Revenue Bureau, and the Customs Bureau.

Nicaragua commemorated International Human Rights Day, December 10, with a march of thousands demanding the comptroller's release. That same day Sweden pulled out of an aid project in Nueva Segovia because of misuse of funds by the government. Edgard Espinoza, who headed the project until dismissed by PLC city government officials, stated that the Swedes discovered that the PLC was using development funds for partisan ends, concluding that Stockholm acted wisely in terminating their participation.[23]

Finally, on Christmas Eve and after forty-four days in jail, all three men were released when an appeals court dismissed the charges against them. Jarquín then called for a referendum on the constitutional amendments that would become the Pact, introduced by Liberals and Sandinistas in the National Assembly, while the comptroller was in jail.[24] He was particularly concerned that the proposals would hobble the CGR and give Arnoldo Alemán immunity from prosecution even after he left the presidency.

The Sandinista Party—Breaks and Cracks

The Sandinista National Liberation Front (FSLN) is, in contrast with the PLC, definitely an ideological party with ideological battles as the basis for many, but not all, of the divisions within it. If, as is often suggested the three most important aspects of Sandinista thought are the ideas of Sandino, Marxism, and Liberation Theology, then their differing interpretations of the theories of Marxism have led to the greatest controversy. Elsewhere, I have maintained that, while a major contribution of the Sandinista revolution was to bring together—in theory and in practice—representative, participatory, and economic democracy, there were many conflicts within the FSLN around these issues. And, in the end, one must question whether that combination of democracy and vanguardism is tenable.

During the years the Sandinistas were in power, many analysts assumed that their collective leadership was less authoritarian than "one-man rule" in other revolutionary countries. The nine men constituting the National Directorate met, arrived at a consensus on the issues, and then sent down their orders. Victor Hugo Tinoco says that, in Nicaragua, the ideas of a vanguard party were combined with a cultural tendency toward caudillismo. He adds that Nicaraguans produced a variation in which "caudillismo of one person was replaced by a caudillismo of nine people. But in the end it was still caudillismo, if a collective one."[25]

With the 1990 electoral defeat, the FSLN party structures opened up. The First Party Congress in July of 1991 made the Sandinista Assembly the highest organ of the party between Congresses. The National Directorate split on important issues—many but not all of them occurring between a social democratic current and a more orthodox, vanguardist current—with consensus harder to reach. In the May 1994 Congress, each democratic reform that was approved was counterbalanced by a decision that reinforced vanguardism. Former vice president Sergio Ramírez was not reelected to the National Directorate. But Henry Ruíz did run unsuccessfully against Daniel Ortega for general secretary of the party, which as Ruíz himself noted, "never happens in a left party."[26]

In October 1994, the Sandinista Assembly voted to remove Carlos Fernando Chamorro from his position as editor of the Sandinista daily, *Barricada*. Other journalists resigned in protest. In January 1995, Sergio Ramírez resigned from the FSLN, followed three weeks later by Dora María Téllez, Luís Carrión, and Mirna Cunningham. On May 21 1995, the Sandinista Renovationist Movement was founded as a political party.

But the break did not mean that ideological controversies within the FSLN disappeared. We can see the differences among Sandinistas as two cross-cutting cleavages. The first is between commitment to the popular classes and openness to multiclass compromise. The second opposes more democratic (negotiation) to more verticalist (command) methods of work. Only one of the four quadrants left the party (those committed to multiclass compromise and democratic methods of work) leaving three others to continue to do battle among themselves. And battle they have.

democratic methods of work

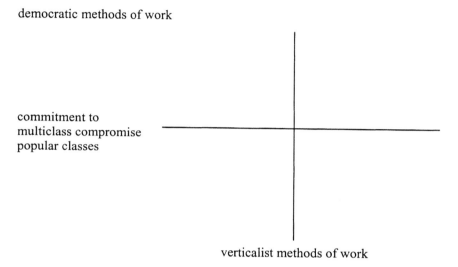

commitment to
multiclass compromise
popular classes

verticalist methods of work

Figure 2.1: The FSLN's Internal Cleavages

While the FSLN lost the 1996 elections with Daniel Ortega at the helm, the party did conserve its base and it remained the largest and best-organized political party in Nicaragua and one of the strongest parties of the left in Latin America. It was the breakaway Sandinista Renovation Movement (MRS), led by Sergio Ramírez, that was unable to gain popular support and achieved only one deputy in the National Assembly. It seemed at the end of 1996 that the FSLN's immediate tasks were to continue its internal democratization and to craft economic proposals to aid the 70 percent of Nicaraguans who live in poverty. Were the Sandinistas able to meet either challenge?

As a result of the primary process, almost all of the FSLN deputies in the National Assembly were new to the job, having been grassroots activists of the party and the popular movements in the departments. According to Victor Hugo Tinoco, head of the Sandinista congressional caucus after the 1996 elections, the FSLN achieved better discipline than the Liberals, because it always thoroughly debated all bills coming before it. The deputies united with nongovernmental organizations representing women to oppose, unsuccessfully, the Alemán initiative to fold the Institute on Women into the new Ministry of the Family. This unity among the deputies was in contrast to the period between 1993 and 1996 when all of the conflicts within the FSLN were being played out in public and alliances within the party were shifting constantly.[27]

In 1997, Nicaragua's chronic economic crisis became acute with large- and medium-scale farmers unable to pay their debts to the banks. Farmers barricaded the principal highways in protest. Many of them still did not have titles to the land they had acquired under the Sandinista agrarian reform, often because the old owner would accept nothing short of the return of his property. Because credit for small farmers and cooperatives was difficult to obtain under conditions imposed by the multilaterals, some Sandinistas feared that if small farmers received legal title to their lands, they would have to sell immediately to feed their families. Property was becoming concentrated again in fewer hands; but now some of the big landholders were Sandinistas.

As the Sandinistas prepared for their party congress scheduled for May of 1998, many stated that the party needed new leadership at all levels as well as new methods for choosing leaders.[28] Manuel Espinoza said that he had asked Daniel Ortega, whom he noted had been called a caudillo, what he thought about the calls for new leadership. Ortega said, "We are ready for the Congress to make this decision. We are not attached to any post. From the moment we enter into the Congress, we leave it in the hands of the Congress, and it is that body which must make the decision."[29] The use of the imperial "we" did not auger well for democratic leadership change!

But any debate on issues was abruptly overshadowed in March 1998 when Ortega's stepdaughter, Zoilamérica Narváez, charged him with sexual abuse, rape, and sexual harassment over a period of twenty years (dating from when she was eleven years old). Because of his parliamentary immunity,[30] Ortega could not be brought to trial, and there was not any possibility that he would lose his immunity. The FSLN leadership accused Narváez of conspiring to destroy Ortega and the party. Lisa Zimmerman notes that "the scandal has served to highlight many of the obstacles that the FSLN faces in carrying out a meaningful transformation: the 'cult of personality'... around Ortega; the failure of established (party) mechanisms ... to deal with charges of ethical failings against its members, and entrenched patriarchal attitudes and values."[31]

At the Congress, Daniel Ortega was unopposed for reelection as general. However, Victor Hugo Tinoco ran against Tomás Borge for vice-general secretary and lost by only twenty-five out of 423 votes. Reportedly, Borge had been outraged that Tinoco challenged him and urged him to withdraw. But Tinoco stayed the course. Only four members of the new National Directorate had served on the previous Directorate: Ortega, Borge, Tinoco, and René Núñez.

Monica Baltodano chose not to run, saying that she "would rather be a dreamer than a killer of dreams."

The questioning of Daniel Ortega's leadership within the party did not stop with his reelection as general secretary, however. Henry Petrie, who was stripped of his post in the FSLN Managua departmental committee for his support of Narváez, said that caudillismo was destroying the party.[32] About the rush to defend Ortega, Alejandro Bendaña said, "'Danielismo' is manipulated to preserve the apparatus, the power, [and] the organization as intact as possible, in other words, not to deal with the underlying problems. The defense of 'Danielismo' is not simply the defense of Daniel but also of those individuals in the FSLN who aspire to a greater share of power.... They see this as a threat, as something that will further weaken the FSLN."[33]

Within a few months the media was full of speculation about a political pact being hammered out between Daniel Ortega and Arnoldo Alemán. In an August interview, Ortega said that there was no comparison between his negotiations with Alemán and the infamous pacts earlier in the century, especially that between Anastasio Somoza Debayle and Conservative Fernando Aguero in 1971. Ortega noted: "First of all, Alemán is not Somoza. The fact is that Somoza disappeared from this country with the revolution of 1979. Alemán represents a government, which, while it is certainly very marked by what was Somocismo, is the fruit of a democratic process that the revolution began.... He is linked to Somocismo, but I insist that he is not Somoza."[34] When reminded that Ortega himself had called Alemán "Somocista," Daniel clarified, "I have said that this government has the vices of Somocismo, but that does not mean it has the power that Somoza had ... This government has the political apparatus ... but it doesn't have either military or economic power, although it has made advances in recovering economic ground."[35]

In January 1999, the Sandinista Assembly and the FSLN legislative caucus decided that Daniel Ortega would assume his seat in the National Assembly for the upcoming legislative session and be their house leader. Ortega had not previously served actively as a deputy. The change was seen as a blow to Victor Hugo Tinoco, who had been the minority leader in the Assembly and who had been mentioned as a possible candidate as the FSLN's 2001 presidential nominee. The FSLN communiqué issued after the meeting explained the change of leadership by saying: "This may be a very difficult year because of the laws to be considered as well as the continuing negotiations with the government."[36]

In summary, the FSLN leadership had three principal reasons for entering into negotiations for a pact with the Alemán forces, according to Marcos Membreño: (1) to preserve Daniel Ortega's parliamentary immunity so that he does not have to stand trial in the sexual abuse case; (2) to ensure that large properties appropriated by the Sandinista leadership after the 1990 electoral defeat, the majority of which have not been completely legalized, are not taken over by the government; and (3) to guarantee positions within the government and on the boards of directors of state-owned enterprises to divide up among their political supporters."[37] As we can see in the case of the bank failures, the FSLN needed protection against charges of corruption and fraud as well. There was very little time or energy among the party's top leadership to address the vital issues of increasing democracy within the party and formulating programs to address poverty.

The Evolution of the Pact

Arnoldo Alemán's first few months in office were marked by protests. Student groups, trade unionists, women, and small farmers' groups took to the streets and put up barricades on highways protesting unemployment, hunger, lack of credit for small farmers, rising costs of living, low salaries, and repression of university students along with what some were calling "growing dictatorial tendencies" of the Alemán government. The latter referred to the issuing of decrees and the steamrolling through the National Assembly of legislation on issues that would normally have involved some sort of national discussion. Included were a new tax law seen to be aimed at helping the return of Miami capital at the cost of local businesses, a decree restricting funding for nongovernmental organizations and others. The April 1997 protest effectively closed down transportation throughout the country. A first round of government-sponsored talks did not produce any results because unions and farmers' groups were not invited. A second round of what the government called "national dialogue" began in July, but the FSLN and several other parties as well as pro-Sandinista organizations boycotted it.

President Alemán spoke of dialogue between political parties at a PLC Convention on July 11, 1998, noting that the foremost group with whom he would be talking would be the FSLN, not with "small political parties." He mentioned the possibility of electoral and constitutional reform which might include the elimination of the prohibition of persons with double citizenship running for office and changes in government funding for political parties and campaigns.[38]

However, the negotiations already had been going on for several months between teams headed up by presidential advisor Jaime Morales and Sandinista advisor Dionisio Marenco. In August rumors had it that a pact, said to include the elimination of the prohibition on immediate presidential reelection, the creation of a Senate and other measures, was ready. Reaction was intense, principally from minority parties left out of the talks. Sergio Ramírez reminded the press that the 1979 revolution was fought precisely to combat this type of bipartisan pact. Conservative leader Noel Vidaurre noted that the Conservatives had made pacts before in Nicaragua's history but that these agreements had never benefited the people. However, Daniel Ortega said that the FSLN was reclaiming lost political space to which it had a right as the second largest party in the country. He stated, "This is not a pact.... It's not secret. It's something legitimate to defend the spaces that others have been taking away from the FSLN."[39]

At the end of September, the parties announced agreement on changes to the electoral law, and PLC deputy Eliseo Nuñez, back in his party's good graces, said that the Liberals and Sandinistas had come to an agreement that would include replacing all the members of the Supreme Electoral Council with members named by the political parties. They also discussed having 90 percent of the electoral council members at the departmental and municipal levels named by the two main parties. Moreover, the reforms would make it harder for a political party to gain legal status.[40]

A number of problems slowed the Pact's progress: questions about the role of Humberto Ortega, Daniel's brother and political power in his own right,[41] and the devastating Hurricane Mitch were the most notable. Yet negotiations but were not suspended. In January Victor Hugo Tinoco noted that the talks between the PLC and the FSLN were causing "strong disagreements" within the FSLN. He said that the Liberals were insistent on the reelection issue and, in general, "There were too many demands that we could not accept." Still, Tinoco admitted that "There is a group within the FSLN which feels that there is too much love for the Liberals."[42]

Daniel Ortega denied that there was a conflict within his party, adding that news reports of an Ortega-Tinoco split were part of a right-wing attempt to weaken the FSLN.[43] However, when talks began again in earnest in June 1999, Tinoco was replaced by Rev. Miguel Angel Casco. Monica Baltodano stated that there was no unity within the Sandinista Assembly about a pact and that a referendum should be held on whether to amend the Constitution. Violeta Chamorro criticized the Pact as an attempt on the part of the Liberals and Sandinistas to either deceive the people or to cover up their "dirty tricks."[44] There began to be rumors about so-called "secret clauses" of the Pact. Among these were "government promises" of "fiscal benevolence" toward Sandinista entrepreneurs and who should replace some unmanipulable functionaries who were to be fired.[45]

By late June, voices from the international community were beginning to be heard. United Nations representative Carmen Angulo said that he hoped that the international community would support the idea of dialogue. In contrast, Ana Quiróz, director of the Emergency Coalition for Transformation and Reconstruction, said she had "heard concerns from the international agencies with whom we work about the results of this dialogue."[46] Within a few weeks, the European Union, the World Bank, and others had expressed concern about the probable enlargement of the Supreme Court from twelve to sixteen justices. Their fear was that, with the appointment of the new judges by the pacting parties, judicial autonomy would be undermined.[47]

The Pact was completed on August 17, 1999. The announcement was made by the spokesmen for the PLC and FSLN, Silvio Calderon and Rev. Miguel Angel Casco, respectively. On the 23rd, a special commission began the task of putting the agreed-upon points into proper legal form.[48] Casco said that even after eleven difficult sessions, the agreement reached was only "partial," meaning, evidently, that the parties were not able to come to agreement on all the points that were put on the table. A few days later, the Sandinista Assembly met for nine hours to discuss and approve all twelve points of the Pact. Even the most controversial point, the seat in the National Assembly for Alemán when he left office, carried 137 to 18.

Ortega applied the whip to the Sandinista caucus, most of whom accepted it. However, some, like Monica Baltadono, refused. The son of the party's founder, Deputy Carlos Fonseca Teran, was adamant in his rejection of the points in the Pact, whatever the political cost to him. Jose González, a deputy from Matagalpa, said that he would oppose the seat in the Assembly for Alemán and would decide soon about his position on the changes in the comptroller's office. And Victor Hugo Tinoco announced that he would criticize the measure but follow the party line in the vote.[49]

One would have thought that the jailing of the comptroller at this very moment would have resulted in the Sandinistas forcing concessions measures from Alemán. The FSLN had, in general, been supportive of Jarquín's anti-corruption efforts. A group of thirty FSLN legislators did see it as an opportunity to demand some changes in the Pact. But when Daniel Ortega returned from an overseas trip he brought everything under control, and not a word of the Pact was changed. Thus, on November 19, 1999, PLC and Sandinista deputies presented to the First Secretary of the National Assembly the proposed Pact. National Assembly president Ivan Escobar Fornos said it "represents a good opportunity for Nicaragua to move forward." Bayardo Arce of the FSLN added that it supported the modernization of the country. All thirty-eight PLC deputies co-sponsored the measure, while twenty-seven of thirty-six Sandinistas signed on.[50]

Leaders of five other Liberal parties, however, distanced themselves. Further, a group of dissident Sandinista deputies held a press conference to declare that they would not vote for the amendments in the Assembly. Speaking for the group, Monica Baltodano stated that the Liberal/Sandinista Pact "makes us Sandinistas appear to be accomplices in the crimes of this government, including the jailing of the comptroller, Agustin Jarquín."[51]

The National Assembly passed the Pact on December 9, 1999, seventy-one to seventeen, with two abstentions. The measure still had to be approved by the next National Assembly session in the new year for the constitutional amendments to take effect. Several Sandinista deputies opposed the Pact: Monica Baltodano, Angelina Rios, Carlos Fonseca, and José González. Fonseca said that the vote was nothing less than the abandonment by the majority of the Sandinista representatives of the very principles for which so many people gave their lives during the revolution and subsequent contra war.[52] Less than a month later, January 18, 2000, the constitutional amendments passed the second required vote in the new session of the National Assembly, with seventy in favor, twelve against, and five abstaining.[53] On the very same day that the constitutional amendments were passed, the National Assembly also passed a new electoral law that put in place the elements of the Pact which dealt with electoral matters. Seventy-five deputies voted in favor of the new law, four voted against it.[54]

In March 2000, Rev. Miguel Angel Casco, who had been the FSLN spokesperson on the Pact after Victor Hugo Tinoco left the negotiations, resigned both from the National Directorate of the FSLN and from the party itself. He joined those who said that the Pact was designed to keep the present leaders in positions of power while justifying their ill-gotten wealth or other abuses.[55]

What's in the Pact?

These are the Pact's main features:

1. The Office of the Comptroller General of the Republic was expanded from one to five officials of equal rank. Agustin Jarquín became one among five, and his vice comptroller, Claudia Frixione, became a mere alternate.
2. Automatic lifetime seats in the National Assembly were granted to outgoing presidents and vice presidents.
3. The number of Supreme Court justices was increased from twelve to sixteen.
4. It would now require a two-thirds vote of the National Assembly to strip a president of the Republic of his or her immunity.
5. The number of magistrates on the Supreme Electoral Council was increased from five to seven.
6. Municipal Electoral Councils were to be established. Their presidents and vice presidents would alternate between the PLC and FSLN. [This was already the case in all Departmental Electoral Councils and all polling centers.]
7. Parties that decided to create an electoral alliance would lose their own legal status if the alliance did not win a certain percentage of votes.
8. Legal standing would only be granted to a party that presented a list of signatures equivalent to at least 3 percent of the last electoral roll.
9. The proportion of votes needed to win the presidency on the first round was reduced from 45 percent to 40 percent. A candidate could win on the first round with as little as 35 percent if the second place candidate had 5 percentage points less than that. A second round would be necessary if these percentages were not met.
10. Popular subscription associations—or petition candidates—would no longer be allowed in local city government elections.[56]

The Pact did not include successive presidential terms, which Alemán had apparently desired. The first five measures amended the Constitution; the second five changed the electoral law.

The Pact Attacked and the Pact Defended

Attacks on the Pact were a constant during the entire period of its negotiation and approval. As early as May 1999, Sergio Garcia Quintero, a member of Alemán's PLC who is a member of the Central American Parliament, offered sixteen reasons for President Alemán's decline in popularity as well as for what he saw as the decline in the party. One reason was the fact that the PLC does not behave like a serious political party, but like a mercantile organization at the service of the private interests of a big boss and his highly questionable clique. Quintero also noted that "the fact that the president of the Republic has gotten into bed with Comandante Daniel Ortega, totally against the desires of Liberals, with no other objectives than to get that Sandinista faction's complicity in the reforms to the Constitution and the Electoral Law and the promulgation of new laws, which in turn have no other ends than to favor the personal, political, and other interests of Arnoldo Alemán and his main cronies."[57] When the contents of the Pact were revealed, Garcia called for demonstrations and a civil disobedience campaign to stop it.

Rank and file Liberals were also outraged. In their number were those in Miami who had supported Alemán, believing that he would help them return to Nicaragua and reclaim their properties without fear of Sandinista reprisals. The president of the Committee of Poor Nicaraguans in Exile said, "Alemán claimed that, once president, he would crush the Sandinistas once and for all, and create thousands of new jobs in Nicaragua so that we could all go home. He said he would be waiting with open arms to greet us … (Instead he) is busy making deals with Daniel Ortega and the other FSLN millionaires."[58]

President Alemán defended the Pact as a "search for points of convergence" with the FSLN. He said that the requirement that a party get 3 percent of the national vote to keep legal status would save citizens from financing the campaigns of small unrepresentative microparties. His supporters said that their leader should hold a legislative seat to let the country benefit from his experience. Making the comptroller general a collegial office was defended as modernizing and strengthening the institution.[59]

But it was from within the FSLN that the criticism of the Pact was the strongest. Human rights leader and former Supreme Court justice Vilma Nuñez was particularly bitter. "The FSLN gained nothing," she said, "not even the elimination of the second round [in presidential elections] and that was their main demand." Regarding enlargement of the comptroller's office, she observed that "the leadership of the FSLN has made itself the accomplices in enthroning corruption in our country."[60] Although she had received threats for opposing the

Pact, Nuñez nevertheless maintained that Sandinista activists had to keep fighting, because "the struggle to rescue the FSLN, transform it and turn it once again into an instrument of popular struggle must take place within (the FSLN, which) belongs to all Sandinistas, not just to the top leadership that has currently kidnapped the party."[61]

To defend the Pact, the FSLN National Directorate argued that the deal was needed to heighten the party's chances for electoral victory. Only then would Nicaragua see progressive policies that would favor the interests of the poor, the workers, young people, and women. But the leadership was not satisfied with this plausible argument. Rather, it had to attack dissidents "who affect the prestige and the honor of the FSLN and its members as well as the coherence, unity, and discipline of the party."[62] The residue of vanguardism is obvious here, but not in the sense of requiring obedience to decisions in support of radical revolutionary policies. Rather, party discipline, even the old Leninist democratic centralism, is being enforced in support of traditional Nicaraguan caudillismo, here that of Daniel Ortega and his closest associates.

Bayardo Gonzalez offers a different line of defense.[63] He suggests that the Pact is more a democratic pact, like Venezuela's Pacto de Punto Fijo (1958), than the dictators' pacts familiar to Nicaraguans. Gonzalez further argues that the Sandinista-Liberal duopoly is the only way to cure the country's proliferation of microparties, and hints that it might even promote fusions to create a third option. Finally, he implies that the Pact will do for Nicaragua what the National Front (1958-1974) did for Colombia, namely prevent a partisan civil war. Though intriguing, the arguments ignore the differences between conditions in contemporary Nicaragua and those that existed in the Andean states four decades ago, not to mention the undesirable outcomes of both pacts. As well, a closer analysis of the Pact's electoral provisions would have revealed that it really was constructed to protect the PLC and FSLN, and not to remedy the ills caused by vanity parties.

None of this convinced dissident Sandinistas. Henry Ruíz, known during his twelve years leading a guerrilla band in Nicaragua's mountains as "Modesto" and who served as minister of planning under the Sandinista government, left the FSLN in March of 2000. He said:

> At this point I don't see any way for the FSLN to put itself back together. Neither my head nor my heart nor my commitments allow me to believe there is any possibility of this. During Violeta Chamorro's government, the FSLN played a more coherent role as an opposition force. We waged a more systematic, more sustained opposition. More recently, facing the Liberal government, the FSLN has not acted as an opposition but rather as a collaborator.... I always maintained and continue to maintain that the current government is a Somocista government, one that seeks to bring back somocismo.... It is inexplicable

that the FSLN leadership has concluded agreements with this government and formed a pact with it.[64]

On December 2, 1999, the Nicaraguan Center for Human Rights (CENIDH), a Sandinista-affiliated human rights group, released an exhaustive critique of the agreements included in the Pact. The document, "Considerations on the Partial Reform of the Constitution Agreed to by the PLC and the FSLN Leadership," recalls that Sandino opposed the Pact of Espino Negro in 1927 and thus began his struggle against U.S. intervention in Nicaragua. Nine years later the forty-five-year Somoza family dictatorship began. Under the Somozas, there were two infamous pacts: the first, signed in 1950, was between Liberal Anastasio Somoza Garcia and Conservative general Emiliano Chamorro; the second, signed in 1971, was between Anastasio Somoza Debayle and Conservative Fernando Agüero Rocha. CENIDH argued that "the greater the 'understanding' or political pacting between the dominant classes—the party in power and the opposition—the smaller is the possibility of true harmony and democracy among Nicaraguans."[65]

The document further notes that the Pact brings legal, political, and economic changes that will benefit only the two caudillos and their closest associates. These changes will keep the two dominant parties in power indefinitely. And though they may alternate in office, both will keep important quotas of power throughout government and thus deny alternative political forces access to influence.[66] CENIDH gave special attention to the provision raising the majority needed to strip a sitting president of immunity from half to two-thirds, suggesting that this is just a device to protect the corrupt. It also expressed grave concern over the politicization of the judicial and electoral branches of government, as well as the comptroller's office, a result of the Pact increasing the number of high-level partisan appointments.[67]

CENIDH's document summarizes the essential criticisms leveled against the Pact. One is tempted to argue, however, that since the Pact does not address the principal economic and social ills that Nicaraguans confront, it does not eliminate the causes of political discontent that could lead to civil war. It just guarantees that the organized force most likely to lead that struggle, and necessary according to social scientists in order for a revolution to actually take over state power, will not take on that leadership mantle, having been neutralized by the Pact.

Many leading public figures (including former president Violeta Chamorro, former vice president Sergio Ramírez, and poets Giaconda Belli and Ernesto Cardenal) called for a referendum on the Pact.[68] It was not until the Pact was signed and the measures putting it into effect were passed by the National Assembly in January 2000, however, that collection of signatures began throughout the country.[69] Public support was there: an October 1999 survey done in Managua by the Instituto de Estudios Nicaragüenses indicated that 67.7 percent of those polled favored a referendum to accept or reject the Pact before it went into effect.[70] Of course, nothing came of this.

The Impact of the Pact on Institutions

The first signals from the enlarged comptroller general's office (CGO) were not encouraging. The Superior Council (SC), as the five-member institution was now called, fired some of the staff working on a number of strategic investigations. Then the SC asked the Supreme Court to quickly resolve all the challenges to accusations of corruption contained in reports filed by Agustín Jarquín when he was comptroller general. According to one analysis, "the idea seems to be to wipe all these cases off the books and start anew, without, of course, finding any of the accused guilty of wrongdoing or recommending their removal from their top posts." All of Agustín Jarquín's functions were taken away from him and he was accused of heading a corrupt administration. Unsurprisingly, he resigned within a few months.[71]

In June, Byron Jerez, director of Nicaragua's Internal Revenue Department, resigned after the collegial comptroller (CC) established that he held "administrative responsibility" for mishandling and misdirecting hundreds of thousands of dollars. But the comptrollers stopped short of accusations of criminal or civil wrongdoing by Jerez. In fact, Jerez stated that he was resigning voluntarily "with my head held high." He added, "I congratulate the Comptrollers on a true and lawful decision."[72] But the media did not agree. *La Prensa* said the newly collegial comptrollers' office had failed its first test. *El Nuevo Diario* called the decision "the height of disgrace."[73]

Soon, however, the CC discovered its backbone. In April 2000, one of the Liberal comptrollers, Luis Angel Montenegro, challenged President Alemán to "justify publicly how a one-time seller of charcoal … should now, after ten short years in public office, be Nicaragua's wealthiest man." Alemán shot back, "Well, he's just a little accountant who always gets hold of the wrong end of the tick." Montenegro then declared, "No one can misappropriate public funds. Our job as comptrollers is to blow the whistle on anyone who appears to be doing wrong."[74] Ten months later, all the magistrates of the CC joined Montenegro in ordering President Alemán to explain why he had a helicopter pad built at one of his ranches and show that its construction did not involve public funds. The unanimous decision pleased Montenegro, who had brought the accusation of presidential impropriety before his colleagues. Alemán said that his security advisors had recommended building the heliport and that its cost, US$35,000, had been met from the president's discretionary funds. The president of the CC, Guillermo Arguello, noted that the body had been also called upon to investigate the construction of another pad at the president's sister's estate.[75]

The Supreme Electoral Council (CSE) was also greatly affected by the Pact. In March 2000, shortly after the Pact came into force, CSE head Rosa Marina

Zelaya, whom the FSLN blamed for their defeat in 1996, and her alternate Cyril Omier challenged the new electoral law, because it shortened their terms of office by a year. They claimed that this was a retroactive law, but the Supreme Court found against them.[76] In July, after the CSE announced that only four parties (the PLC, the FSLN, the Conservative Party [PC] and the Nicaraguan Christian Way [CCN]) could run candidates in that November's municipal elections, Cardinal Obando y Bravo spoke out against the new electoral law, arguing that "everyone should have a chance to compete in the elections."[77]

The CSE was busy in July 2000, dissolving twenty-six parties that failed to meet the newly stringent stipulations. The law demands that an official party be endorsed by 3 percent of those on the electoral rolls, thus about 76,000 people, and that no one can endorse more than one party. Several parties appealed, claiming that they had met the requirement, but to no avail. In October, FSLN and PLC leaders asked the CSE to deny legal recognition to the political parties of retired general and former Sandinista Joaquin Cuadra, the Movement for National Unity, and Jose Alvarado, who had held the defense and education portfolios in Alemán's cabinet, the Liberal Democratic Party. This would keep Cuadra and Alvarado out of the 2001 presidential race.[78]

Former CSE president (1984-1996), Mariano Fiallos, identified two key weaknesses in the new electoral law: it politicized the CSE and it closed off political participation. He explains that the body applied the rules selectively, based on partisan calculations. In the case of the Conservatives and the other parties that gathered signatures, Fiallos argued that the Liberals and Sandinistas originally intended to declare that none of them met the test. But protests, including from abroad, led to recognizing the Conservative claim.[79]

Electoral Consequences

The Pact paid its first political dividends in the 2000 municipal elections, the first ever held independently of national general elections and the first to be conducted under the electoral law amended by the Pact. Although the PLC won a majority of the mayoral elections and a plurality of the votes cast, the party lost Managua and several other key cities.[80] With only a year to go before elections for a new president, National Assembly, and representatives to the Central American Parliament, the governing party was concerned.

During the run-up to the November 2000 local elections, political parties in Nicaragua had to register and secure official recognition. Only the FSLN and the CCN received automatic approval, due to their 1996 performances. Because it had run as part of an alliance in the last national elections, even the PLC had to collect signatures from a minimum of 3 percent of the country's registered voters and have party organizations in place in all 151 municipalities to meet the new stipulations. Many parties, including the MRS, failed to meet the exigent and perhaps arbitrarily applied standards of the pacted electoral law. In fact, the only other party to fulfill the requirements was the Conservatives (PC). From over twenty parties in 1996, Nicaragua was down to four.

Although the elections themselves went reasonably well, the CSE took a month to certify the results. Even then the Sandinistas had to apply pressure to get their victories officially recognized. This produced a strong suspicion that the governing party was trying to use its majority on the CSE to improve its showing. In fact, Mariano Fiallos suggests that the delays came from behind-the-scenes partisan negotiations.[81] Either explanation is consistent with the Pact's dynamics.

But the municipal races were just a tune-up for the main event in 2001. The FSLN worked hard to reduce the pluralities needed for a first round presidential election to 40 percent, and as low as 35 percent, if the runner-up is at least five points back. Yet this makes no sense in light of the Pact's push toward a Liberal-Sandinista duopoly. For the 40 percent floor to work there should be at least three strong parties, each capable of getting at least a fifth of the vote; the 35 + 5 percent provision probably requires four serious parties, if not five. We do not know what the FSLN traded away to get this chimera, but if they gave up much they were snookered.

The elections themselves in one sense followed the script from 1996: The FSLN moved into a virtual tie for the lead with a month left, only to lose by a landslide. But where the 1996 result owed a great deal to interventions by Cardinal Obando y Bravo, the 2001 race felt the presence of Washington.

After the September 11 terrorist attacks on the United States, the Bolaños campaign began continuous attacks against Daniel Ortega, labeling him a "friend of terrorists" based on his visits to Libya and Iraq, even though some Sandinistas pointed out that Osama bin Laden had evidently provided support to the contras in the 1980s. On October 29, *La Prensa* carried a full-page paid ad for the PLC's Enrique Bolaños signed by Florida governor Jeb Bush, the brother of U.S. president George W. Bush. The page had at the top in small letters: "The Brother of the President of the United States." Then, in a massive headline: "GEORGE W. BUSH SUPPORTS ENRIQUE BOLANOS." The body of the ad said, "Daniel Ortega is an enemy of everything the United States represents. Further, he is a friend of our enemies. Ortega has a relationship of more than thirty years with states and individuals who shelter and condone international terrorism. By contrast Enrique Bolaños is a man whose past promises a future of freedom."[82] On November 4, Bolaños defeated Ortega by 14 percentage points, 56 percent to 42 percent. The Conservatives received only 1.4 percent of the vote.

But the outcome could have been different.[83] Four days before the election, on October 31, Bolaños met with Gabriel Solórzono, head of Ética y Transparencia (ET), Nicaragua's electoral observer organization, and claimed that Alemán and Ortega agreed to hand the presidency to Ortega by stealing votes from Bolaños. The margin was to be 7 percent. A declaration of a state of emergency would provide the cover for the fraud; the decree was already signed and ready for promulgation. And the now highly partisan CSE was onside.

The worst appeared to be happening when, at ten p.m. on election night, November 4, the CSE's computer system and satellite links went down. Visions of the historic 1988 Mexican electoral fraud loomed large. ET had done a quick count of the results and presented its data to the CSE at 1:30 in the morning. These showed Bolaños with a landslide victory. A few hours later ET met with former U.S. president Jimmy Carter, whose Carter Center was also observing the election. However, the first official results began to arrive and, shortly thereafter, Daniel Ortega conceded.

This would have been the Pact's crowning shame.[84] One can only guess what Alemán demanded from the FSLN in return for throwing them the election. Only luck, the alertness of Gabriel Solórzano, and perhaps the pragmatism of Daniel Ortega avoided electoral catastrophe.

Conclusion

Democracy is not in danger of collapsing in Nicaragua. But, the Liberal-Sandinista Pact of August 1999, which was made possible by the power of two caudillos, Arnoldo Alemán and Daniel Ortega, over their own parties, contributed to the strengthening of that old strain of caudillismo within Nicaragua and thus to the weakening of democracy. Particularly disturbing were the measures within the Pact that were added simply in order to have more high-salaried patronage positions, which the nation can ill afford. Most political parties have some patronage at their disposal. But in Nicaragua, the term "the spoils of office" describes a situation that is truly spoiled and rotten, especially when the standard of living of the officeholders is compared to that of 70 percent of the population that survives on less than $2 per day.

Even after the arrest of former president Alemán, the Pact still exists in amendments to the constitution and electoral law, which politicized the Supreme Court and Supreme Electoral Council, as well as local electoral councils, and made the comptroller general a five-member body. Will the pact provide stability to Nicaragua, or will it merely be a vehicle for corruption? With no specific measures yet passed to prevent corruption and two-party division of "the spoils of office" still in place, the latter is certainly possible.

Will the main parties now be able to alternate in office through free and fair elections instead of through violent overthrow of the government as in the past? This certainly seems likely, but the tradition was established in 1990, when the Sandinistas turned power over to Mrs. Chamorro. The Pact was not necessary to reinforce it. The changes to the electoral system as a result of the Pact were designed to strengthen a two-party system, but some analysts speculated that they could contribute to the rise of a strong third force. This might happen more easily now with the weakening of the Liberals.

The Alemán–Ortega Pact was frequently compared to the pacts of the Somoza years. But there was a big difference. The Somoza era pacts were between one very strong political force and one segment of a much weaker political force which was willing to be used by the stronger for a specific political purpose in return for certain limited favors. The Alemán–Ortega Pact was between roughly equal leaders, equal both in power and, perhaps, in vulnerability. But, as it turned out, Alemán was much more vulnerable, and the person who brought him down was his own vice president, Enrique Bolaños, aided by the Pact's co-signers, the Sandinistas.

Notes

1. An earlier version of this paper was presented to the 2001 Congress of the Latin American Studies Association, Washington, D.C.

2. Katherine Hoyt, "Alemán Holds Press Conference in DC," *Nicaragua Monitor* (April 1996): 7.

3. "Where has Liberalism Come?" *Envío* (August 1999): 8.

4. David Close, "Arnoldo Alemán: Forward to the Past," *Nicaragua Monitor* (April 1996): 6.

5. Close, "Arnoldo Alemán," 6; David R. Dye with Jack Spence and George Vickers, *Patchwork Democracy: Nicaraguan Politics Ten Years after the Fall* (Cambridge, MA: Hemisphere Initiatives, 2000), 12.

6. Marcos Membreño, interview by Midge Quandt, *Voices of Sandinismo in Post Election Nicaragua* (Washington, DC: Nicaragua Network Education Fund, 1997), 66.

7. Victoria Gonzalez, "'The Devil Took Her:' Sex and the Nicaraguan Nation, 1855-1979," paper presented to the 22nd Congress of the Latin American Studies Association, Miami, March 2000, p. 3.

8. Victor Hugo Tinoco, interview by Midge Quandt, *Voices of Sandinismo in Post Election Nicaragua* (Washington, DC: Nicaragua Network Education Fund, 1997), 76-78.

9. "Liberals Plan for Power Until 2016," *Nicaragua Monitor* (June-July 1997): 4 (reprinted from *Envío*, May 1997).

10. "Liberals Plan for Power Until 2016," *Nicaragua Monitor*.

11. Dye, et al., *Patchwork Democracy*, 13.

12. *Nicaragua News Service* (NNS) (April 26-May 2, 1998), 4; Dye, et al., *Patchwork Democracy*, 13.

13. Equipo Nitlapan-Envío, "Mitch: 100 Días Después," *Conyuntura—Nicaragua* (February 2000), 5. [José Cuadra, an outspoken foe of the Pact, was later murdered on his farm outside Matagalpa. Politics did not seem to be involved.]

14. According to the United Nations, 44 percent of the population survives on less than a dollar a day in income, while other figures put the percentage of those living on less than $2 per day at over 70 percent. See, NNS, September 6-12, 1998.

15. Dye, et al., *Patchwork*, 19.

16. NNS (August 30-September 5, 1998), 2.

17. NNS (January 17-23, 1999), 2, 3.

18. NNS (February 7-13, 1999), 2.

19. "Presidente acorralado," *El Nuevo Diario*, 26 February 1999; "Fortuna es inverosímil," *El Nuevo Diario*, February 27, 1999.

20. NNS (March 14-20, 1999), 3. The police investigation found enough evidence existed to prosecute Lacayo.

21. Nitlapan-Envío team, "Is the Game All Sewn Up? Questions and Contradictions," *Envío* (September 1999): 7.

22. Interview with Agustin Jarquín, "Bipartidismo y Dictadura," *Confidencial* (November 14-20, 1999).

23. NNS (December 5-11, 1999), 4-5.

24. NNS (December 20-26, 1999), 1.

25. Interview by the author, cited in Katherine Hoyt, *The Many Faces of Sandinista Democracy* (Athens: Ohio University Press, 1997), 158.

26. Cited in Hoyt, 175.

27. Manuel Espinoza Rivera, "Debate interno garantiza unidad: Una bancada sólida y comprometida," *Visión Sandinista* (November 1997), 2-3.

28. Manuel Espinoza Rivera, "El congreso de mayo y sus expectativas: Oportunidad histórica para cambiar y vencer," *Visión Sandinista* (December 1997), 4-5.

29. Espinoza Rivera, "El congreso de mayo," 5.

30. He acquired legislative immunity when he was given a seat in the National Assembly as a former candidate for president in the 1996 elections.

31. Lisa Zimmerman, "FSLN Congress Re-Elects Ortega," *Nicaragua Monitor* (June 1998), 1.

32. Midge Quandt, "Interview with Henry Petrie," *The Crisis in the FSLN and the Future of the Left in Nicaragua,* Occasional Paper (Washington, DC: Nicaragua Network, 1998), 13.

33. Quandt, "Interview with Alejandro Bendaña," *The Crisis in the FSLN*, 7.

34. NNS (August 23-29, 1998), 1.

35. NNS (August 23-29, 1998).

36. NNS (January 17-24, 1999), 1. Some believed, however, that Ortega took his seat in the Assembly to guarantee his immunity against his stepdaughter's charges, and it was suggested that a deputy could lose immunity by lack of attendance at legislative sessions.

37. Lisa Zimmerman, "NLM Discusses Future Solidarity," *Nicaragua Monitor* (July 1999), 1, 10.

38. "Government to dialogue with FSLN," NNS (July 12-18, 1998), 3.

39. "FSLN—PLC Pact," NNS (August 16-22, 1998), 1-2.

40. NNS (September 27-October 3, 1998), 1.

41. "Humberto Ortega allegedly involved in PLC-FSLN pact negotiations," *Nicaragua News Service* (October 18-24, 1998), 4.

42. NNS (January 31-February 6, 1999), 4.

43. NNS (February 7-13, 1999), 1.

44. NNS (June 6-12, 1999), 2.

45. "First Impacts of a Devils' Pact," *Envío* (August 1999): 3.

46. NNS (June 21-27, 1999), 1-2.

47. Carlos Fernando Chamorro, "Pacto está 'cocinado,'" *Confidencial* (August 8-14, 1999).

48. "Pactos consumados," *El Nuevo Diario*, August 18, 1999.

49. "Sin sorpresas en Asamblea Sandinista," *El Nuevo Diario*, August 30, 1999.

50. NNS (November 14-21, 1999), 3-4.

51. NNS (November 14-21, 1999).

52. "Legalizan dictatura," *La Tribuna,* December 10, 1999.

53. Commentators noted that the amendments could face a constitutional challenge because an addition had been made between the first and second vote. A clause was added that increased from one to two years the amount of time that a candidate must live in a municipality before running for mayor of that town. This was a transparent attempt to prevent Pedro Solorzano from running for mayor of Managua in 2000. This change, plus the Pact's division of Managua into three cities (Managua, El Crucero, and Ciudad Sandino), prohibited Solorzano, who lives in El Crucero, from running.

54. NNS (January 17-23, 2000), 2.

55. NNS (March 20-26, 2000), 4.

56. NNS (December 5-11, 1999), 1.

57. Cited in Nitlapan-Envío team, "After Stockholm and Before the Pact," *Envío* (June 1999): 10.

58. NNS (February 14-20, 2000), 6.

59. "First Impact of a Devil's Pact," 9-10.

60. "Pacto enterró la democracia," *El Nuevo Diario*, August 19, 1999.

61. Vilma Nuñez de Escorcia, "The Deep Crisis of Sandinismo," *Against the Current* (July-August 2000): 26.

62. "Comunicado de la Dirección Nacional del Frente Sandinista emitido el 24 de septiembre de 1999," e-mail from Cristianos Nicaragüenses por los Pobres, September 30, 1999.

63. Bayardo González, "Forum for Discussion: The Y2Pact," *Nicaragua Monitor* (January-February 2000): 2-3.

64. Henry Ruíz, "The FSLN Has Lost the Strong Ethical Basis that Motivated Us," *Envío* (May 2000): 17.

65. "Consideraciones del CENIDH sobre el proyecto de reforma parcial a la constitution política acordado por el PLC y la dirigencia del FSLN," photocopy, 1.

66. "Consideraciones del CENIDH," 4.

67. "Consideraciones del CENIDH," 6 and 8.

68. NNS (July 5-12, 1999), 2-3.

69. NNS (January 10-16, 2000), 3.

70. Carlos Fernando Chamorro, "Opinión dividida sobre 'bondades' del pacto," *Confidencial* (October 10-16, 1999).

71. The Scandinavian countries reacted by freezing US$3 million in aid that they had intended to donate in 2000 to Nicaragua to strengthen the comptroller's office. Nitlapan-Envío team, "The Pact's First Offspring," *Envío* (March 2000), 7.

72. NNS (June 5-11, 2000), 1.

73. NNS (June 5-11, 2000), 1. Two minority opinions were issued by Agustin Jarquín who, even with diminished functions, still took part in decisions, and by Sandinista comptroller Jose Pasos.

74. NNS (April 16-22, 2000), 5.

75. NNS (April 23-29, 2001), 3.

76. NNS (March 13-19, 2000), 4.

77. NNS (July 31-August 6, 2000), 3-4.

78. NNS (October 2-8, 2000), 2-3.

79. Interview with Mariano Fiallos, "Ley Electoral partidizó CSE y cerró participación," *Confidencial* (December 3-9, 2000).

80. Results are found on the CSE Web site at www.cse.gob.ni/elecciones/2000/escru/index.html

81. Interview with Mariano Fiallos, "Ley Electoral partidizó CSE y cerró participación," *Confidencial* (December 3-9, 2000).

82. *La Prensa*, October 29, 2001.

83. Material in this section comes from *La Prensa,* February 13, 2003.

84. The parties to the Pact gave finding a crowning shame one more try. In the week before Alemán was sentenced to twenty years for corruption, the Nicaraguan media were abuzz with talk of a "re-pacto," a second pact, that would have freed Alemán in return for more Sandinistas on the Supreme Court. This failed when the PLC refused to budge on the Court, leading the Sandinistas to declare that "setting Alemán at liberty was not up for negotiation." See, "Pact Falters, Alemán Sentenced, Elections Agreement Collapses," *Nicaragua Network Hotline*, December 8, 2003.

Chapter 3

The Assault on Pluralism

Kalowatie Deonandan

The democratic project in Nicaragua has historically been one plagued with set-backs. Whether the mission of socialist leaders or liberal democratic ones, the results were not always dissimilar. The rule of Arnoldo Alemán and his Consti-tutional Liberal Party (PLC) from 1997 to 2001, provides new insights into how democracy can be undone under the guise of electoralism. Alemán's strategy was to weaken democracy from within, by maintaining its formal institutional structures while undermining the foundations on which these institutions were constructed, often by turning democracy on itself. Manipulation of legislation, restrictions on the party system, exploitation of state institutions, and outright corruption were some of the weapons in his arsenal. This form of rule is remi-niscent of the era of caudillismo or strongman rule which prevailed in the early years of the nation's history.

In this chapter it is argued that Alemán's brand of caudillismo undermined genuine pluralism and consequently contributed to the undoing of democracy in Nicaragua. This thesis will be demonstrated by examining the government's approach to dealing with pluralist groups, specifically the unions, women's rights groups, nongovernmental organizations (NGOs), and the media. Instead of practicing inclusiveness and attempting to resolve social conflicts through compromise or negotiations, part of the foundations of a genuine democracy, the Alemán administration chose to exclude or marginalize those groups opposing its policies.

Driving this assault on pluralism was the neoliberal imperative of a coop-erative or pliant social sector to ensure the success of market reforms. Impor-tantly too was the desire for personal gain, a process ironically encouraged by neoliberalism which provided opportunities which state managers could exploit. Such corruption and abuse of state power within a democratic framework added to the imperative of restraining genuine pluralism. Analyzing this process of control is a crucial step toward understanding how democracy has been undone in Nicaragua. To demonstrate its thesis, this chapter is organized into four sections: the first explains the key concepts—pluralism and caudillismo—used in this analysis; the second outlines the terms of the neoliberal strategy of development advocated by Nicaragua's international creditors, the political imperatives of this model of development, and the location of civil society within it; the third discusses the campaign against civil sectors by focusing on the regime's attack on labor organizations, women's organizations, NGOs, the media, and also the role corruption played in this process; and the final section speculates briefly on democracy in Nicaragua post-Alemán.

Concepts

Pluralism

Although both the definition of civil society as well as its role in promoting democracy have long been subjects of academic debate, these topics have regained currency in the last decade in light of the prominent role played by civil society actors in ousting authoritarian regimes across the globe, and by the current significance accorded them by international institutions in promoting democratic governance. However, when social science, official development agencies, and international financial institutions rediscovered civil society, they forgot about the concept's older and more inclusive kinds: pluralism and pluralist democracy. Pluralism acknowledges the existence of divisions within society. These can be vertical, as with classes, or horizontal, as with gender; they can reinforce or cut across one another, and they can either strengthen or weaken society. Pluralist democracy demands that there be centers of independent authority outside the state and these can parallel a society's plural cleavages though they need not.

Theories of pluralism and civil society share the foregoing. They diverge, however, over what kinds of organizations to emphasize. Civil society perspectives privilege autonomous, often ad hoc, groupings such as NGOs, without links to formally organized economic or political groups. Pluralism casts its net wider. Unions, trade associations, pressure groups, political parties, the media, all of which rigorous definitions of civil society would exclude, are part of the pluralist universe. This chapter examines how Alemán dealt with pluralist groups as well as those traditionally defined as part of civil society. Because the analysis adopts a more broad-based approach, the terms "civil society" and "pluralism" are used interchangeably. All these organizations or groups regardless of their classification are vital to a well-functioning constitutional democracy and all can be very inconvenient to political leaders aspiring to the status of caudillos, free from any system of accountability.

The role of pluralist groups is not an issue of contention in this analysis though the author acknowledges that this is a highly controversial subject.[1] For purposes here it is accepted that they are an important element in fostering democratic rule and in ensuring "the health of established democracy."[2] Their importance is rooted in their twofold function, encouraging citizen participation[3] and ensuring state accountability, such as with the media.[4] In contemporary Nicaragua, both functions have been evident. The growth of pluralist organizations there, especially NGOs, largely began in the mid-80s and did not parallel the process elsewhere in the region where they emerged primarily in opposition to the state. Instead, their expansion was rooted in a deliberate campaign by the governing Sandinista National Liberation Front (FSLN) to promote grassroots democracy and to ensure support for its policies. Consequently, "the line between the state and civil society became difficult to discern."[5] Change in this relationship, however, began with the 1990 election of the National Opposition Union (UNO) under Violeta Chamorro, and the divide widened the subsequent election of Arnoldo Alemán. Ironically, as the opposition between the state and civil society intensified there was concurrently an explosion in the growth of civil sector organizations. This was due largely to the end of the Cold War and to the calls by international organizations such as the International Monetary Fund (IMF) for the inclusion of societal actors in state decision making. An added impetus has been the fact that many Sandinistas searching for an alternative to the formal party structures and perhaps even employment opportunities in the wake of their electoral loss turned to establishing their own NGOs, raising questions about the credibility and independence of these organizations from the party. Indeed the historical association between the FSLN and the NGO sector has been part of the motivation behind Alemán's campaign against the latter.

Caudillismo

Alemán's approach to governing in many respects represented a return to the age of caudillo politics. Prevalent in Latin America in the nineteenth and early twentieth centuries (and always present to varying degrees in the region's politics), caudillismo recently witnessed a revival in the form of such modern-day equivalents as Peru's Alberto Fujimori who, according to Philip Mauceri, followed a purposeful effort to weaken democratic institutions and accountability while further centralizing decision making.[6] Common to the politics of caudillismo are centralization, personalism, verticalism, oppression, corruption, patron-client bonds, and the willingness to resort to extralegal practices.[7] In his assault on Nicaraguan democracy many of these same tactics were evident in Alemán's arsenal. New in the caudillismo of Alemán and his contemporaries was that it was imposed within the frameworks of electoral democracy and of neoliberalism. Further, where old-style caudillos relied on the military and strong-arm tactics to achieve their objectives, the new caudillos opted more for the manipulation of the political and legal apparatuses of the state, such as the formation of political pacts, with only rare resort to the military or police powers. This is not surprising given the need to maintain the facade of democracy.

The Economic and Political Framework of the
New Caudillismo

Alemán's campaign against civil society and democracy is rooted in the failure of the socialist project (as evidenced by the fall of the former Soviet Union and the demise of revolutionary experiments around the globe, including Nicaragua), the exploding debt crisis in the nation (and the region), and the concomitant triumph of neoliberalism. Accompanying this victory has been the acceptance by all parties, including those at the center and even on the left, of the basic principles of the neoliberal program. Implicitly providing the groundwork for caudillo rule and the assault against pluralism have been the international lending institutions whose prescriptions for financial reforms, decentralization, and market liberalization, have created the imperative for a strong state apparatus to combat protests from below, from the sectors harmed by the economic recovery packages. At the same time these same institutions call for inclusion of the civil sectors in policy making in order to strengthen democratic governance. The IMF, for example, in its analysis of the roots of the crises within the southern economies has concluded that the problem lies, in part, in the lack of transparency and good governance. Consequently, southern governments were directed to implement policies promoting transparency and to promote best practices, including strengthening the participation of civil society in governance. The stated rationale is that empowerment of local communities will strengthen oversight of government policy, thus ensuring stability and democracy. However, as Mohan and Stokke caution, this call for local inclusion is misleading as it represents not empowerment, but rather a strategic re-envisioning of the role of the "local" to that of support mechanisms for market efficiency.[8] Further, they argue, this perspective detracts attention from "local social inequalities" and situates the "local" in isolation from broader economic and political structures.[9]

Similarly, Susanne Soederberg suggests that the IMF's "drive for increased forms of transparency symbolizes the attempts to bolster the ideological commitment of neoliberal restructuring in the global South while promoting a move toward a form of legal obligation between states."[10] In other words, by stressing surveillance requirements, the Fund aims to increase transparency, to bind states legally to play by the rules of the market, and thus avoid economic market disasters such as the 1995 Mexican peso crisis.[11] Among the transparency requirements is an enhanced role for civil society, but only insofar as this supports market efficiency.

Admittedly, while the liberalizing of Nicaragua's economy did not begin with Alemán, his government played a central role in accelerating the process, beginning with its consenting to and extending the IMF's Enhanced Structural Adjustment Fund (ESAF II) in 1998, an extension of ESAF I which had been signed by the UNO administration. These were standard economic stabilization packages applied to developing countries throughout the world. Among the policy prescriptions were calls for reductions in public-sector spending and employment, improvements in the system of tax collection, privatization of state-owned enterprises, and restrictions in credit. Admittedly as a result, some macroeconomic gains were realized, but Nicaragua's economic status remained precarious as Dye and Close have shown in this volume. By 2001, it was still Central America's most indebted nation and with one of Latin America's highest per capita debts, with over 50 percent of the national population living below the poverty line,[12] and with an unemployment rate stalled at approximately 60 percent (a problem aggravated by the dismissal of almost 5,000 state workers during Alemán's tenure).[13] The process of wealth concentration was accelerated as those who could not service their debts (primarily campesinos, owners of cooperatives, small farmers, and businesspersons) were compelled to sell their holdings to larger operations at drastically reduced prices. It was reported that agricultural cooperatives declined by almost 90 percent between 1990 and 1999, from 3,800 to 400.[14] At the same time, the allocation of state resources continued to favor large-scale enterprises to the detriment of small farms and businesses.

Given the social costs accompanying the restructuring, it was critical to the program's success that there be a strong state to contain social mobilization. Hence the ground was prepared for the emergence of the new caudillos. This is particularly crucial in the Nicaraguan context given the nation's history of revolutionary social mobilization. Important to the strengthening of the state was the deal forged through the signing of the Liberal-Sandinista Pact (El Pacto)[15] between Alemán and Daniel Ortega, leader of revolutionary FSLN. The Pact, discussed in more detail by Hoyt in this volume, was a deal between the two leaders to guarantee that they and their parties retained power. It also enshrined the centralization of power through constitutional amendments and through the politicization and corruption of electoral, judicial, and other state institutions. Further, it has eliminated diversity in political expression, suffocated the institutions responsible for ensuring state accountability, and marginalized citizen participation in the political process.

In light of the FSLN's historical ties with civil society organizations, this Pact was a strategic move for the Alemán regime. It meant that the government would have the implicit and explicit consent of the FSLN in its control of civil activism, regardless of the impact on these groups of the economic hardships of neoliberalism. Commenting on the convergence in the political position between the two men, one critic observed that Alemán and Ortega must confuse themselves in the mirror, not knowing who is the man and who the reflection as both symbolize the new Somocismo.[16]

Pluralism under Attack

The Facade of Inclusiveness

The campaign against the various social sectors was innovative in that it involved what seemed to be concessions to or even inclusion of the "local." These, however, were only at the level of rhetoric and formal institution building and were geared to winning the approval of international creditors. In policy formulation, for example, the president sometimes consulted with societal groups as was the case in June 1997, his first year in office. Responding to a series of national strikes which brought the economy to a halt and which exposed the gaping polarization within the nation, he initiated a National Dialogue which included representatives from civil society. The process, however, was denounced because of its limited input from below. Detractors pointed out that the government had five representatives, each legal political party had two each, and the rest of civil society was represented by only two persons. Further, they charged, the government turned a deaf ear to the concerns of the civil sector and that the "dialogue" was a show for the international financial institutions concerned about the country's lack of political stability and thus its suitability for aid and investments.[17] A similar response greeted the establishment of the National Council of Economic and Social Planning which was created as part of the government's signing on to the Stockholm Declaration, an agreement designed to foster dialogue among civil society, government, and the international community.[18]

Still aiming to win the approval of the international lenders and donors, the administration also adopted several institutional frameworks to demonstrate its commitment to transparent governance. In 1999, it ratified the Inter-American Convention Against Corruption and established an Anti-Corruption Commission, in effect an officially created NGO headed by then vice president Enrique Bolaños, and which also included representation from other state agencies as well as the Catholic Church and civil society. Its mandate was to promote integrity in governance and its approach was to organize National Integrity Workshops funded by the World Bank Institute. Given the rampant corruption scandals which plagued the regime and the fact that Alemán himself is now under indictment for corruption, it is obvious that this agency was basically impotent in promoting its mandate. As the director of the Americas' Accountability/Anticorruption Project (AAA) cynically observed, "'the corruption eruption and the anti-corruption eruption' are both trends sweeping the region."[19]

Undermining Labor Protections

While at the level of rhetoric, as seen above, the administration practiced a version of "inclusion" to contain social mobilization, more favored strategies, such as those against labor, involved the use of force, manipulation of legislation, and collusion with employers. Largely driving the official approach to dealing with labor unrest was the neoliberal requirement for a quiescent workforce. A second motivation, however, and one described by Cuadra was the authoritarian perception held by the regime that all social conflicts were illegitimate and threatened the nation's stability. Based on this line of reasoning, such threats must therefore be forcibly suppressed.

It can be said that the relationship between the Alemán government and pluralist groups was encapsulated in the long list of protests and strikes[20] against the regime, the first within just a hundred days of its being in office. The common thread linking these actions, be they by workers, producers, or students, was the hardship resulting from both the austerity package imposed as part of the debt reduction strategy (and this link often meant that supporters of different political ilk were united in their opposition to the regime) and from the corruption within the regime. A few of these strikes were eventually settled, some after lengthy periods. The majority, however, either resulted in violence, or in attempts by the administration to criminalize strike activities, or they were dismissed as illegal. Among the first of the strikes[21] during the Alemán presidency was that organized in April 1997 by the National Union of Farmers and Ranchers (UNAG) and several other agricultural groups, to demand government assistance in alleviating the economic burdens of falling incomes, rising costs, and escalating debts. The fate of coffee producers is illustrative of the hardships faced by this sector. Their livelihoods were devastated by the dramatic decline in the global price of their commodity which was brought on by the recovery of Brazilian coffee production after its destruction by frost, the increased competition from new producers such as Vietnam, and crop loss due to droughts, floods, and later Hurricane Mitch. Worst affected were the landless farmers. Estimated at between 10 and 20 percent of the rural population, and among the nation's poorest, they were completely reliant on larger, wealthier farmers for their employment and their survival. Deprived of work and income, their situation was worsened by the rising food costs and the market reforms which called for the state to retreat from providing social services.

The plight of the farmers and rural workers resonated with thousands of others who joined their strike in solidarity. These included government employees facing layoffs, small farmers fearing abrogation of their land titles (granted during the FSLN and Chamorro years), transport workers fearing privatization of their industry, small property owners dealing with debts and rising costs, the unemployed, and many others who opposed the government's free-market program. Estimates placed the number of protesters from 5,000 to 10,000. During the course of the strike, a few hundred protesters built barricades from paving stones, tree trunks, old buses, and burning tires at dozens of points along the highways leading into the major cities. In addition to Managua, cities in the departments of Leon, Matagalpa, Boaco, Estelí, Jinotega, and Masaya were all targeted with blockades. An interesting dimension of this strike, as with many later ones, was that protesters came from a number of political groups, and were not just FSLN supporters, as the government frequently claimed. As observers noted, it was the Nicaraguan flag that they carried, not the FSLN banner.

The government threatened to use the police against the strikers but countermanded the order after UNAG threatened that it would intensify its activities if force were used. In light of mounting financial costs, as well as food and fuel shortages, the government could not afford an escalation in strike activities. A compromise was negotiated with the FSLN (which then called off the strike) whereby the government committed to introducing legislation limiting public sector layoffs (to 3,000 instead of the original 14,000, though about 5,000 were eventually let go) and to suspend for three months campesino evictions from disputed lands. Additionally, there were agreements to set up a bilateral group to negotiate the bank debts of producers (a critical issue in the strike) and to establish several other commissions to address other issues of contention. However, approximately two months later, once the crisis had abated, the government flexed its muscles and introduced legislation designed to preempt future strike action by criminalizing certain types of strikes and protests. It amended the penal code to allow for fines and even jail terms for protests that involved roadblocks or gatherings "in a tumultuous manner in clear challenge to authority."[22] According to Sandinista deputy Victor Hugo Tinoco, with this bill the government not only revealed its repressive nature, but it was also "making prisoners" of those segments of the population most detrimentally affected by the social and economic crisis.[23] The legislative apparatus of the state was used to undermine democracy. A second major strike that illustrates the regime's willingness to use force to subdue labor was the April 1999 Managua transport workers' dispute (which was also joined by students protesting cutbacks in university funding). This struggle grew from the government's plans to privatize the industry and to eliminate fuel subsidies. When negotiations failed, over 10,000 trucks blocked highways across the country. The president's response was to send the army in against the striking civilians and to threaten to arrest, sue, or imprison strikers. In the resulting showdown, marked by sixty days of confrontation, several demonstrators were wounded and over a dozen arrested. In an interview with *Confidencial*, the then head of the military, General Joaquín Cuadra Lacayo, stated that he advised the president against such a move. However, Alemán and the hardliners surrounding him advocated the more forceful option, arguing that it was within the law and the only way to control the protesters. [24]

The conclusion came with the government's agreement to shelve its privatization plans, roll back the price of diesel fuel, and increase the university budget. That concessions were granted may seem surprising in light of the government's overall attitude to labor, but it becomes less so when placed in context. The administration was scheduled to meet with Nicaragua's international creditors in May (just weeks before the strike ended) to discuss disaster relief for victims of Hurricane Mitch. It was the fear that a massive and ongoing labor dispute would be viewed unfavorably by foreign donors that impelled the government to settle, not recognition of the legitimacy of the strike demands.

Manipulation of the labor code, especially as it pertains to workers in the free trade zones (FTZs) has been another favorite tactic of the regime to undermine labor rights. Under the articles of the Nicaraguan Constitution, particularly in the new labor code which took effect in 1996 (replacing the code of 1944) workers have a protected right to organize, form unions, and strike. However, before a strike can be deemed legal, unions must follow several predetermined steps, which would require approximately six months of completing according to the Labor Ministry's own estimate. For critics, the process is excessively onerous and lengthy, and precludes many legitimate strikes.[25] To meet the standards of a legal work stoppage, among other stipulations of the code, a union's strike call must receive the approval of the Labor Ministry and the endorsement of a majority of all the workers in the enterprise. To secure the Ministry's approval, however, the union must first have undertaken what the Ministry determines to be good faith bargaining with management to avoid the strike. The requirement that a strike action receive the vote of a majority of the workers in the plant, while seemingly logical, is a challenging process stacked against workers as many enterprises have competing unions existing simultaneously. While this may be seen as enhancing plurality, it also undermines the independence of the union movement as employers often dominate one union and can sign separate agreements with the different unions. In such instances, the difficulty of getting a majority of workers in an enterprise to vote for strike action becomes evident. Compounding the problem for workers is the fact that many, especially those in the FTZs are not even aware of the rights they do have.[26]

The demanding and complex nature of the strike terms have meant that between 1996 and 2001, only three of the many strikes which have taken place have been deemed legal. And, though the labor code prohibits any retaliation against strikers or the union leaders, these protections are withdrawn if a strike does not meet the standards for legality. Under these conditions, workers and union organizers can then be fired, and they often are.

Furthermore, strikes are preempted by mechanisms in place to control union organization and leadership. The code prohibits union leaders from being fired, but companies can easily bypass this restriction if they can show just cause to the Labor Ministry, and rare is the occasion when the state does not concur with the business's decision. This practice is particularly evident in the FTZs to where many of the Ministry's own lawyers have moved in search of more lucrative rewards. Familiar with the workings of the Ministry they are adept at manipulating the language of the legislation to meet Ministry's standards. One of the most disturbing failings in the code from the employee's perspective is that it permits the dismissal of any worker, including union leaders and members, providing the employee is paid double the normal severance to which he/she is entitled. This loophole has been extensively and successfully exploited to block union organization and is one the factors accounting for the steady decline in union membership. Eliminating payroll deductions for union dues has been another strategy tried by the government to undermine unions and this has been attempted not just in the private sector but also the public sector unions such as the National Association of Educators of Nicaragua (ANDEN) and the Federation of Health Workers (FETSALUD).

As noted above, the campaign against labor is particularly explicit in the FTZs, the symbols of market dominance and of Nicaragua's commitment to eliminating barriers to trade and investment. According to one critic of the *zonas francas*, Nicaragua is a nation where workers are vulnerable and where the government is complicit in deepening this vulnerability[27] in the interest of international investors from Taiwan, Japan, the United States, and elsewhere. Many of the major companies in the FTZs were accused of violating workers' rights regarding such guarantees as freedom of association, collective bargaining, and the prohibition against forced labor.[28] Workers claimed that they were coerced into renouncing their union membership with threats of dismissal.[29] Companies countered that the dismissals were based on their failure to fulfill their employment duties.[30] Strikes to combat labor code violations were usually deemed illegal by the companies and strikers were frequently fired, with union leaders especially targeted. Complaints by workers to the Ministry of Labor (MITRAB) inevitably resulted in the latter siding with the corporations and ruling the strikes illegal.[31] Once a strike has been deemed illegal the company is then within its legal rights to fire the striking workers.

The workers' struggle at Chentex Garments, a subsidiary of the Taiwanese giant Nien Hsing Consortium, and one of the biggest investors in the Las Mercedes Free Trade Zone (employing approximately 200 people, mostly single women), graphically illustrates managements' repressive tactics. In April 2000 the Sandinista Workers Central (CST) sought permission from MITRAB to initiate strike action against the company on the grounds that the company failed to respect the terms of the collective agreement relating to increase in the minimum wage, and that negotiations failed to address the issue satisfactorily. Reportedly, approximately fifty workers took part in the strike. Management responded, with MITRAB's approval, by firing eleven of thirteen union board members on the grounds that they had participated in an illegal work stoppage,[32] a decision later upheld by a labor court.[33] The company then tried to decertify the union, arguing that with the firings, the union no longer met minimum membership requirements. While there was some further "to and fro" on the issue with some rehirings (based on a later appellate court ruling and pressure from the International Labor Organization), some resignations of rehired workers (who argued that their presence was not welcomed by the opposing union, the Confederation of Nicaraguan Workers [CTN] believed to be employer controlled), and further firings (some with severance packages), in the end the CST lost its status at the factory due to its inadequate membership. The company's argument was that workers were leaving voluntarily in order to take advantage of the severance package (a claim scoffed at by labor and human rights activists in light of the staggering unemployment rate in the country). It is interesting to note here that the Taiwanese government is a significant aid donor to Nicaragua, apparently an expression of gratitude for the country having supported its readmission to the United Nations.[34] In addition, Taiwanese money is reportedly responsible for financing the building of Alemán's office as well as the complex for the Foreign Ministry.[35]

A similar situation as with Chentex's prevailed throughout 2000 at the Mil Colores textile factory. Here again MITRAB voted with the company, acquiescing to the request to fire fifty workers as part of a cost-cutting measure. Interestingly, among those dismissed were twenty-four of thirty-six workers who had sought recognition for the CST at the factory.[36] At the same time, the Ministry denied the workers' request for union certification arguing that with the firings, the union lacked the requisite membership.[37] This situation turned violent as workers accused the company and the Ministry of collusion. They charged that the company had backdated the dismissal request to indicate that approval for this measure was sought prior to the workers' request for unionization. In the ensuing conflict between police and protesters over two dozen people were injured and several arrested. As with Chentex, while some rehiring eventually took place and the union was certified, by the end of the year several of the workers had "resigned" and the CST lost its union status at the factory.

Another antilabor tactic practiced by employers in the FTZs, with the support of the government, is to threaten plant closure. This is a strategy used particularly against workers considering unionization, and it often has the implicit support of the government.[38] Citing weak economic performance, the company would argue that the situation has made it impossible for it to maintain its contractual commitments to labor and that survival of the enterprise demands that workers take a salary cut. According to Article 45 of the labor code, plans to dismiss workers based on the company's inability to maintain them must be reported to MITRAB. In 2001, workers at Chentex and Chu Sing Garment, (another company in the FTZ) were led to believe that plant closure was imminent due to economic downturn (and according to the code under these circumstances they would not be entitled to severance pay). To add credence to claims of impending closure, Chentex even implored its labor force to demonstrate in its support and demand that the government prevent the closure. Meanwhile MITRAB confessed to the media that none of the businesses had actually approached the Ministry about plant closures, only that they were studying the possibility of reducing the workers' contracts to ensure economic survival. Many workers, however, charged that failure to participate in this show demonstration would have resulted in their being fired.[39] Of course, as women form a large sector of the workforce in the FTZs, they are the ones who suffered most under these repressive labor tactics.

Undermining Women's Rights

Women were also targeted in more direct ways as the regime tried to roll back earlier political gains they had made. The developmental paradigm endorsed by the Alemán administration prescribed a particular role for women, one designed to return them to the more traditional and private spheres—a strategy begun under the Chamorro administration and one influenced strongly by the Roman Catholic Church led by Cardinal Obando y Bravo. Relegating women to the realm of the private absolves the states of many responsibilities—including employment and childcare. The approach combined legislation with religion to frame women's roles in terms of family values and tradition, that is, in terms of their functions as wife and mother. The establishment of the Ministry of the Family is the institutional manifestation of this strategy. As the former first lady stated in a speech before the UN General Assembly session on "Beijing+5," the Ministry's mandate was to protect the institution of the family, defined as the nuclear family and deemed the core of society.[40] Within this framework, the role of women was to strengthen the family (by procreating) in order to strengthen society.[41] This articulation of women's role narrows the definition of what constitutes "a family" and perfectly mirrors the Catholic Church's teachings. However, it bears little resemblance to the Nicaraguan reality with its varied family structures where divorce, common-law relationships, single mothers, and homosexual relationships are all commonplace. Furthermore, while the law prescribes the appropriate role for women, it fails to address issues of pressing importance to them such as domestic violence, poverty, maternal mortality, and a crumbling social infrastructure, particularly in the areas of health and education.

This traditional interpretation also has implications for the state's approach to women's reproductive rights. Theoretically, the law does allow for therapeutic abortions. Reforms to the penal code, however, have tightened the restrictions permitting abortions only when medically vital as determined by no less than three doctors. Critics have denounced this policy on many fronts, one being that conditions such as rape, incest, or malformation of the fetus are not deemed acceptable grounds for termination. Another is that it penalizes poor women, many of whom live in rural areas with access to no doctors, or at best one. Furthermore, their poverty precludes their being able to consult even with one doctor, assuming geography was not a problem.[42]

Problematic too is that while, on the one hand, this legislation seemingly does provide a limited opening for abortion rights, on the other it seems to exclude them completely because the law also threatens all medical personnel practicing abortions with imprisonment, loss of license, and closure of their clinics.[43] The harassment of *Si Mujer,* an NGO working in the area of women's health, and which is discussed by Kampwirth, provides vivid evidence of this and it also demonstrates that even when the evidence is lacking, medical personnel can be menaced by the authorities.

Controlling NGOs

The *Sí Mujer* example points to another dimension of the government's attack on democracy and civil society—its attempts to control NGOs. Since the economic agenda of the state demands its retreat from the social sphere, from programs and services relied upon by the lower sectors, it therefore fell to the voluntary agencies to fill the consequent void. Not surprisingly, as economic conditions worsened there was a significant increase in the number of NGOs,[44] especially those working with women and children. They were the voice of the underclass and, along with other nonstate institutions such as the media, served the role of unofficial opposition to the government as the official opposition party was compromised through its pacted relationship with the governing administration. However, though NGOs are vocal opponents of free-market policies, their growing numbers and their expanding fields of work among the poor unintentionally assist the neoliberal state by relieving it of many of its social responsibilities. Their work also contributes to a reduction in social tensions as these are likely to occur if social problems remain unattended. As such, one would expect the state to encourage NGO activities. Certainly in the more developed liberal democratic states there has been a great push to promote the voluntary sector.

However, while the Alemán government recognized the benefits accruing to it from the existence of the NGO sector (and hence its calls for consultations with it), it nevertheless viewed this sector predominantly with hostility, seeing it as an ideological opponent to be subordinated and rendered ineffective. Also, as many NGOs are linked to the progressive sectors, work with women, and are active lobbyists for women's rights, they were deemed threatening to the state's (and by extension the Church's) vision of society, the family, and the role of women within these. Further, the anti-NGO campaign was also likely rooted in partisan politics, given the historical ties between the NGO community and the FSLN. Finally, attacking the NGO community by accusing them of corruption or of undermining Nicaragua's social mores (such as by promoting women's rights) deflected attention from the problems of corruption within the state and also the government's inability to address the nation's many desperate problems.

The government used a familiar tactic, namely legal, passing legislation to ensure state oversight of their activities. Organizations working with women and children were required to obtain the approval of the Ministry of the Family, an agency strongly linked to the Roman Catholic hierarchy. Other types of NGOs had to register with the Ministry of Governance, which also is responsible for prisons and the police. The implication here is that they are in some way a threat to the social order and hence must be monitored. NGOs soliciting funds abroad had to get the permission of the Ministry of External Cooperation. As it did with other organizational critics such as the media, the state also practiced a strategy which came to be known as "fiscal terrorism" against NGOs whereby they were financially harassed by being subjected to taxation (even on aid for humanitarian assistance) and other forms of monetary pressures. By obstructing their access to resources, the administration hoped to undermine their effectiveness, and thus their legitimacy among the population. An added dimension of this strategy was the stipulation that NGOs must give evidence of being self-sustaining; they must raise matching funds domestically for those coming in from international agencies. Realistically, given Nicaragua's poverty, it would be virtually impossible for NGOs to meet this criterion.

Not only did the administration try to limit the ideological space and the financial support of independent NGOs or those with FSLN affiliation, but it also ensured that its own ideological message was being transmitted by encouraging the formation of NGOs loyal to the Liberal Party. Admittedly this was not official policy but rather unofficial practice. This strategy reflects the perception by the administration that NGOs are among its political competitors and therefore must be checked where possible. Just as an alternative vision must be advanced to counter that of an opposing political party so too must one be presented to challenge the NGOs.

Many bureaucrats, former government ministers, party deputies, and activists, along with the president's daughter, María Dolores Alemán,[45] as well as the Catholic Church, all established their own NGOs, with the objective, according to Ms. Alemán, of taking "the ideological struggle to the level of civil society," and to compete with the pro-Sandinista voluntary sector.[46] Ms. Alemán, who was first lady[47] at the time of Mitch, was then the conduit through which hundreds of thousands of dollars of international aid funds flowed. In this position, she gained extensive insights into foreign donors' preferences, observing their partiality toward the voluntary organizations over a scandal-plagued government. Capitalizing on this insight and on the growing credibility and expansion of the NGO sector, Ms. Alemán and others created their own opportunistic organizations as a lucrative means of tapping into the international aid dollars. Adopting the language of the established NGOs, all the newly formed organizations declared themselves to be without political motivations and to be working in the interest of women, children, or the poor (the target groups of international donor aid). Endowing themselves with progressive-sounding titles such as the Women's Association for Peace and Development and the Foundation for Economic and Social Development, they ensured that they would have the same credibility and legitimacy as their more progressive counterparts. For the average Nicaraguan who may have depended on the services of NGOs, and for international donors for that matter, the differences between the two groups then were not immediately obvious as they were both using a similar vocabulary. Their political agenda, of course, differed dramatically.

One of the telling features of the Liberal-affiliated NGOs was their disregard for the requirement that they have legal recognition. When questioned about this they responded that the juridical standing of the organization was irrelevant as long as the NGO was committed to building civil society, to helping those in need and not caught up in political or bureaucratic competition.[48] Rationalization aside, the fact is that not seeking legal standing placed them beyond governmental supervision. At the same time, and to no one's surprise, the state did not seem particularly concerned with enforcing the legislation as far as these particular NGOs were concerned.

This lack of accountability, combined with the mercenary nature of these organizations, reflected the endemic corruption within the regime. Furthermore, the entire approach to the NGO sector demonstrated the government's strategy of suffocating genuine pluralism. This strategy was again in evidence in its treatment of the media.

Controlling the Media

A free press is critical to a true democracy. It is one of the instruments promoting transparency and accountability within the state. In performing these functions the Nicaraguan media brought to light a mind-numbing array of corruption allegations against the government. Like the NGOs, the media too found themselves serving in the role of surrogate political opposition, given the relationship engendered between the FSLN and the PLC by the Pact and the overall weakness of the party system within the state. As a consequence, they faced vehement retaliations—legal reprisals, financial penalties, and personal harassments. Unlike the approach used against labor unrest, which involved invoking police powers against the media, it was primarily judicial and administrative forms of coercion. Nevertheless, the tactics were no less repressive, and the objectives were similar—to silence opponents.

Additionally, against the media, the motivation to limit their powers also had a personal dimension. News organizations were not only critical of the types of public policy being implemented, but they were also accusing the leader directly of corruption. Hence, by trying to delegitimize them or by making their operations difficult, the Alemán regime was also ensuring that its neopatrimonial practices would be unhindered by media oversight.

Foremost among the challenges to press freedom was legislation adopted in 2000 to regulate the profession of journalism. Among its requirements, the law called for the establishment of a national professional guild to which all journalists must belong in order to gain professional certification. Those caught working without appropriate credentials would be subject to fines or imprisonment. The legislation left ill-defined the government's role in controlling such an association in determining the criteria for professional licensing and in setting salaries, but implied that it would have some role. Another stipulation concerned the guarantee of minimum wages for print, radio, and television journalists. While this can be interpreted as advancing workers' rights, it was really a Machiavellian strategy to close many media outlets, as the smaller ones would not be able to meet such added costs.

Coming on the heels of a series of damaging media exposés of government corruption, this legislation with its calls for increased government intervention in the profession, represented a deliberate assault on press freedom and on the principles of democracy. The law contravened various international legal instruments, including the Declaration of Principles on Freedom of Expression as outlined by the Inter-American Commission on Human Rights, which specifies that membership in any such association cannot be made compulsory.[49] In the end, the guild was never established. Nevertheless the passage of the legislation demonstrated how far the administration was willing to go to control media critical of its activities.

Another stratagem against press freedom was the same "fiscal terrorism" used against NGOs. In the case of the media, it entailed financial audits, on the grounds that these were necessary to ensure the organizations' compliance with the nation's tax laws. Nevertheless, only independent media were scrutinized, not the government-controlled outlets.[50] *El Nuevo Diario*, the left-leaning daily which spearheaded many of the corruption revelations, became the target of a tax audit by the national revenue agency (Dirección General de Ingresos—DGI). So too did its more conservative competitor, *La Prensa*, which also played an energetic role in reporting government malfeasance. As a consequence of the audit, the DGI accused the latter of failing to pay over six million córdobas in taxes.[51] *La Prensa* countered that the charge was politically motivated, driven by its revelations about the corruption within the DGI (the paper had helped oust the DGI's previous head, Byron Jerez, by revealing his abuse of office for financial gain). In a similar vein, Channel 2, the country's largest television station, which had done several exposés on corruption, was also the object of a tax audit and became entangled in a confrontation with the DGI over alleged nonpayment of employees' social security fees.[52] The independent media complained that the audits not only hindered their operations and made it difficult for them to purchase necessary equipment and supplies from abroad, but the aim behind them was to intimidate the press and limit its freedom.[53]

Aside from legislative and financial machinations, there were also more direct methods of intimidation, reminiscent of the traditional caudillos. One of the more prominent cases involved the journalist Eloísa Ibarra of *El Nuevo Diario*. The situation began while journalists were questioning the president about the various corruption allegations. Angered by the nature of the interview, Alemán approached Ibarra, grabbed her forcefully, pushed her, and shouted at her to stop questioning him. The personal dimension of the assault was shocking. Press personnel from across the country, along with a host of organizations representing workers, women, and others, joined in denouncing his actions. For women's groups, the attack was not only against freedom of the press, but also against women's rights. As public outrage against the president mounted, Ibarra reported that she feared for her and her family's safety as she believed the regime would find some way to retaliate against her.[54] While no harm came to Ibarra, Alemán's actions showed not only his lack of regard for one of the fundamental institutions of a democracy, but the vehemence and personal nature of the attack confirmed the popular perception that he thought himself above the law, a strongman accountable to none. Commenting on the president's onslaught against the press, Hugo Holmann Chamorro, one of the editors of *La Prensa*, wrote that the campaign against press freedom has ensured that the Alemán era has been one of the worst in the newspaper's seventy-five-year history (even taking into consideration the Somoza murder of his uncle and former editor of the paper, Pedro Chamorro).[55]

Corruption and the Assault on Pluralism

As alluded to throughout this paper, one of the most disturbing features of the Alemán administration was the pandemic corruption which scarred it from the top down. This too had severe implications for civil society and democracy. As Mitchell Seligson found in his survey of four Latin American countries, including Nicaragua, corruption breeds distrust among the citizenry, undermines the legitimacy of the political system, and thus subverts democracy.[56] Political participation is undermined as citizens become alienated from the system, believing that the corruption is so deeply rooted that they are unable to effect change. This theme of corruption and its harm to democracy was echoed in 2001 by Latin American and Caribbean heads of state and governments who asserted that "corruption undermines core democratic values."[57]

The plague of corruption within the Alemán regime was in part related to the very processes of development which are being encouraged by international creditors. The emphasis on privatization and liberalization sets in place the conditions for the rise of official misconduct. The sale of the state-owned Nicaraguan Bank of Industry and Commerce (BANIC), a move encouraged by the World Bank, serves as a good example of the manipulation by the ruling elites of the privatization process. Comptroller General Agustin Jarquín charged that this sale was fraught with irregularities. Supposedly, BANIC was sold to a bank based in Florida, but according to Jarquín's allegations, the owners of the Florida enterprise were actually BANIC executives acting under pseudonyms, and Alemán and members of his family gained favors and benefits for supporting the sale.[58]

The list of corruption charges by the comptroller general did not end here. However, this analysis does not seek to detail them all as they are discussed in length in various chapters throughout. The objective is to demonstrate that corruption weakens civil society and pluralism and thus weakens democracy as it leads to a citizenry "disaffected" by the system. According to one poll conducted on the corruption question, 77 percent of Nicaraguans expressed doubts about Alemán's integrity[59] and another revealed that 85.6 percent believed that the corruption had had an impact on them.[60] Corruption undermines civil society in a variety of ways. With state resources directed toward private accumulation by state managers, the public interest and hence democracy is undermined. Furthermore, corruption directly affects people's livelihoods through its impact on the economy. Economists have often warned that corruption "increases transaction costs, reduces investment incentives, and ultimately results in reduced economic growth."[61] As the vice president of UNAG, the farmers' and ranchers' union, complained, state corruption and the national obsession with it meant that attention had been detracted from the very critical problems facing the country, such as the crisis facing farmers—their growing impoverishment, their lack of access to credit, and the loss of confidence of international investors who had been adopting a wait-and-see approach in light of the various scandals rocking the country.[62] The deepening economic crisis in turn could negatively affect political participation as citizens concentrate on meeting immediate survival needs.

One infrequently discussed impact of corruption on civil society is its corruption of civil society. As James Mittelman and Robertson Johnston observed, the theoretical claims in support of a strong society is that it is a countervailing force to state power, however, "the very idea of civil society is becoming corrupted, torn away from the theories that spawned it."[63] What is becoming increasingly evident is that an array of players, including both public entities (state and interstate agencies) and private organizations, "seek to develop civil society, to appropriate not only the concept but also the real activities juxtaposed to the public sphere."[64] To see the relevance of this to the Nicaraguan context, reference can be made to the earlier section of this analysis which discussed attempts by various actors within the state apparatus to establish their own NGOs to take the ideological battle to the level of civil society and to the international agencies which stress the development of civil society, yet who promote policies antithetical to this objective.

Conclusion

The hallmark of a healthy democracy is the existence of genuine pluralism, a healthy civil sector free to challenge executive authority within the allowed legal channels, and an executive accountable to the people and transparent in its conduct of the state's business. This fundamental principle was consistently undermined in Nicaragua under Alemán. The assault on pluralism engineered within the context of electoralism was perpetrated by governing strategies consistent with caudillo rule—centralization of authority, manipulation of the legislative and judicial processes, exploitation of state agencies, and harassment and intimidation of critics.

The underlying objectives of this challenge to Nicaraguan democracy was to ensure the personal accumulation of Alemán and his cohorts, as well as to guarantee the smooth implementation of market liberalization. The result, of course, was that the democratic project in Nicaragua suffered a serious setback. It is now up to the new administration of Enrique Bolaños to ensure that the fragile democratic foundations are strengthened. Given that Bolaños, too, and all foreseeable administration will have to face the demands from international creditors for greater market liberalization, the fate of Nicaraguan democracy is open to question. Nevertheless, any administration in which personal greed and corruption are not its hallmarks will be an advance on that of Arnoldo Alemán.

Notes

1. While it is generally accepted that societal groups played a positive role in the democratization process, there is also a more dangerous side to its activities, though analyzing this dimension is not part of the objective here. Examples of such groups, as Richard and Booth point out, could be the Ku Klux Klan in the United States and, in light of the 11 September 2001 attack on the World Trade Center, extremist religious organizations such as Osama bin Laden's Al Qaeda. See Patricia Bayer Richard and John A. Booth, "Civil Society and Democratic Transition," in Thomas Walker and Ariel C. Harmony, eds., *Repression, Resistance and Democratic Transition in Central America* (Wilmington, DE: Scholarly Resources Inc., 2000), 235.

2. Michael Foley and Bob Edwards, "The Paradox of Civil Society," *Journal of Democracy* 7, no. 3 (July 1996): 38.

3. William A. Galston, "Civil Society and the 'Art of Association,'" *Journal of Democracy* 11, no. 1 (January 2000): 68.

4. Foley and Edwards, "The Paradox of Civil Society," p. 38. Their analysis makes a distinction between these two functions and argue that several implications follow from this difference, among them, the types of organizations which can be classified as part of the civil sector.

5. Christina Ewig, "The Strengths and Limits of the NGO Women's Movement Model: Shaping Nicaragua's Democratic Institutions," *Latin American Research Review* 34, no. 3 (1999): 75-102.

6. Philip Mauceri, "Return of the caudillo: Autocratic Democracy in Peru," *Third World Quarterly* 18, no. 5 (December 1997): 900.

7. For a study of caudillismo, see John Lynch, *Caudillos in Spanish America, 1880-1850* (New York: Oxford University Press, 1992).

8. Giles Mohan and Kristian Stokke, "Participatory Development and Empowerment: The Dangers of Localism," *Third World Quarterly* 21, no. 2 (April 2000): 251.

9. Mohan and Stokke, "Participatory Development," 251.

10. Susanne Soederberg, "Grafting Stability onto Globalisation? Deconstructing the IMF's recent Bid for Transparency," *Third World Quarterly* 22, no. 5 (October 2001): 856.

11. Soederberg, "Grafting Stability onto Globalisation?" 850.

12. See UNDP, *Human Development Report, 2001* and World Bank Group, *World Development Indicators Database 2002* Inweb18.worldbank.org.

13. Katherine Isbester, "Nicaragua 1996-2001: Sex, Corruption, and Other Natural Disasters," *International Journal* 56, no. 4 (Autumn 2001): 638.

14. *Envío*, July 1999, 10.

15. El Pacto entailed a series of seventeen amendments to the articles of the Nicaraguan constitution. Some of these changes include: the expansion of the Supreme Court from twelve to sixteen judges; the substitution of a single comptroller general with the five-person body empowered with the authority to investigate financial or other charges of wrongdoing by government officials; the guarantee that the outgoing president and vice president automatically receive a seat in the National Assembly; the requirement that the voting criteria for removing presidential immunity be two-thirds, rather than the previous qualified majority; and changes in the types of requirements a presidential candidate must adhere to in order to preclude a second run-off election. Importantly too, the amendments state that in order for a party to maintain its legal status, it must receive at least 4 percent of the vote in a general election.

16. Mario Mairena Martinez, "Alemán y Ortega se confunder en el espejo," *El Nuevo Diario*, May 11, 2000.

17. *Weekly News Update*, June 7, 1997.

18. This body was created in response to the 1999 Stockholm Declaration which stemmed from a meeting of the Consultative Group for the Reconstruction and Transformation of Central America (CG). The Stockholm Declaration mandated the governments of the region to promote "good governance and social development."

19. Quoted in Transparency International, *Global Corruption Report 2001*, p. 162. www.globalcorruptionreport.org.

20. Among the strikes were an FSLN-led national strike (April 1997) to denounce property and economic austerity measures; a farmers' and ranchers' strike (April 1997) called to demand support for the economic hardships of agricultural producers and workers; a student strike (May 1997 and again in May 1999) to force the government to abide by its constitutional obligations regarding funding for education; a bus strike (August 1997) to protest against salary freezes and minimum wages which were far below the cost of living; a health workers' strike (February 1998) to demand job security; a four-month-long doctors' strike (April-July 1998) to demand better wages; a banana workers' strike (October 1998) against wage freezes; a truckers' strike (May 1999) to fight back against the increase in fuel costs and against plans to deregulate the industry; a coffee producers' strike (April 2001) to draw attention to the hardships endured by this sector due to falling coffee prices; and a transport workers' strike (June 2001), to protest against privatization plans and the decision to eliminate gas subsidies. Among other things, what this list of strike action eloquently communicates is the polarization between the state and society in Nicaragua.

21. Recall that the first strike was that which the FSLN had called earlier in April, (and one which lasted five days) to protest against the government's socioeconomic policies.

22. Quoted in Toby Mailman, "Anti-Protest Bill Recalls Somoza's Regime," *Weekly News Update*, June 7, 1997.

23. Quoted in Mailman, "Anti-Protest Bill Recalls Somoza's Regime."

24. Quoted in Oliver Bodán, "En el filo de la navaja," *Confidencial*, no. 179 (February 13-19, 2000).

25. This assessment of the labor code is based on the reports of the U.S. State Department. See specifically, U.S. Department of State, *Country Reports on Human Rights Practices (2001): Nicaragua*, (Section 6a), March 2002, www.state.gove/g/drl/rls/hrrpt/2001/wha/8315.htm.

26. Some unions such as the Nicaraguan Public Services Trade Union (UNE) is offering legal training on the labor code, a program funded by some British unions.

27. Quoted in Joaquín Tórrez A. "Gobierno es culpable de violaciones 'maquiladas,'" *La Prensa*, February 16, 2001.

28. Milagros Sanchez and Gabriela Roa, "CST pedirá suspensión de nueve maquiladoras," *La Prensa*, December 15, 2001.

29. Janelys Carillo Barrios and Gabriela Roa, "Chentex inica negociación," *La Prensa,* April 18, 2001.

30. Carillo Barrios and Roa, *La Prensa*, April 18, 2001.

31. Gabriela Roa, "Situación laboral con altos y bajos," *La Prensa*, November 16, 2001.

32. U.S. Department of State, *Country Reports on Human Rights Practices (2001): Nicaragua* (Section 6b) March 2002, www.state.gove/g/drl/rls/hrrpt/2001/wha/8315.htm.

33. In August of 2001, the company, along with two others, requested permission from MITRAB to dismiss 800 workers arguing that this step is necessary due to economic slowdown. See Gabriela Roa Romero and Mariela Ocán Rodriguez, "Denuncian cierre de tres maquiladoras," *El Nuevo Diario*, August 21, 2001.

34. David Gonzalez, "Nicaragua's Trade Zone: Battleground for Unions," *New York Times* (electronic version), September 16, 2000.

35. Gonzalez, "Nicaragua's Trade Zone," *New York Times*.

36. U.S. Department of State, *Country Reports on Human Rights Practices* (section 6b).

37. U.S. Department of State, *Country Reports on Human Rights Practices* (section 6b).

38. See Gabriela Roa Romero and Mariela Ocán Rodriguez, "Denuncian cierre de tres maquiladoras," *El Nuevo Diario*, August 21, 2001, and Rafael Lara, "Trabajadores de Chentex obligados y accareados," *El Nuevo Diario*, January 13, 2001.

39. Lara, *El Nuevo Diario*, January 13, 2001

40. Maria Fernanda Flores de Alemán, "Women 2000: Gender Equality: Development and Peace for the Twenty-First Century," speech during the General Debate of the Twenty-third Special Session of the United Nations General Assembly, New York, June 8, 2000.

41. Flores de Aleman, "Women 2000."

42. *La Boletita*, no. 47 (August 2001): 5.

43. *La Boletita*, no. 47, 5.

44. As will be discussed later, not all NGOs have a progressive agenda as there has also been a significant increase in NGOs linked to the conservative factions.

45. Valeria Imhof, *"Liberales forman ONG,"* *Confidencial*, no. 184 (March 19-25, 2000). Among the Liberal Party members who established NGOs were: Liberal deputy and president of the Commission of Defense and Governance; Wilfrid Navarro, former Minister of employment and mayoral candidate for the PLC in Managua; Pedro Joaquín Ríos, Liberal deputy, Georgina Lupiac, president of the PLC in Madriz, and Johana Moncada, PLC mayoral candidate in Somoto.

46. Imhof, *Confidencial*, no. 184

47. She served as the first lady until Alemán, who had been a widower, remarried in 1999.

48. Imhof, *Confidencial*, no. 184.

49. "Amenaza a la libertad de expresión," *El Nuevo Diario*, November 28, 2000, and "La CIDH y la colegiación de periodistas," *El Nuevo Diario*, December 19, 2000.

50. "DGI sólo audita a medios independientes," *La Prensa*, August 24, 2000.

51. "DGI sólo audita," *La Prensa*, August 24, 2000.

52. Commission on Human Rights, A Department of State Human Rights Reports for 2000, U.S. Department of State, February 2001. www.humanrightsusa.net/reprots/nicaragua.html.

53. "Crece Solidaridad con Eloísa," *El Nuevo Diario*, December 7, 2000.

54. Rafael Lara, "Amenazada y temer por su familia," *El Nuevo Diario*, December 7, 2000.

55. Hugo Holmann Chamorro, "Opinión," *La Prensa*, January 27, 2001.

56. Mitchell Seligson, "The Impact of Corruption on Regime Legitimacy: A Comparative Study of Four Latin American Countries," *Journal of Politics* 64, no. 2 (May 2002): 418.

57. Quoted in Transparency International, *Global Corruption Report 2001*, 161. www.globalcorruptionreport.org.

58. Isbester, "Nicaragua 1996-2001," 636. The comptroller general eventually annulled the sale.

59. Infopress Central America, *Central America Report*, May 14, 1999, p. 2.

60. Infopress Central America, *Central America Report*, May 12, 2000, p. 8.

61. Seligson, "The Impact of Corruption," 409.

62. Erving Sanchez Rizo, "Lucha anti-corrupción no debe postrar la Economía," *El Nuevo Diario*, May 10, 2002. In early 2001, for example, the Dutch suspended their aid to the municipality of Chinandega after it came to light that public funds were improperly used.

63. James H. Mittelman and Robert Johnston, "The Globalization of Organized Crime, the Courtesan State and the Corruption of Civil Society," *Global Governance* 5, no. 1 (January-March 1999): 119.

64. Mittelman and Johnston, "The Globalization of Organized Crime," 119.

Chapter 4

Alemán's War on the NGO Community[1]

Karen Kampwirth

Throughout his political career, Arnoldo Alemán often framed political dilemmas in stark and simplistic terms, as a battle between good and evil, us and them, insider and outsider. In doing this he drew on a long tradition of populist politics in Latin America in general and in Nicaragua itself, a tradition in which often-dictatorial leadership was justified in reference to an excluded and long-suffering "people."

> Although the populist emphasis on "the people" is a common denominator—so low that it is not confined to populism—it does carry some further connotations. Invocation of "the people" is regularly and logically associated with a dichotomisation of "people" and the permutations are endless—the "non-people," "anti-people," "the other," "the oligarchy," the "elite," foreigners, Jews, and traitors.[2]

Like revolutionaries, populists spoke to the real anger felt by the traditionally excluded. But unlike revolutionaries, they did not seek to mobilize that anger to overturn the system and transform it into a new political order characterized by more justice and less exploitation. Instead, classic populists promised inclusion without revolution, an inclusion that was material as well as symbolic.[3]

But Arnoldo Alemán, who served as president of Nicaragua from 1997 to 2002, is not a man of the classic populist age, an age that reached its peak in Latin America in the 1940s. Instead, since the 1980s, he and other Latin American politicians faced a new set of dilemmas, making the new populism significantly different from classic populism. Understanding the new populism required distinguishing "between electoral movements that seek power, and political movements that already hold power."[4] Politicians like Alberto Fujimori of Peru and Carlos Menem of Argentina were much like the classic populists in their early phases, and quite unlike them once they held presidential power.[5]

Arnoldo Alemán was also far more populist in approach as a candidate than as president.[6]

The same pattern of populist campaigning followed by sharp reversals once in office can be observed across the region, in countries that otherwise differ in significant ways. The prevalence of this style therefore cannot be explained solely in terms of the personal characteristics of a given politician or of national issues but, at least partly, in terms of changes in the international system. These changes include the end of the Cold War (which had given classic populists, as long as they were anticommunist, some leverage with the United States), the rise of the international debt (with its concomitant pressures to enact neoliberal austerity measures), the increasing dominance of the ideology of free trade, and the exponential growth of the informal sector of the economy, largely in response to the scarcity of formal sector jobs. At the dawn of the twenty-first century, it was difficult for a symbolically inclusive populist candidate to become a practically inclusive populist president, even when the politician was so inclined.[7] Growing poverty and social inequality coincided with the democratic openings that began in many Latin American countries, including Nicaragua, in the 1980s. That created a dilemma for those who sought to govern. According to Carlos Vilas, "the very tension between an economy that marginalizes and a political system that requires integration, leads to the need for a new sort of leadership."[8] Whether democracy is understood in a thin electoral sense or a thicker social sense, "democracy always implies a system of integration. In contrast, poverty implies exclusion and inequality."[9] In the era of neoliberal pressures to exclude citizens economically (by eliminating formal sector jobs and public services) at the same time that they are to be included politically (by mobilizing them electorally), politicians of various sorts find themselves promoting (or at least accepting) neoliberal policies that contribute to the impoverishment of the very citizens whose votes they seek. This was even true for the party of the revolution, the Sandinista National Liberation Front (FSLN), in the 1996 campaign that led to Alemán's election as president.[10] Thus, in the age of neoliberalism, populist strategies are needed more than ever by politicians who wish to instill hope in the electorate, at least enough hope to get them to vote every few years. Any framework that can explain the roots of voters' poverty and imply a clear solution is better than the status quo. It can be argued that Nicaragua's two largest parties, the FSLN and Alemán's Constitutional Liberal Party (PLC), promoted one such framework, and excluded electoral competitors, through the 1999 agreement Nicaraguans called "the Pact," which Hoyt analyzes in chapter 2.

Alemán's campaign against organized competitors was also waged on other fronts, including what Nicaraguans often called his war against non-governmental organizations, or NGOs. In particular, he targeted prominent NGO figures who were often foreign-born and always female. Alemán's chosen targets must also be explained with reference to the specifics of Nicaraguan civil society, especially the importance of feminism during that period. This chapter argues that the consequences of Alemán's political choices, targeting the NGO sector in general and its feminist leaders in particular, contributed to the undoing of democracy in Nicaragua.

Civil Society, Foreigners, and the New Populism

Populism can be understood as an approach to politics rather than as a set of policies. While the policies traditionally associated with Latin American populism have shifted in the new circumstances of the post—Cold War, neoliberal era, there are continuities if populism is understood as does Kurt Weyland, as a political strategy through which a personalistic leader seeks or exercises government power based on direct, unmediated, uninstitutionalized support from large numbers of mostly unorganized followers;[11] or as does Alan Knight, who writes that "populism is best defined in terms of a particular political style, characteristically involving a self-proclaimed rapport with 'the people,' a 'them-and-us mentality,' and (often, though not necessarily) a period of crisis and mobilization."[12]

In his analysis of neopopulist strategies in Argentina, Brazil, and Peru, Weyland argues that populist strategies and neoliberal strategies were quite compatible. Menem, Collor, and Fujimori all sought to bypass organized civil society, weaken or subordinate intermediary organizations, and attack privileged groups and the "political class," at least rhetorically. And as populist political tactics furthered structural reform, those reforms in turn strengthened populist leaders because they weakened organized interest groups and parties that sought to hem in the leaders' latitude.[13]

It can be argued that both the Pact and the attacks on the NGOs enhanced Alemán's power by weakening organized groups that might have limited his ability to implement neoliberal policies. Moreover, the Pact and the attacks on the NGOs made it easier for him to use the state for his own personal economic benefit or that of his cronies. The NGO sector also was useful, from Alemán's perspective, as a scapegoat for the economic misery that faced most Nicaraguans. To the extent that those who were involved with the NGOs were foreigners (as were most of the funders and some of the local workers), Alemán had an opportunity to draw on the populist tradition of blaming outsiders for domestic problems, of setting up a stark "us and them" dichotomy in which select foreigners were "them" and Alemán himself was the spokesperson for "us."

While it might have been more logical to blame the foreign proponents of neoliberal policies for the effects of those policies, the proponents—international agencies like the International Monetary Fund and the World Bank, and First World states, specially the United States—were powerful. Politicians like Alemán depended on those powerful foreigners for both political support and debt relief (in exchange for neoliberal cuts in social services and state employment).[14] So the classic populist strategy of identifying the international bankers and imperialist states as the foreign roots of domestic problems was not an option for new populists.

This does not mean that it was impossible to blame foreigners for domestic problems; simply that new sorts of foreigners had to be found. The new foreigners were those who either visited or lived in Nicaragua to work with NGOs, foreigners who apparently were trying to address poverty and inequality and whose efforts had not worked, at least to the extent that Nicaragua remained poor.

One explanation for the NGOs' apparent failure to eliminate poverty was that the problems were far too deeply rooted and complicated to be resolved by a few nongovernmental development projects. While those projects helped, long-term solutions for Nicaragua's economic problems would have to be coordinated and funded at national and international levels. But this explanation laid the blame on the most powerful: local and international elites whose actions (cutting spending on basic social services like education; opposing a living wage or organizing rights for the majority) reduced the possibility that there would ever be a more prosperous and equitable Nicaragua. Luckily for the beneficiaries of neoliberal policies, there was a simpler explanation: NGO workers must be dishonest and interested only in helping themselves.

Early Attacks on the NGOs

The NGO sector, and especially foreign-born NGO workers, became one of Alemán's targets at least as early as his presidential campaign.

> If with the millions of dollars that have been sent in the past as aid or "subsidies" for hundreds of "projects," that have perhaps made Nicaragua the country that "has the most projects in the world," if only a very few [of those dollars] had been channeled and carried out adequately, with honesty, plausible and transparent realism, surely we would have made significant and visible advances in many areas. But where are the results and the realities? We don't want to continue to be a "project." Nor do we want to be anybody's place for "experimentation and dumping garbage"![15]

Accusing the NGO workers of being dishonest, deceitful, and unrealistic was a good strategy, for it implied a fairly easy solution: if only the NGO sector would become more honest (or if only a politician like Arnoldo Alemán could force that sector to become more honest), then the many projects in the country might have a great effect on reducing poverty in the near future. Accusing the NGOs of being the cause of Nicaragua's poverty offered hope, and might have seemed plausible to some people. Average Nicaraguans certainly knew that many foreign-financed projects were under way in the country and that most of them had access to the sorts of resources (cars, telephones, computers, air conditioning) that were beyond the economic reach of most citizens.

Asserting that NGO workers caused Nicaragua's poverty also deflected attention from the real relationships of power and wealth. Although those who worked in a women's clinic with a car to transport patients or in an air conditioned human rights office were certainly privileged in the Nicaraguan context, they were hardly wealthy compared to those who worked in the international institutions that promoted fiscal austerity for Nicaragua. Similarly, the sort of waste and corruption that might have slipped by in the NGO sector (which typically was carefully audited by donor agencies) was minuscule compared to the corruption of Nicaraguan politicians like Alemán himself.[16] But perhaps the fairly visible small privileges of the NGO workers generated more resentment than the huge privileges of national and international elites precisely because most NGO offices were open to the poorest of the poor, something that was not true for institutions like the World Bank, located far away in Washington, or the U.S. embassy in Managua, surrounded by high walls.

Changing the Rules of the Game

During his first year in office, President Alemán announced plans for a series of organizational and legal changes that affected NGOs. The Nicaraguan Women's Institute (INIM) would no longer be a distinct state agency, but would be subsumed under the newly created Ministry of the Family. This ministry's role was to "defend" the institution of the family, defined as the nuclear family, even though most Nicaraguans did not live in such an arrangement.[17] Among other things, to defend the family meant "to help people in common-law marriages to formalize their relationship through matrimony,"[18] even though defacto polygamy—men with second and even third wives and children—was common. According to the law that created the new ministry, the purpose of those nuclear families was "procreation," a purpose the state was committed to defending.[19] For the Alemán administration, to defend procreation meant "to defend life from its conception in the maternal womb":[20] while it was less explicit regarding the contradiction between access to contraception and defense of procreation, logically even contraception would be a threat to this model of family life.

Perhaps the most important aspect of the proposed Ministry of the Family from the NGOs' perspective was the language that would define their relationship. One of the duties of the proposed ministry was to "'oversee and coordinate' the actions of all governmental and nongovernmental organizations that work with children, women, youth, the family, elderly people, and disabled people."[21] Through that phrase, the balance between the state and civil society was to be tilted in favor of the state.

That same year, the Alemán administration proposed that Article 147 of the civil code, the 1992 law regulating the relationship between NGOs and the state, be revised to increase state control over the funding and programming of all NGOs, establishing that "no Nongovernmental Organization (NGO) will be able to request funds from foreign sources, except with the proper authorization of the government."[22] Another law proposed in 1997, the Ley de Justicia Tributaria, permitted the state to tax donations to nonprofit organizations, including donations of goods and cash. After a series of protests from organizations in Nicaragua as well as foreign funding agencies, all these legal changes ultimately were passed, but in watered-down versions that, according to multiple sources, were typically more of a threat than a reality, to be applied selectively if at all.[23]

A Turning Point: Hurricane Mitch

Although the legal screws were tightening on the NGOs, a public campaign against prominent NGO leaders did not begin until after the worst natural disaster to hit Nicaragua during the Alemán administration: massive flooding as a result of Hurricane Mitch in late 1998 and early 1999, which resulted in about 3,500 deaths and hundreds of millions of dollars in damage.[24]

While Hurricane Mitch was a tragedy for most Nicaraguans, for President Alemán it was both an opportunity and a great political risk. It was an opportunity in that, as is typical in the wake of natural disasters, relief aid arrived in the country, donations that the Alemán government sought to tax and control. A week after Mitch hit Nicaragua, "[a] number of major donations from international organizations [had] already been channeled through the First Lady, the president's daughter, Maria Dolores Alemán ... approximately 20 cargo containers [were] impounded by Nicaraguan customs, with the government demanding that the nongovernmental recipients of the shipments pay exorbitant taxes on this previously tax-exempt aid."[25] The new "taxes ranged from 40 percent to over 100 percent of the estimated value of the aid."[26]

But while Hurricane Mitch presented new opportunities to control foreign aid and limit the resources available to NGOs, it also presented great political risks for the administration. A corrupt governmental response to an earlier natural disaster—the Somoza family's response to the 1972 earthquake in Managua—had been a turning point that consolidated the anti-Somoza coalition and led to the Sandinistas' 1979 overthrow of the government. It is likely that Arnoldo Alemán was aware of that historical precedent and concerned that his response to Hurricane Mitch might contribute to his own downfall.

Accelerating the campaign against the NGOs was logical, given the administration's goals: to capitalize on opportunities while minimizing the political risks associated with Hurricane Mitch. To the extent that aid could be channeled through the government, or at least withheld from the NGOs, Alemán would look good politically, while the NGOs would be unable to respond effectively to the crisis and would thus look bad. One way to minimize the risks in this strategy was to try to quiet dissidents in Nicaragua, especially those who might communicate with international aid organizations. So when an e-mail message written by Julie Noble, an American who had lived in Nicaragua for six years administering USAID funds, in which she repeated local news reports criticizing the president's handling of the crisis, was forwarded to Alemán's brother in Wisconsin, Noble was promptly expelled from the country.[27] Had the threat from foreign aid workers been limited to a few individuals like Noble, the president probably would not have begun a concerted campaign against the NGO sector, because it was politically easier to deal with such problems on an individual basis. But the NGO sector itself became transformed as a result of Mitch, forming a Civil Coordinator (Coordinadora Civil) in November 1998 that comprised more than three hundred NGOs, associations, and social move-ments.[28] Once the NGO sector had united in the Civil Coordinator, it was less vulnerable to tactics aimed at individual NGO workers because Coordinator members could organize and publicize their activities. They also could carry out careful studies of the unmet needs of people in regions hit by Hurricane Mitch, studies that clearly irritated Alemán.[29]

Alemán, furthermore, could not have been pleased to realize that many foreign funders seemed to deem the groups that belonged to the Civil Coordinator more trustworthy than his own administration. According to Ana Quirós, national liaison for the Civil Coordinator and president of the Federation of NGOs in Nicaragua, "for the government, the level of international aid that came last year was in the range of $600 million ... more or less the average in the last 3 or 4 years. [This] means that Mitch didn't do much—I mean, if we compare just the amount—in raising the amount of international aid. Which is completely different in the case of the NGOs. Last year, we in the NGO community managed about $300 million. So there was not as much aid through the government as was expected."[30]

According to Quirós, the main reason the international community tried to channel relief through the NGOs rather than the government was "the attitude of this government toward the international community. They had problems with the European Union. They had problems with the Swedes. They had problems with the Norwegians. And so on."[31] Alemán might have relied on the tried and true populist strategy of blaming powerful foreigners for the country's problems responding to the devastation of Hurricane Mitch, especially the members of the European Union. Earlier he had criticized some donor countries that asked for explanations following the 1999 pact.[32] In general, however, Hurricane Mitch led him to accelerate his attacks on the less powerful local foreigners, the prominent members of the NGO sector; though in the years following Mitch, government officials consistently denied that such a campaign was taking place.[33]

Individual Attacks on NGO Workers

One of the most concerted attacks was directed at the spokesperson for the Civil Coordinator, Ana Quirós. Quirós was born in Mexico to Costa Rican parents and, after two decades as a Nicaraguan resident, naturalized as a Nicaraguan citizen during the Alemán administration. Beginning in February 2000, the administration denounced her for participating in Nicaraguan politics through her elected position as spokesperson for the Coordinator organizations, asserting that she had no right to do so as a "foreigner," a claim that was inconsistent with the Nicaraguan Constitution.[34] That attack was followed by an eventually unsuccessful campaign to strip away her Nicaraguan citizenship and then (most observers assumed) deport her.

In some ways, the campaign against Quirós can be seen as an attack against the Civil Coordinator and its affiliated organizations. By the beginning of 2000, Alemán had already spent several years criticizing the NGO sector. He claimed that it was controlled by wealthy, corrupt foreigners who controlled large amounts of money, although, according to Quirós, the organizations that belonged to the Coordinator did not control nearly as much money as the state; the difference was that those organizations were far more efficient. Quirós thought that because of their greater efficiency, state officials might have gotten the impression that they had much larger budgets than they actually had.[35] Another reason for attacking the NGO sector, and the Coordinator in particular, was that Alemán perceived the NGOs as being FSLN fronts; indeed, many of them had been founded by people who traced their political roots back to the revolutionary period. But by February 2000, when the attacks on Ana Quirós began, the relationship between the FSLN and most NGO activists, including those with historical ties to the Sandinistas, had changed. Just a few weeks earlier, the political pact between the FSLN and the Liberal Party had been finalized. The Civil Coordinator, through its spokesperson, had been very critical of the pact, along with other policies of the Alemán administration. This demonstrated that the Coordinator member groups were hardly FSLN fronts, as Alemán had claimed, and served to unite the FSLN leadership with that of the Liberal Party in the campaign against the Coordinator.

On another level, the attack on Ana Quirós can be seen as an attack on her as an individual. As someone who was foreign-born, she was more vulnerable to attack than a native-born Nicaraguan. She was also someone with open ties to the feminist movement as assistant director of CISAS, a health-care advocacy group that participated in the Network for Women's Health. Being a feminist was a characteristic she shared, perhaps not coincidentally, with all the other people who would become targets of Alemán's attacks in the months that followed.[36]

Toward the end of June 2000, the next verbal shot was fired against a prominent, foreign-born, feminist NGO professional, Dr. Ana Maria Pizarro, born in Argentina and a resident of Nicaragua for decades. On a series of programs on the state television station hosted by a government spokesperson, Luis Mora, several representatives of political parties linked to evangelical churches accused Sí Mujer, the women's clinic Dr. Pizarro directed, of performing illegal abortions. Mora's guests called for the elimination of Sí Mujer's legal standing (*personaria juridica*), which would have made it impossible for the clinic to continue to serve low-income women, for it would no longer have the right to seek outside funding or to publish reports. They also called for Dr. Pizarro's arrest on the charge of murder.

Because none of her accusers could offer evidence that the staff of Sí Mujer performed abortions, they instead went on to accuse her, and two other doctors who worked at the clinic, of malpractice in the case of a woman who became infected after giving birth by Cesarean, also a dubious accusation.[37] Supporters of Dr. Pizarro and Sí Mujer thought the underlying issue was that the Alemán administration (and its allies in the Catholic and Evangelical Protestant churches) were in the middle of a campaign to eliminate the right to therapeutic abortion; the symbolism of that right was important to people on both sides of the debate. One major impediment to the administration's attempts to eliminate therapeutic abortion rights were people like Dr. Pizarro, who, along with most other women's health providers in Nicaragua, supported the right to safe abortion.[38]

On November 14, 2000, less than a month before her seventieth birthday, Dorothy Granada became the next target of the anti-NGO campaign. Granada was a U.S. citizen and registered nurse who, in 1989, had settled in Mulukukú, a small town in the northern mountains, where she had helped found the Maria Luisa Ortiz Women's Cooperative. On that day in 2000, at a public event in Mulukukú, Alemán accused the cooperative staff of serving only Sandinistas (a charge that cooperative members later refuted) and promised to close down the clinic and jail its workers.[39] Two days later, government workers arrived in Mulukukú to go over the documents that demonstrated Dorothy Granada's legal right to live in Nicaragua. Although the documents were in order, fifteen armed police officers returned with government officials on December 7 intending to seize Granada and deport her, having already reserved for her a one-way ticket out of the country.

As it happened, Granada was in the capital that day; so instead of returning to work in Mulukukú, she went into hiding for two months. At the same time, government officials threatened Swiss Workers' Aid, one of the international NGOs that funded the cooperative's work. The children's food program and the clinic were forced to close, leaving most of Mulukukú's residents with no source of health care.[40]

After shutting down the clinic on the grounds that it served patients in a politicized way, the Alemán administration added the charge that Granada and the cooperative's other fifty-one members performed abortions. According to Enoc Rueda, the PLC mayor of a neighboring community, "we have witnesses to prove that abortions were performed and also [to prove Granada's] disrespect for Liberals. The foreigner should go."[41] But the evidence presented by the Alemán administration, that a woman named Elba Rosa Hernandez had received an abortion at the clinic, was refuted by Hernandez herself at a press conference with human rights activist Vilma Nuñez, where she held the young child who had supposedly been aborted. Furthermore, a study by the Institute of Legal Medicine done at the government's request found no evidence that abortions had ever been performed at the clinic.

When the first accusations fell through, the administration accused Granada of having provided medical attention to members of the Andres Castro United Front (FUAC), an armed group of former Sandinistas that was active in the region where the clinic was located. This charge was similarly unsubstantiated. But although lower courts consistently ruled in Granada's favor, and despite a massive national and international campaign in her support, the administration persisted in its attempts to deport her.[42] When the Supreme Court failed to rule on her case by the time her resident visa expired on September 9, 2001, Granada was forced to leave the country.[43] The campaigns against Quirós, Pizarro, and Granada received a great deal of attention from both the Nicaraguan press and the international solidarity community. In contrast, another campaign that began in 2000 against the agricultural development support group Nochari Association and its president, María Eugenia Morales, received very little attention, although it ultimately was far more damaging as Nochari was shut down for ten months, from September 2000 to July 2001.

Why did Nochari's case receive so little attention? One reason may be that the campaign against Nochari was not personalized as other campaigns had been; instead of publicly attacking an individual, the organization as a whole was criticized. So that campaign may have been less interesting to reporters, who, in Nicaragua as elsewhere, tend to prefer stories that can be personalized. Another reason may be that foreign-born administrators (who often can draw on networks of international supporters) were not directly targeted. Unlike the campaigns against Pizarro and Granada, and to a greater extent than that against Quirós, moreover, the campaign against Nochari was carried out by the Alemán administration with the direct support of its ally in the Pact, the FSLN. FSLN loyalists therefore were unlikely to object to the campaign against Nochari, though many of them objected vociferously to Alemán's other anti-NGO campaigns.

The FSLN joined the Alemán administration against Nochari because María Eugenia Morales was a threat to the FSLN in particular and to the pact's two-party logic in general. Although Morales had never formally belonged to the Sandinista party, she had been identified with it and had been known as a Sandinista. But she became increasingly unhappy with the FSLN starting in 1998 when Zoilamérica Narváez, the stepdaughter of Daniel Ortega, accused him of having sexually abused her since she was eleven years old. Morales's disillusionment only deepened as party officials closed ranks around Ortega, dismissing the accusations of abuse (although the sexual relationship had been an open secret for years). Morales actively and publicly supported Narváez's quest to have her case heard in court.

Local Sandinista officials in Nandaime nevertheless thought Morales, a well-known and well-respected development worker, would make a good candidate for mayor. But she turned them down: "I couldn't live with someone like Daniel Ortega. To continue covering up for Daniel Ortega is to continue covering up men's violence."[44] Not only did she turn down the FSLN, she accepted the Conservative Party's invitation to be its candidate. This angered FSLN leaders so much that they filed a complaint claiming that she had no right to direct an NGO and run for office, a claim without legal basis. Nevertheless, the Alemán administration proceeded to suspend Nochari's projects and to withdraw its legal standing. The effort finally failed, however, when Nochari workers returned to their work after the NGO had been closed for ten months.[45]

Only a few individuals and organizations in the NGO sector ever had to confront the sort of direct public attacks that Quirós, Pizarro, Granada, and Morales faced. But many did have to contend with another strategy that the Alemán administration used. That quieter strategy was known in the NGO community as fiscal terrorism (*terrorismo fiscal*). Many organizations were audited repeatedly by state agencies; in one of the more extreme cases, auditors spent three months in the offices of the agricultural support group CIPRES, carefully combing the books for small errors, finally fining the agency 75,000 córdobas (about US $10,000) because it could not produce a receipt for a purchase of ten chickens.[46]

Most, although not all, agencies that experienced fiscal terrorism could trace their roots to the Sandinista revolution.[47] One of the most prominent cases concerned the Popol Na Foundation, a community development organization that worked on credit and gender issues. Along with other organizations, Popol Na was the subject of ongoing audits in late 2000 and early 2001, though government officials singled out Popol Na as uncooperative for refusing to authorize audits going back to 1997 until the initial audit of the books from 2000-2001 was completed.

Considering that months of audits yielded nothing, many in the press and the NGO community suspected that the target of the audits was not Popol Na itself but the organization's director, Monica Baltodano, a woman with a long history of involvement in opposition politics. During the struggle against the Somoza dictatorship in the 1970s, Baltodano had risen to the rank of guerrilla commander in the FSLN. A Sandinista in the National Assembly during the Alemán years, she was one of the most vocal critics of the Pact.

But while Baltodano was an unusually prominent Sandinista critic of the Pact, she was not the only one. Another FSLN congressional critic, Jose "Chepe" González, was also the director of an NGO. Yet for some reason his NGO was not targeted for repeated audits. Ana Quirós suggests that the distinction was not coincidental: "given a choice between a man and a woman they are going to choose a woman," especially if that woman was known to be sympathetic to the feminist movement.[48]

Baltodano, like all the other women who were targets of Alemán's campaign, was publicly defended by Dr. Vilma Nuñez, executive director of what was probably the most prominent human rights organization in Nicaragua, the

Centro Nicaraguense de Derechos Humanos (CENIDH). In April and May 2001, Nuñez herself was accused by Alemán's chief of staff, Jose Marenco, of being an accomplice of the Andrés Castro United Front (FUAC), a band of armed former Sandinistas who had been involved in a series of kidnappings and murders. When it turned out that Marenco's evidence was a report written by someone in his office and some communications between Nuñez and FUAC members as part of a mediation effort, the case was dismissed.[49] NGO workers and their supporters abroad had to devote considerable energy, and resources to resisting the campaigns against all these women, energy and resources that they could have used to carry out the original goals of those organizations. Those battles also threatened the NGOs' ability to attract foreign funding. Over the course of the Alemán years, foreign donors often expressed dismay at the president's efforts to consolidate his personal power and that of his party through actions such as the campaign against the NGOs, the pact with Daniel Ortega's FSLN, and the use of development funds for political purposes. In one case that, atypically, was covered in the press, a European Union-funded housing project, donors even withdrew from works in progress rather than allow the Alemán administration to control them.[50] Other NGO workers found that many foreign funders were no longer willing to give grants to projects in Nicaragua. According to one, "Nicaragua is drying up."[51]

Church, State, and the Feminist Threat

The attacks on the NGOs and their individual female leaders reflected another aspect of Nicaraguan civil society in the 1990s, the explosive growth of feminist organizing. During the Alemán years, Nicaragua had the most significant feminist movement in Central America and one of the most significant in Latin America as a whole.[52]

In addition to the prominent feminists Alemán targeted, "the more than 200 private medical clinics that offer services to low-income women were chosen for harassment and investigation" "under the pretext that abortions were carried out there," according to Ana Quirós.[53] Many Nicaraguan feminists supported the right to safe, legal abortion for public health reasons. Although the Alemán administration never found evidence that any of those centers performed abortions, the campaign against women's health providers was not primarily a campaign against their actions but a campaign against their ideas (that is, their belief in reproductive rights).

In the campaign against the NGOs, Alemán united the church and state on one side, while he and his allies conflated foreigners and feminists on the other side.[54] Another illustration of the president's close ties to the church was his declaration (formally published in the press) that March 25, 2000, and all subsequent years would be the National Day of the Unborn Child (Dia Nacional del Nino por Nacer), the date of the Catholic feast of the Annunciation.[55]

Supporters of banning abortion under all circumstances asserted that the church and the Alemán administration were the real Nicaraguans, not those NGO activists who defended women's right to life. According to "Dr. Rafael Cabrera of the Catholic University [Universidad Americana], the NGOs 'are foreigners who do not represent Nicaraguans, feminist movements that promote lesbianism and organizations that promote sexual licentiousness and homosexuality.' "[56]

Journalist Sofía Montenegro has suggested that of all the sectors of civil society, the feminist movement is the most threatening to the interests of the Catholic Church. According to Montenegro, "the church has demanded the head of the feminist movement" as part of its pursuit of the "reevangelization of the continent [which is necessitated] by secularization and, on the other hand, [by] competition with the Protestants." She suggests that the very close ties between the Alemán administration and the church hierarchy can be seen as an unofficial pact, with the ultimate goal of forming a hegemonic alliance between the Liberal Party, the FSLN, and the church. Given that the 1999 pact between the Liberals and the FSLN undercut all other parties' ability to compete, and given the weakness of private enterprise and the unions in neoliberal Nicaragua, the main impediments to the Liberal-FSLN-church alliance were the feminist movement and the press.[57]

Through Alemán's campaign against the NGOs, Nicaragua saw further unification of church and state—a violation of its own secular constitution—via the rhetoric of antifeminism. This unity suggests that the most significant threat of the revolutionary legacy (from the perspective of Alemán, his supporters in the Liberal Party, and the hierarchy of the Catholic Church) was the feminist movement, an offshoot of the revolution, not the FSLN, the party of the revolution. For by the end of his administration, Alemán had largely succeeded in co-opting and controlling the FSLN through the Pact. In contrast, the feminists were not so easily co-opted or controlled.

Weakening Democracy

Attacks on the NGO sector like those Alemán made during his years as president would damage democracy in any country. Making the unsubstantiated claim that development projects did not eliminate poverty because development workers were corrupt was another way of suggesting that all people are corrupt. If corruption is universal, then it is not a political problem but rather a fundamental part of human nature. Such accusations minimized the massive corruption of the Alemán administration itself, implying that as long as Alemán "got things done" there was little harm in his enriching himself at the expense of taxpayers and foreign donors.

The attacks on the legitimacy of NGO efforts to study social problems and take positions regarding social controversies tended to undermine democracy, for the significance of electoral democracy is diminished to the extent that ideas cannot be freely exchanged. But the campaign against the NGOs was even more troubling, for that campaign was not aimed at all NGO leaders. The leaders who were attacked—Ana Quirós, Ana Maria Pizarro, Dorothy Granada, María Eugenia Morales, Monica Baltodano, Vilma Nuñez—shared a number of characteristics. Many of them were foreign-born and were targeted as such, a campaign that, this study has argued, is consistent with the new populism. All of them were women, even though the majority of Nicaraguan NGOs were directed by men.[58] They were, moreover, all connected with the women's movement, either as open sympathizers or as active participants in feminist NGOs or social movements.

Alemán's decision to target prominent feminist NGO activists for harassment, and his close ties to the church, illustrate how much the president was willing to rework the liberal tradition in Nicaragua. Victoria González has argued that in the course of rebuilding the Liberal Party, Alemán embraced positions on women and families that, during the Somoza era, were promoted by the Liberal Party's main opponent, the Conservative Party.[59]

González identifies a number of possible reasons why Alemán's liberalism differs from the liberalism of the Somoza family: "Unlike the Somozas, who consolidated the modern Nicaraguan state and incorporated urban women into that process by offering them state employment, the Alemán administration [had] no economic incentives to offer women and no need for them to become involved in formal sectors of the economy."[60] González's argument regarding the evolution of liberalism and women is consistent with the argument in this article regarding the evolution of Nicaraguan populism. In a neoliberal world, the old populism, with its clientelistic promises, is no longer possible in most countries. The dilemma for all politicians in highly indebted countries with electoral rule is how to incorporate people politically through voting at the same time that they are excluded economically through neoliberal austerity measures.

But just because all politicians in countries like Nicaragua face similar dilemmas does not mean that they resolve those dilemmas in similar ways. González offers clues as to why Alemán chose his particular strategy, seeking to mobilize populist feelings of "us versus them" by casting NGO activists, especially those who were either foreign-born or feminist, as "them." Blaming such activists made sense to Alemán's constituents (and probably to Alemán himself), for "the Nicaraguan right has been heavily influenced by socially conservative (and Catholic fundamentalist) right-wing forces in the United States during the last twenty years, forces which place great importance on the family and family values."[61]

Politics of both left and right were transformed during the twenty years of revolutionary and counterrevolutionary upheaval with which Nicaragua concluded the twentieth century. As a result, many right-wing women found themselves marginalized:

> [T]he militarization of Nicaraguan politics during the 1970s and 1980s ... diminished the role women played within the Nicaraguan Liberal right. In exile, many Somocista women retreated into domestic affairs ... while Somocista men took over the task of envisioning the type of government that would eventually replace the Sandinistas.[62]

Additionally, targeting the NGO activists who were foreign-born or feminist made sense for Alemán because they represented a political threat. "Alemán has to contend with a politically and economically strong feminist movement, while the Somozas were able to co-opt and weaken the early twentieth-century feminist movement that existed in Nicaragua when they came to power in 1936."[63] The leaders of the feminist movement of Alemán's day, unlike some of the leaders of the first wave feminist movement or of the Sandinista party, could not be co-opted but instead were some of the key political figures demanding that Nicaraguan democracy be respected and extended, demands that often directly threatened Alemán's agenda. For instance, the feminist movement was at the forefront of efforts to oppose the pact between Alemán's Liberals and Ortega's Sandinistas.[64]

A final part of the explanation may be found in the logic of the new populism. Like classic populists, new populists tend to reject political parties and other political organizations; when they belong to a traditional political party, as Alemán did, they tend to use that party as a personal vehicle, without great concern for upholding the party's historical values.

Alemán's antifeminist words and deeds may be one more example of the ideological flexibility of populism. Had a new strategic opportunity presented itself, Alemán might have chosen to cut his ties to the church or even to build an alliance with civil society. While such an alliance may seem unlikely, an alliance with the FSLN, such as the pact, seemed at least as unlikely not too long ago. If the NGO sector were willing to be co-opted in the way that the FSLN leadership was, Alemán would have had little reason to reject such a relationship. Such an alliance might have required that he moderate his rhetoric toward the feminists, foreigners, and foreign-born feminists of the NGO sector. It might even have required that he look elsewhere for an "elite" that he could attack in the name of "the people." But that would not be too much of a problem for a creative politician like Alemán.

Notes

1. This chapter is a revised version of Karen Kampwirth "Arnoldo Alemán Takes on the NGOs: Antifeminism and the New Populism in Nicaragua," *Latin American Politics and Society* 45, no. 2 (Summer 2003): 133-70. It is reprinted with the permission of *Latin American Politics and Society.*

2. Alan Knight, "Populism and Neo-populism in Latin America, especially Mexico," *Journal of Latin American Studies* 30, 2 (1998): 229.

3. Michael Conniff, "Introduction," in *Populism in Latin America*, ed. Michael Conniff (Tuscaloosa: University of Alabama Press, 1999), 4-7.

4. Felipe Burbano de Lara, "A modo de introducción: el impertinente populismo," in *El fantasma del populismo: aproximación a un tema [siempre] actual,* ed. Felipe Burbano de Lara (Caracas: Nueva Sociedad, 1998), 12.

5. Burbano de Lara, "A modo de introducción," 12-14.

6. This distinction between the campaign and the presidency may not be entirely new. After considering the careers of a number of classic populists, Knight notes a possible pattern: "it could be argued that the more durable variants, as they experience the 'routinisation of populism,' shift from being confrontational experiences, often the product of crisis, embodying strong, affective appeals to dissident groups, and move in the direction of a machine politics, premised on government patronage and a lingering but less red-blooded populist style" (Knight, "Populism and Neo-populism," 231-32). The shift between the rhetoric of the campaign and the reality of the presidency is nonetheless distinctive for the new populists, because whereas the old populists had economic goods to channel through political machines, the realities of neoliberalism mean that the new populists are often just as stingy as less populist presidents.

7. Hugo Chavez of Venezuela seems to be an exception to this rule, a populist candidate who has not gone on to be a neoliberal president. This exception may be explained by Venezuela's role as a major oil producer, which makes it more effectively sovereign than its neighbors.

8. Carlos Vilas, "Entre la democracia y el neoliberalismo: los caudillos electorales de la posmodernidad," *Socialismo y Participación* 69 (March 1994): 32.

9. Vilas, "Entre la democracia y el neoliberalismo," 33.

10. "[T]he Sandinistas' economic program differed little from Alemán's—reactivate the economy by luring foreign investment and increasing exports. The Sandinistas even brought in a former IMF official to draw up theirs, which emphasized the principal role of the private sector. Still, they vowed that social programs would accompany growth policies.... How the Sandinistas would have funded such programs was another question." Douglas W. Payne, "Nicaragua: Bottomed Out," *Dissent* 44 (Spring 1997): 39.

11. Kurt Weyland, "Neopopulism and Market Reform in Argentina, Brazil, Peru, and Venezuela" (paper presented at the 22nd meeting of the Latin American Studies Association, Miami, March 16-18, 2000), 5.

12. Knight, "Populism and Neo-populism," 223. Caster contributes one of the many analyses that note the continuities in the populist tradition in Nicaragua. "[L]ike Somoza before him, Alemán developed a popular base and a formidable political machine that reeks of traditional clientelism.... But in a country where corruption is a tradition and ordinary people fear unemployment above all other ills, many forgave Alemán's sins because he was perceived as doing something for them." Mark Caster, "The Return of Somocismo? The Rise of Arnoldo Alemán," *NACLA Report on the Americas* 30, 2 (September-October 1996): 8. On Alemán's similarity to the Somozas, see Edwin Sanchez, "Somoza era 'mis fino': Alejando Serrano Caldera lamenta 'burdas reformas,'" *El Nuevo Diario*, January 20, 2000; on Anastasio Somoza Garcia's use of populist strategies in the 1930s and 1940s, see Jeffrey Gould, *To Lead as Equals: Rural Protest and Political Con-*

sciousness in Chinandega, Nicaragua, 1912-1979 (Chapel Hill: University of North Carolina Press), 15-16 and 79-81; and Walter, *The Regime of Anastasio Somoza*, 44-47.

13. Weyland, "Neopopulism and Market Reform," 4. On neoliberalism and the new populism, see also Kenneth Roberts, "Neoliberalism and the Transformation of Populism in Latin America: The Peruvian Case," *World Politics* 48, no. 1 (October 1995): 82-116.

14. Although the U.S. government may have supported Alemán and his Liberal Party less directly than it did Somoza and his Liberal Party, the relationship was still close. For instance, during the 2001 campaign, "U.S. Ambassador Oliver Garza's various expressions of 'concern' about a possible FSLN victory [were] a welcome addition to the Liberal script, as are similar statements issued by top officials of the Bush ... administration. Both the U.S. spokespeople and their Nicaraguan Liberal counterparts know the electoral value of reminding the Nicaraguans that a government without U.S. endorsement will not be allowed to govern." *Envío*, "An Election Script with Heavy-handed Special Effects," *Envío* 20, 238 (May 2001): 1-8.

15. Liberal Alliance, *Asi piensa Arnoldo*, 1996 www.nfdd.org/Book/Socied.htm.

16. Chapters 7 and 9 examine Alemán's wealth.

17. "Los puntos en agenda del 'Ministerio de la Familia,'" *La Boletina*, no. 30 (April-May-June 1997): 12-19.

18. Presidencia de la Republica, "Ley de organización, competencias y procedimientos del poder ejecutivo," Article 28, Point (d). Draft law. Unpublished document, 1997.

19. "Los puntos en agenda del 'Ministerio de la Familia'," *La Boletina*, 14.

20. Presidencia de la Republica, "Ley de organización," Article 28, Point (e).

21. "Los puntos en agenda del 'Ministerio de la Familia'," *La Boletina*, 15.

22. Quoted in "Hablemos no de 'controlar' si no de construir propuestas," *La Boletina*, no. 30 (April-May-June 1997): 5.

23. Denis Darce and Ana Quirós Viquez, "La historia de las ONG's en Nicaragua y su relacion con los gobiernos de los anos 70s a nuestros dias," unpublished ms., 2000; "Hablemos no de 'controlar' *La Boletina*, 1-11; "Los puntos en agenda del 'Ministerio de la Familia'," *La Boletina*, 12-19; "En tiempos de sobrevivencia...," editorial, *La Boletina* no. 31 (July-August, 1997): 1-4;" Ministerio de la Familia: No todo lo que brilla es oro!" *La Boletina* no. 31 (July-August, 1997): 21-30; Presidencia de la Republica, "Ley de organización"; author interviews, Managua, January and February 1997, June and July 1998, April 2000, August 2001.

24. Glenn Garvin, "American Aid Worker Expelled by Nicaragua," *Miami Herald*, 9 November 1998.

25. Nicaragua Network, *Hurricane Mitch Alert*, no. 1 (November 2, 1998): 4 www.nicanet.org.

26. Nicaragua Network Midwest, *Nicaragua Alert* 16 (November 1998): 3.

27. Garvin, "American Aid Worker Expelled."

28. Midge Quandt, *Nicaragua: The Promise of the New Politics and of Civil Society?* (Washington, DC: Nicaragua Network, 2000), 1.

29. Among others, see Esteban Solís R., "Alemán inaugura, descalifica y politiquea: termina gira por Las Segovias," *El Nuevo Diario*, June 23, 2000.

30. Quoted in Quandt, Nicaragua, 6.

31. Quoted in Quandt, Nicaragua, 6.

32. "Yesterday, President Alemán reacted violently against recent demands for good government conditions that were authored by foreign development organizations, to the point that he asked them to leave the country if they were not satisfied with politics in Nicaragua. 'We are open to them, but when they reach the point of wanting to get themselves involved in topics like constitutional reforms or the electoral laws, I say to them just one minute, go back to your own countries to make those sorts of comments.' " Humberto Meza, "Alemán regana a donantes," *La Prensa*, January 27, 2000; see also Barbarena S., "Alemán contra medios" and Walter Treminio, "Alemán reitera sus ataques a donantes," *El Nuevo Diario*, January 29, 2000.

33. See, for example, Lourdes Arroliga, "Aborto terapéutico a debate hasta en próxima legislatura? Mayor distanciamiento entre clero y movimiento pro mujeres," *Confidencial* 5, 239 (May 6-12, 2001).

34. According to a newspaper article that reported the campaign against Quirós, Article 30 of the Nicaraguan Constitution, which addresses duties and rights, reads, "'a Nicaraguan has the right to freely express his or her thinking in public or in private, as an individual or collectively, in oral, written, or other form.' While Article 15 says that anyone who was born in Nicaragua or naturalized is Nicaraguan." Rafael Lara, "Ana Quiroz amenazada: gobierno quiere quitarle nacionalidad," *El Nuevo Diario*, February 16, 2000.

35. Quirós gave an example of a mayor in the Nandaime region who proposed to construct a bridge for $25,000 to $30,000. Instead, by drawing support from the community, the NGO Nochari (a member of the Coordinator and a target of Alemán's campaign) managed to construct the same bridge for $5,000. "From this perspective, obviously it would seem to them that we control a great deal of money," author interview with Ana Quirós, Managua, August 6, 2001.

36. Sergio Aguirre Aragon, "Terrorismo de estado contra ONGs: funcionarios de Coordinadora Civil define y denuncia," *El Nuevo Diario*, February, 2000; Lara, "Ana Quiroz amenazada"; Rafael Lara, "Ana Quiroz amparada: tribunal requiere a Migración a Gobernación," *El Nuevo Diario*, February 19, 2000. Author interviews with Ana Quirós, Managua, March 29, 2000 and August 6, 2001.

37. Mario Mariena Martínez, "Oscurantismo y perversidad: 'Si Mujer' se defiende y denuncia conspiración; Niegan abortos anticonceptivos y prueban su notable colaboración con la salud de Ia mujer; Intención [*sic*] integral reconocida nacional e internacionalmente," *El Nuevo Diario*, June 29, 2000.

38. Mario Mairena Martínez, "Caceria medieval: acoso contra Si Mujer y aborto terapéutico." *El Nuevo Diario*, June 28, 2000; and Mariena Martínez, "Oscurantismo y pervasidad." Illegal abortions (estimated at 36,000 per year) contributed to one of the highest rates of maternal mortality in Central America, 106 deaths per 100,000 live births. Scarlet Cuadra, "Tintes políticos en la polémica sobre el aborto en Nicaragua: unidos, la iglesia y el presidente Alemán," *Proceso*, no. 1246 (September 17, 2000): 3-4, www.proceso.com.mx/1246/1246n23.html. Article 165 of the Constitution, a 129- year-old civil code provision, made therapeutic abortion legal when three doctors from the Ministry of Health determined that the pregnant woman's life was in danger. Such abortions were rarely performed; based on conversations with health-care activists, my understanding is that it was hard to find three doctors willing to take the politically risky position of recommending a therapeutic abortion. In the political climate that prevailed in Nicaragua from 1990 on, poor women who were dependent on the public health-care

system, and whose pregnancies endangered their lives, were effectively condemned to death.

39. Granada's response to the accusation was to invite government officials to the record room, which keeps active records for 23,000 patients, whereas there are only about 6,000 Sandinistas in the region (quoted in Lourdes Arroliga "Alemán ordena intervenir cooperativa y ONG suiza," *Confidencial* 5, 221 (December 10-16, 2000). The quantitative evidence in the clinic files was supported by statements from people who identified themselves as members of the former Resistance [the Contras], Sandinistas, Liberals, Evangelicals, or Catholics all of whom testified that they had been served by the clinic's staff. Roberto Collado Narváez, "El helicóptero es de Alemán," *El Nuevo Diario*, April 22, 2000.

40. When Dorothy Granada was able to return to Mulukukú two months later and the clinic reopened (on March 8, International Women's Day), many local residents from a variety of political parties, including the president's Liberal Party and former Contras, participated in the reopening celebration. Many of the speakers noted that the clinic was their only source of health care. They included a woman holding a small boy who said that the boy's twin brother had died of asthma recently because the clinic was not open. Jill Winegardner, "Solidarity in Times of Internet," *Envío* 20, 237 (April 2001): 28.

41. Quoted in Collado Narváez, "El helicóptero es de Alemán."

42. The national campaign, which mobilized human rights groups, women's groups, peasant organizations, and NGOs in support of Granada's right to continue to serve the health-care needs of poor rural dwellers, was most dramatically illustrated by a march of ten thousand people in Managua. Outside Nicaragua, the campaign was headed by solidarity groups and eventually involved pressures from the U.S. Congress and Amnesty International. Winegardner, "Solidarity in Times of Internet," 22-29.

43. She was permitted to return to Nicaragua in February 2002, a month after Alemán stepped down as president, with an offer of Nicaraguan citizenship. This seemed to be a way for newly inaugurated President Enrique Bolaños to distance himself from Alemán, whom he had served as vice president. Arroliga, "Alemán ordena intervenir"; Lizbeth Garcia, "Dorotea confía en la Corte Suprema: plazo es al 9 de septiembre," *El Nuevo Diario*, August 14, 2001; Oliver Gómez, "Dorotea llega y llora: 'Gracias mi Nicaraguita,' exclama al recibir documentos," *El Nuevo Diario*, February 23, 2002; "Dorotea Granada: 'Me dice feminista porque odio la violencia,'" *La Boletita*, no. 46 (February-May 2001): 62-69; Nicaragua Network Midwest 2001, 7; Nicaragua Network Midwest, *Nicaragua Alert* 16, 7; Ary Pantojo, "Todo el estado contra Dorotea," *La Prensa*, December 18, 2000; Consuelo Sandoval, "Solicitaran nacionalidad para Dorotea Granada," *La Prensa*, 30 June 2001; and Winegardner, "Solidarity in Times of Internet," 22-29.

44. Author interview with María Eugenia Morales, Nandaime, August 9, 2001.

45. Coordinadora Civil para la Emergencia y la Reconstrucción (CCER), *Visión de país*, January 2001: 1-12; Humberto Meza, "Guerra a los ONGs," *El Nuevo Diario*, December 16, 2000, 2001; author interview with Quirós, August 6, 2001; and author interview with Morales, August 9, 2001.

46. Author interview with Quirós, August 6, 2001.

47. Even those who did not identify with the Sandinistas recognized the anti-Sandinista focus of Alemán's battle with the NGOs. The authors of an article published in *La Prensa*, a newspaper well known for its opposition to the Sandinistas during their

decade in office, noted on April 4, 2001, "The Ministry of State (MIGOB) and the Non Governmental Organizations (NGOs) are beginning a new round in an endless fight that began in 1997 and that continues today." The article also noted that organizations targeted for multiple audits included even those with Sandinista roots that were critical of the current Sandinista leadership. Juan Rodríguez, Gabriela Roa Romero, and Consuelo Sandoval, "Gobernación y ONG libran nuevo round: practican auditorias de las asociaciones civiles dirigidas por sectores críticos al 'orteguismo,' *La Prensa*, April 4, 2001.

48. Author interview with Quirós, August 6; Centro de Apoyo a Programas y Proyectos (CAPRI), Directorio ONG de Nicaragua, 1999-2000 (Managua: Centro de Capacitación Profesional Nicaragüense Alemán, 1999), 194; Octavio Enríquez, "Resurge guerra contra Los ONG: ahora van con POPOL-NAH," *El Nuevo Diario*, April 4, 2001; Octavio Enríquez, "Amenazan a los ONG rebeldes," *El Nuevo Diario*, April 4, 2001; and Rodríguez et al., "Gobernación y ONG libran nuevo round."

49. Octavio Enríquez, "Dra. Nuñez exonerada," *El Nuevo Diario*, May 9, 2001; and *Envío*, "An Election Script with Heavy-handed Special Effects," 2.

50. This case was newsworthy because the Alemán administration was unusually open in defending the use of foreign development funds for its own political purposes. Vice President Bolaños told a reporter, "in any civilized country if one is going to construct 800 houses and ... the president says 'look, give me one, two, three, ten, twenty so that, within the parameters that you give me ... I can choose some people who will get houses,' don't you think this would be a nice courtesy for the President of the Republic?" Solis, "Alemán inaugura, descalifica y politiquea."

51. Personal communication, August 2001.

52. Florence Babb, *After the Revolution: Mapping Gender and Cultural Politics in Sandinista Nicaragua* (Austin: University of Texas Press, 2001); Maria Teresa Blandon, "The Coalicion Nacional de Mujeres: An Alliance of Left-Wing Women, Right-Wing Women and Radical Feminists in Nicaragua," in *Radical Women in Latin America: Left and Right*, ed. Victoria González and Karen Kampwirth (University Park: Pennsylvania State University Press, 2001), 111-31; Norma Stoltz Chinchilla, "Feminism, Revolution, and Democratic Transitions in Nicaragua," in *The Women's Movement in Latin America*, ed. Jane Jaquette. (Boulder, CO: Westview Press, 1994), 177-97; Ana Criquillon, "The Nicaraguan Women's Movement: Feminist Reflections from Within," in *The New Politics of Survival: Grassroots Movements in Central America*, ed. Minor Sinclair (New York: Monthly Review Press, 1995), 209-37; Katherine Isbester, *Still Fighting: The Nicaraguan Women's Movement, 1977-2000* (Pittsburgh: University of Pittsburgh Press, 2001); Karen Kampwirth, "Confronting Adversity with Experience: The Emergence of Feminism in Nicaragua," *Social Politics* 3, 2-3 (Summer-Fall 1996): 136-58; and Sofia Montenegro, ed., *Movimiento de mujeres en Centroamerica* (Managua: Programa Regional La Corriente, 1997).

53. Quoted in Cuadra, "Tintes políticos en la polémica sobre el aborto," 5.

54. In the face of lobbying efforts by women's rights activists, Article 165 was put off until the subsequent legislative session. Lourdes Arroliga, "Aborto terapéutico a debate hasta en próxima legislatura? Mayor distanciamiento entre clero y movimiento pro mujeres," *Confidencial* 5, 239 (May 6-12, 2001).

55. Asael Perez Marín, "Iglesia celebrara el Día del Niño por Nacer," *La Prensa*, 18 March 2000.

56. Infopress Central America, "NGOs Under Attack," *Central American Report* (CAR), March 10, 2000: 2, www.infopressca.com/CAE/magizi/2710-2.htm.

57. Author interview with Sofia Montenegro, Managua, August 7, 2001.While they go beyond the scope of this article, the number of efforts to curtail the press that were carried out during the Alemán years ranged from legal changes in the regulations as to who could work as a journalist to physical attacks on one female journalist by President Alemán himself when he did not like her questions. Eloisa Ibarra, "Alemán agrede a Eloisa: borracho vociferaba como un energumeno," *El Nuevo Diario*, August 2, 2001; Octavio Enríquez, "Alemán huye de la SIP," *El Nuevo Diario*, July 5, 2001; Rafael Lara, "Alemán confronta y agrede a la prensa," *El Nuevo Diario*, July 5, 2001; and Rafael Lara, "Cobarde agresion de Alemán," *El Nuevo Diario*, December 5, 2000.

58. The Directorio ONG de Nicaragua, 1999-2000, which is the most complete source on the nongovernmental sector, gives information regarding 218 NGOs, including the names of the executives of those organizations. In eighty-three of the cases the executive is a woman, in 134 of the cases the executive is a man, and in one case a man and a woman are listed as coexecutives. CAPRI, Directorio ONG de Nicaragua, 27-244.

59. Victoria González, "'The Devil Took Her': Sex and the Nicaraguan Nation, 1855-1979" (paper presented at the 22nd meeting of the Latin American Studies Association, Miami, March 16-18, 2000).

60. González, "The Devil Took Her," 3.

61. González, "The Devil Took Her," 2.

62. González, "The Devil Took Her," 3-4.

63. González, "The Devil Took Her," 3-4.

64. The thousands who protested the Pact in Managua on July 8, 1999, were led by representatives of the National Feminist Committee and the Women's Network Against Violence, among them Daniel Ortega's stepdaughter, Zoilamérica Narváez, who helped carry a banner reading "Sexual abuse should not be negotiated or pacted, no to impunity." Quoted in Mario Mairena Martínez, "Contra el pacto, contra corrupción," *El Nuevo Diario*, July 9, 1999; see also Joaquín Torrez, "Marcha resumió esperanzas populares," *El Nuevo Diario*, July 9, 12, 1999.

Chapter 5

Unholy Alliance: Church and the State in Nicaragua (1996-2002)

Andrés Pérez-Baltodano

The process of democratic experimentation that Nicaragua initiated in 1990 came to a halt during the Liberal government of Arnoldo Alemán (1996-2002). A "pact" reached by the Frente Sandinista de Liberación Nacional (FSLN) and the Partido Liberal Constitucionalista (PLC), gave these two parties almost absolute control of the Nicaraguan electoral and judicial systems.[1]

Moreover, administrative corruption and abuses of power by government officers reached endemic proportions during the Alemán presidency. The Corruption Perception Index published by Transparency International in 2001 placed Nicaragua among the fifteen most corrupt countries of the world and as the third most corrupt country of Latin America.[2] On August 7, 2002, Arnoldo Alemán and several members of his family and government were formally accused by the new administration of Enrique Bolaños of the misappropriation of more than one hundred million dollars.[3]

Official corruption was one of the factors responsible for the dismal socioeconomic conditions of Nicaragua during the Alemán presidency. A study released by the United Nations Food and Agriculture Organization (FAO) in June of 2002—five months after the end of the Alemán government—shows Nicaragua as the country with the worst levels of malnutrition in Latin America.[4] Despite the deplorable political, social, and economic conditions of Nicaraguan society during the period 1996-2002, the Nicaraguan Catholic Church maintained unwavering support for the Alemán government, defended it against accusations of corruption and abuses of power, and even attacked and condemned those who denounced it. This chapter analyzes the politics of the Nicaraguan Catholic Church during the period 1996-2002 and assesses the main arguments used by the Church to reject, deflect, and downplay both accusations of corruption and abuses of power against the Alemán administration, and public criticism of the nature of church-state relations during this period.

In defending the regime, the Church in fact provided the moral legitimacy for the undoing of democracy by Arnoldo Alemán, and through this role it became one of the pillars of Alemán's caudillismo. The other pillar, as has been discussed elsewhere in this volume by Hoyt, was the FSLN, which despite its political and ideological differences with Alemán and the PLC also facilitated the reign of caudillismo by virtue of the Ortega-Alemán pact. Given the fragility of Nicaragua's democratic institutions, this triumvirate of FSLN-Alemán-Church was to have a powerful impact in rolling back the process of democratic consolidation in Nicaragua. The objective here is to focus on the Church's role in this process.

From Doctrinal Principles to Pragmatism

In the mid 1970s, the Nicaraguan Catholic Church transformed itself from a silent participant in the reproduction of the power structures of Somocismo, to a vocal critic of the government of Anastasio Somoza Debayle. Inspired by the doctrinal teachings of the Second Vatican Council, the Latin American Bishops' Second Conference at Medellin in 1968 and the reinterpretation of Christian values and principles articulated by Liberation Theology, the Nicaraguan Catholic Church proclaimed the historical and political relevancy of Christianity, and demanded the initiation of a radical process of structural changes to bring freedom and justice to Nicaraguan society.[5] In 1979, less than a year after the celebration of the Latin American Bishops' Third Conference at Puebla, the Nicaraguan bishops went as far as to proclaim the legitimacy of the armed popular insurrection against Somoza.[6]

During the revolutionary decade of the 1980s, the Nicaraguan Catholic Church opposed the centralist political project and materialistic philosophy of the FSLN and it became the most important institutional expression of the opposition against the Sandinista regime. With the uncompromising anticommunist position of Pope John Paul II, and the gradual institutionalization of his conservative religious doctrines within the Church, the critical position of the Nicaraguan bishops concerning the nature and orientation of the Sandinista Revolution hardened. The clearest indication of the level of congruency between the position of the Nicaraguan Catholic Church vis-à-vis the Sandinista Revolution and the Vatican's view of socialism was the appointment of Archbishop Miguel Obando y Bravo as cardinal in 1985.

The Church interpreted the electoral defeat of the FSLN and the beginning of a democratization process in 1990 in the same way it had interpreted the fall of the Soviet Union and communism in Eastern Europe. For the Church, the collapse of the Berlin Wall and its aftermath were determined by Divine Providence; that is, by the intervention of "digitus Dei."[7] The Pope himself proclaimed the intervention of Divine Providence in the ending of the Sandinista regime when in his second visit to Nicaragua in February 1996 he declared, "Thirteen years ago, it seemed that you, Nicaragua, and you, Central America, were only a superpowers' shooting range. Today it seems that you are the subject of your own human sovereignty: Christian and Nicaraguan. I remember the celebration of thirteen years ago. It had a place in the darkness, in a deep dark night. Today we had the same Eucharistic celebration. It is clear that Divine Providence is acting its designs on the history of the nations of all of humanity."[8]

Despite the Pope's optimistic assessment of post-Sandinista Nicaragua, democracy in this Central American country was a fragile procedural arrangement that was not based on a legitimized consensus regarding the organization of the social, political, and economic life of Nicaraguans. Even after the defeat of the FSLN in the elections of 1990, Nicaraguans were sharply divided into Sandinista and anti-Sandinista camps representing and advocating two radically different visions of the proper relationship between the state, the economy, and society.

The Nicaraguan Catholic Church understood the fragility of the Nicaraguan democratic experiment and recognized the potential for a Sandinista resurgence in the country. Afraid of the consolidation of the power of the FSLN in post-revolutionary Nicaragua, the Church deplored the influential positions that Sandinistas retained in the Nicaraguan political system during the Chamorro government and repeatedly demanded that Sandinista leaders respond for the cases of corruption and violations of human rights during the 1980s.

The position of the Church was at odds with that of the Chamorro government, which had formally adopted a policy of national reconciliation, which necessarily included the FSLN—the largest and most powerful political party in the country. By 1993, the Church was openly opposed to the politics of the Chamorro government vis-à-vis the FSLN.[9]

Despite their references to Catholic doctrines and principles, the pastoral letters and official notices of the Conferencia Episcopal de Nicaragua after 1990 reflected the predominant political concerns of the Nicaraguan Catholic Church. In these documents, the conventional diplomatic and metaphorical language normally used by the Church to deal with "temporal matters" was abandoned in favor of very direct and aggressive language against the Sandinistas.

At the same time, Cardinal Obando y Bravo began to systematically express his opinion on all kind of political and economic issues confronted by the Chamorro government. From his position, he was able to tap on a strong reservoir of anti-Sandinista feelings among Nicaraguans to become the most influential personality in post-Sandinista Nicaragua.

During the campaign for the presidential elections of 1996 the FSLN, led by Daniel Ortega, was involved in a tight race with the Alianza Liberal led by Arnoldo Alemán. The possible return of the FSLN to power induced Cardinal Obando y Bravo to use his considerable authority in an openly partisan manner.

On October 17, three days before the elections, Cardinal Obando y Bravo celebrated a mass and delivered a sermon—broadcast by radio throughout Nicaragua—in which he invented a biblical passage about a treacherous snake that has killed an innocent man who naively believed that snakes could be trusted. Every Nicaraguan understood that the invented biblical passage was a reference to the Sandinista candidate Daniel Ortega. Arnoldo Alemán, the Liberal candidate—who was present at the mass—had referred to the FSLN as a "black and red snake" during the campaign.

After the mass, Cardinal Obando y Bravo offered his blessing to the liberal presidential candidate. The picture of a pious Arnoldo Alemán receiving Cardinal Obando y Bravo's blessing was published in color and distributed by *La Prensa* on election day.[10]

Alemán won the elections and the Catholic Church established itself as the indisputable arbiter of Nicaraguan politics. However, the power achieved by the Church as a result of the political role that it began to play after 1990 had a price. By immersing itself in the ruthless and contradictory political process of Nicaraguan society, the Nicaraguan Catholic Church was forced to adopt a pragmatic position congruent with the opportunistic and instrumental values that dominate Nicaraguan politics. By pragmatism we mean a position devoid of principles and guided predominantly by expediency.[11]

The dangers of pragmatism would become evident during the six-year presidency of Arnoldo Alemán. During this period, the Church subordinated doctrinal consistency to political convenience to neutralize the power of the FSLN and to consolidate its institutional position within Nicaraguan society. By 2002, the pragmatic position adopted by the Nicaraguan bishops had transformed the Church into a virtual accomplice of the Alemán government.[12]

The Presidency of Arnoldo Alemán (1996-1997)

In February 1999, three years after the inauguration of the presidency of Arnoldo Alemán, the Contraloría General de la República (CGR) released Alemán's probity declarations corresponding to 1990, the year when Alemán was elected mayor of Managua; 1995, the year when Alemán resigned his position as mayor to run for the presidency; and 1996, the year when Alemán became president. These documents show that from 1990 to 1996 Alemán's personal wealth had increased by 900 percent. Alemán provided vague explanations for the astonishing growth of his personal patrimony, and refused to provide the CGR with detailed information concerning his personal businesses.[13]

New evidence of corruption against President Alemán mounted quickly during the first half of his mandate. Almost daily, the media provided information concerning Alemán's vigorous purchase of land and his systematic use of public resources and services to improve his private properties. The intricate relationship between the state and Alemán's personal business became painfully clear when it was revealed that the director of the Rural Development Institute (IDR)—a public sector institution—was in charge of the administration of Alemán's farms.[14]

Corruption and abuses of power by the Alemán government attracted international attention. In June 2000 *The Economist* reported that political scandals in Nicaragua were approaching mythic levels. In the last year of the Alemán presidency the international reputation of the Nicaraguan government was in a shambles. That year, President Jimmy Carter pointed out that: "the general assessment by international organizations is that Alemán's is one of the most corrupt administrations in the hemisphere."[15]

The Nicaraguan Catholic Church, however, publicly defended Alemán and his government against documented accusations of abuses of power and corruption. In the face of all this, many Nicaraguans—Catholics in particular—were trying to make sense of the relationship between the Church and the government of Arnoldo Alemán.

The Unholy Position of the Church

During the period 1996-2002, the Catholic Church consistently deplored poverty and corruption in Nicaragua.[16] Using explicit and implicit arguments, however, the Church contended: that the root causes of poverty and corruption lay in the revolutionary experiment of the 1980s; that corruption was a general societal moral problem and, by implication, not a sin or a crime that could be directly attributed to the Alemán government; that the solution to corruption and poverty was moral and spiritual and, by implication, not political or legal; and finally, that the problem of corruption and abuses of power during the Alemán government was a fabrication of the Nicaraguan media.

Blaming the (Sandinista) Past

The Church acknowledged the contribution of Somocismo to the dismal social conditions of Nicaragua during the 1990s. It even assigned some responsibility for the reproduction of these conditions to the Chamorro and the Alemán governments.[17] However, the Church consistently maintained that the main cause of poverty and corruption in Nicaragua lay in the revolutionary experiment led by the FSLN from 1979 to 1990.

The official messages of the Nicaraguan Catholic Church during the period 1996-2002 systematically reminded Nicaraguans of what Pope John Paul II referred to during his second visit to Nicaragua as "the dark night" of Sandinista rule in the 1980s. Moreover, the bishops repeatedly demanded that the abuses of power and violations of human rights that took place during the Sandinista regime be punished. They argued that those who in the past committed injustices and crimes should "humbly recognize" and repair their actions.[18]

Nicaragua's "suffering," according to the Nicaraguan Catholic bishops, went back to 1972, which was the year when Managua was destroyed by an earthquake. Since then, the bishops pointed out, "selfishness, personal and group's ambitions, social insensitivity (particularly of those who own most of the economic and cultural capital), hatred, and *the hypocrisy of many politicians and pseudorevolutionaries*" have been responsible for the persistence of suffering in the country.[19]

The Nicaraguan bishops also argued that poverty and social inequality were the result of past actions and more specifically of "the ambitions, selfishness, and corruption of those who have controlled wealth and power."[20] The bishops also demanded that those who "brought the country to beggary and taught people to obtain goods and things without working should accept and redeem their guilty."[21] This message was a reference to the Sandinistas and the socialist and populist policies and programs they promoted in the 1980s.

Writing in the past tense, the bishops added: "Wealth and power were used for personal gains or for the benefits of groups and parties that enriched themselves at the expense of the misery of everybody else. If on top of this we add the hatred and political divisions that created the conditions for war, the huge backwardness of the country is not surprising."[22] Nevertheless, the bishops pointed out, "the country has enjoyed progress over the last years."[23]

The optimism of the Nicaraguan Catholic bishops regarding the "progress" enjoyed by Nicaragua over the "last years" was not supported by reality, and was not shared by most observers. By 1999 a mounting body of evidence implicated the Alemán government in systematic corruption and abuses of power. Fraudulent privatization schemes, illegal transfers of money from government institutions to private accounts, double salaries and unjustified extra-incomes for high ranking government officers, and the misappropriation of international donations and loans received by Nicaragua after Hurricane Mitch for the personal benefit of government officers, were exposed by the Nicaraguan press at the same time that the Nicaraguan Catholic Church was blaming the past and celebrating the present. In this, the Church was out of touch with most Nicaraguans.[24]

One survey carried out in 1999 showed that 45.2 percent of the population considered the Alemán government as the most corrupt government in the history of Nicaragua.[25] Another study conducted in March 2000 showed that 89 percent of the population defined the Alemán government as "corrupt."[26] The authorities of the Nicaraguan Catholic Church downplayed the results of these studies. Monsignor Eddy Montenegro, the vicar general of the archdiocese of Managua, for example, pointed out that corruption "was a problem that existed all over the world."[27]

Socializing Corruption

Ambiguity was one of the rhetorical resources used by the Church to discuss the problem of corruption without assigning direct responsibility to the Alemán government. In the pastoral letters of the Conferencia Episcopal de Nicaragua as well as in press conferences offered by the authorities of the Church, corruption was portrayed as a "societal problem" caused by general erosion of moral values in Nicaraguan society.

The generic and abstract nature of corruption, according to the Church, made it difficult to establish direct and concrete responsibility for its occurrence. In their message "Justicia y Paz con occasion de las Fiestas Patrias" of 1988 the bishops pointed out: "The vice of corruption erodes the social, political, and economic development of any nation and must be combated decisively."[28] While the Church acknowledged that government corruption had a negative impact on development, it also argued that "Corruption is difficult to fight against because it adopts multiple forms."[29]

The multiple forms that the Church made reference to in its message "Justicia y Paz" included all forms of misguided and criminal behavior by all members of society, regardless of the position, age, and social responsibility of the culprits, or the consequences and implications of their actions. The Nicaraguan bishops pointed out: "There exists a generalized culture of corruption that covers almost all sectors of our society. This culture continues despite the Church's constant denunciations against it."[30] "We are," the bishops argued, "in the presence of a morally sick society that needs to be cured through its conversion, that is, through its return to Lord Jesus."[31]

Following the publication of the "Justicia y Paz" message, the secretary of the Conferencia Episcopal de Nicaragua, Father Ariel Ortega Gasteazoro, reinforced the Church's portrayal of corruption as a societal and generic problem that indiscriminately included all kinds of wrongdoings regardless of their nature, scale, and consequences. Father Gasteazoro argued that "sometimes we forget that the student that cheats is corrupt, or that a person that pretends to be sick is corrupt. Corrupt is the teacher that does not teach properly and also the owner of the convenience store who falsifies the price of his merchandise."[32]

The generic, abstract, and indiscriminate view of corruption portrayed by the Church became a convenient way for the government to avoid political and legal punishment. Using the rationale and the arguments articulated by the former to conceptualize and explain corruption, Vice Presidente Enrique Bolaños —who headed the Comité Nacional de Integridad (National Committee on Integrity)—quickly pointed out, "we are all sick."[33]

Spiritualizing (and Decriminalizing) Corruption

Consistent with its portrayal of corruption as a general moral problem the Church proposed spiritual solutions to this problem. In their "Mensaje de Pentecostés" of 1997, the Nicaraguan bishops acknowledge that that social, political, and economic condition of the country was "critical and difficult" and that "profound changes" were necessary to resolve them. Moreover, the bishops recommended the organization of an undefined "social economy" and "the rule of law" as ways of confronting the challenges of Nicaraguan society. However, they pointed out that these institutional and structural changes were secondary to, and dependent on, the "spiritual renovation" of Nicaraguan society. Social, political, and economic changes, the Nicaraguan bishops argued, "will not take place unless there is a change of hearts and minds among Nicaraguans."[34]

In their "Mensaje con Motivo del Inicio de Adviento," the Church proposed once again a spiritual solution to the political and social problems of Nicaraguan society. Nicaraguan Catholics, the Church argued, needed to confront the "environment of uncertainty" within which the country operated by promoting "the virtue of hope" so that they "do not lose sight of their definitive encounter with Jesus."[35]

The Church's position regarding the need for a spiritual solution to the social and political crisis of Nicaraguan society was reaffirmed in the communiqué "Justicia y Paz con occasión de las Fiestas Patrias" of 1998. The solution to this crisis, the Church argued, required "a personal *metanoia*: a change of attitude."[36] This change, according to the Church, "would be the beginning of a structural renovation that will allow Nicaraguans to live in harmony and peace."[37]

Following their view of corruption as a moral problem that demanded, first and foremost, a spiritual solution, the Church asked the rich and the powerful "to be compassionate" so that they could "see the misery of those around them." The rich and the powerful, the bishops argued, should "exercise all their ethical and religious energy to overcome all situations of injustice and inequality."[38]

The official position of the Conferencia Episcopal de Nicaragua concerning the nature of the problem of corruption and its solution were reinforced by public statements and sermons offered by authorities of the Church. On May 25, 2000, for example, Obando y Bravo declared that the elimination of corruption demanded the spiritual conversion of "the whole of society."[39]

By proposing a spiritual solution to the crises confronted by Nicaraguan society during the Alemán presidency, the Nicaraguan Catholic Church promoted the decriminalization of government corruption. "Spiritual conversion before legal and political action" was the implicit message sent by the Nicaraguan bishops to the Nicaraguan people. This message was quickly adopted by Vice President Bolaños who declared that the solution to the problem of corruption was "the cure and moralization of the whole Nicaraguan society."[40]

Shooting the Messenger

The relationship between the Nicaraguan media and the Nicaraguan Catholic Church during the presidency of Arnoldo Alemán stands in sharp contrast with the one that existed between the Church and the government during the last years of the Somocista regime. In 1978, the Church raised its voice to protect freedom of press against the dictatorship of Anastasio Somoza Debayle: "We cannot remain silent," the Nicaraguan bishops stated, "when freedom of expression is not complete and when people's right to receive true information is suffocated with fines and threats."[41] During the Alemán presidency, however, the Church not only remained silent about the threats and intimidations made by President Alemán against the Nicaraguan media, but it also became the media's most vocal enemy.

During the first years of the Alemán presidency, the Nicaraguan Catholic Church repeatedly accused the Nicaraguan media for "sensationalizing" and "exaggerating" the problems of corruption and abuses of power by the government.[42] Toward the end of the Alemán presidency, the position of the Church vis-à-vis the media had deteriorated to the point of hostility.

By 1999, denunciations of corruption by the main Nicaraguan newspapers were portrayed by the Church as expressions of "envy" and "irresponsibility."[43] In their "Comunicado Ante la Realidad Nacimal" of June 2001, the bishops went as far as to suggest that the "media's lack of objectivity and sincerity" could be part of a "perfectly elaborated plan to create chaos, anarchy, uncertainty, and destabilization with electoral and political motives."[44]

The position of the Conferencia Episcopal de Nicaragua was reiterated by the bishop of León, César Bosco Vivas Robelo, in a personal letter to President Alemán. In this letter, Bishop Vivas Robelo praised Alemán for his performance as president, and he accused the media of trying "to destroy and discredit him [Alemán] and his government." Vivas Robelo stated that: "It is sad ... that the media did not constructively criticize the government for those mistakes that members of the government—human as they are—could have made during your presidency."[45] Concurrently, Cardinal Obando y Bravo declared to *La Prensa* that the media had "exaggerated" the problem of corruption during the Alemán presidency. "There has been mistakes," the cardinal pointed out, "but we have to recognize that the government has created public works that did not exist before."[46]

By May 2002, four months after the end of the Alemán presidency and amid a growing mountain of evidence of corruption and abuses of power against the Alemán government, the Church launched its strongest attack against the Nicaraguan media. In its message of May 11, 2002, the Church argued that the media had "manipulated" the public to create an artificial crisis.[47] In this message, the Church also asked the new government of Enrique Bolaños—the former vice president and head of the Integrity Committee during the Alemán government—"to forgive" and to establish a dialogue "with all other political forces."[48] To the surprise of many, President Bolaños had declared a "war against corruption" and had begun to investigate Alemán, members of his family, and associates.

Ironically, the Church that had blamed "the past" for poverty and corruption during the Alemán government, and that has demanded that the "sins of the past" be accounted for by the Sandinistas, was now calling on the Bolaños government to forgive and forget the Alemán past and to concentrate its attention on the present and the future. "We need," the Church stated, "to overcome the injuries of the past that have caused so much suffering to the Nicaraguan society and family."[49] Therefore, the Church argued that it was necessary to promote a process of reconciliation and consensus between the new government and all other political forces, so that the country could confront the great challenges of the present moment.[50]

The Pragmatism of the Catholic Church and the Future of Nicaraguan Democracy

The political position of the Church during the period 1996-2002 can be characterized as *pragmatic*. During this period, the Nicaraguan bishops ignored and even contradicted the doctrinal position of the Church regarding the moral responsibilities of government. At the most basic level the seventh commandment forbids theft. The catechism of the Catholic Church is more specific and includes as "theft" a list of "morally illicit" actions that reads as a description of the charges made by the Nicaraguan press and the government of Enrique Bolaños against the government of Arnoldo Alemán: "speculation in which one contrives to manipulate the price of goods artificially in order to gain an advantage to the detriment of others; corruption in which one influences the judgment of those who must make decisions according to law; appropriation and use for private purposes of the common goods of an enterprise; work poorly done; tax evasion; forgery of checks and invoices; excessive expenses and waste. Willfully damaging private or public property is contrary to the moral law and requires reparation."[51]

The position of the Nicaraguan Catholic Church regarding government corruption during the Alemán presidency was also in contradiction with the teachings of the Consejo Episcopal Latinoamericano (CELAM).[52] In 1997, the Latin American bishops invited the media to actively participate in the struggle against corruption: "We ask the builders of society, especially those responsible for the mass media, to help us to promote authentic Christian values and to eradicate corruption from the life of our nations."[53]

The position of the Church concerning corruption during the Alemán presidency was a far cry from the courageous position adopted by the Nicaraguan bishops—including Cardinal Obando y Bravo himself—in 1978 when the abuses of power of Anastasio Somoza Debayle led them to declare: "We cannot remain silent: When the majority of the population live in inhuman conditions as a result of an evidently unfair distribution of wealth [...] when public officers use their power to enrich themselves, forgetting their responsibility to the people that they are suppose to represent [...] when administrative corruption remains unsanctioned despite repeated scandals that erode public morality [...] when the national budget does not help the poorest sectors of [Nicaraguan] society."[54]

The reasons behind the pragmatization of the Nicaraguan Catholic Church from the late 1970s to the 1990s are complex. This chapter has argued that the Church's political position during the period 1996-2002 was mainly motivated by the Church's desire to neutralize the power of the FSLN. It is also possible to argue that the Nicaraguan Catholic Church supported the Alemán government in order to maintain and develop its political influence in the fields of reproductive health, family, and education policies.[55] Furthermore, it is possible to contend that the Nicaraguan Catholic Church supported the Alemán government in order to secure government financial and other forms of material support to confront the rapid expansion of different forms of Protestantism in the country.[56]

Questions have been raised about the Church's direct involvement in government corruption. At the time of the writing of this chapter, the Comisión de Promoción Social Arquidiocesana (COPROSA), the main Catholic organization for social services in Nicaragua was under investigation for allegations of corruption. Several high-ranking members of the Catholic clergy have also been mentioned as possible beneficiaries of illegal government operations during the Alemán presidency.[57]

There are also less tangible reasons that need to be taken into consideration before a full explanation of the Church's position of support to the Alemán government can be articulated. After the virtual elimination of the influence of the members of the "Popular Church" that supported the Sandinista Revolution in the 1980s, the Nicaraguan Catholic Church became one of the most intellectually backward churches of the Latin American region. From this perspective, the pragmatism of the Nicaraguan bishops during the Alemán presidency could be the result of the Nicaraguan bishops' inability to strike an adequate balance between the Church's political needs and its religious and doctrinal compromises and obligations.

The Nicaraguan Catholic Church's intellectual poverty is probably the most important impediment for the necessary reconstitution of this important religious organization in the aftermath of the Alemán presidency. To overcome the shortcomings of the pragmatic position adopted by the Nicaraguan bishops during the presidency of Arnoldo Alemán, the Nicaraguan Catholic Church needs to reestablish its doctrinal foundation. In turn, this transformation requires a level of commitment to philosophical and theological analysis that seems to be beyond the vision and capacity of the current leadership of the Nicaraguan Catholic Church.

The inability of the Nicaraguan Catholic Church to reestablish its doctrinal and moral foundation can only have a negative effect on the future of Nicaraguan democracy. Despite its declining institutional legitimacy,[58] the Nicaraguan Catholic Church continues to exercise enormous influence in a country whose political culture is dominated by a predominantly religious vision of politics and power.

Notes

1. Emilio Alvarez Montalván, *Cultura Política Nicaragüense* (Managua: Hispamer, 2000), 296-99.

2. Transparency International, "Corruption Perception Index, 2001," www.transparency.org.

3. "Y después de abrir la huaca qué?" *La Prensa*, August 8, 2002, www.laprensa.com.ni; "Corrupto y Traidor," *El Nuevo Diario*, September 8, 2002, www.elnuevodiario.com.ni.

4. "Nicaragua Encabeza Lista de Países con más Desnutrición", *La Prensa*, June 9, 2002, www.laprensa.com.ni.

5. Conferencia Episcopal de Nicaragua, "Mensaje al Pueblo Nicaragüense," *Documentos Conferencia Episcopal de Nicaragua*, January 20, 1979, www.tmx.com. ni/~cen.

6. Conferencia Episcopal de Nicaragua, 1979.

7. Vittorio Messori, ed., *Crossing the Threshold of Hope (by His Holiness John Paul II)* (Toronto: Alfred A. Knopf, 1994), 127.

8. John Paul II, "Homilía en la Eucaristía Concelebrada en Managua," *Documentos Conferencia Episcopal de Nicaragua*, 1996, www.tmx.com.ni/~cen.

9. Conferencia Episcopal de Nicaragua, "Segundo Concilio Provincial de Nicaragua," *Documentos Conferencia Episcopal de Nicaragua*, no. 132, 1992-1993, www.tmx.com.ni/~cen.

10. "El Nuevo Escenario Nacional," *Envío* (November-December, 1996), www.uca.edu.ni/publicaciones/revistas/envío.

11. John Patrick Diggins, *The Promise of Pragmatism: Modernism and the Crisis of Knowledge and Authority* (Chicago: University of Chicago Press, 1994).

12. "Y después de abrir la huaca qué?" *La Prensa.*

13. "En el Vórtice de otro Huracán: La Corrupción," *Envío* (March 1999), www.uca.edu.ni/publicaciones/revistas/envío.

14. *Envío*, "En el Vórtice de otro Huracán."

15. Jimmy Carter, quoted in Mary Jordan, "Nicaraguan Election Draws High Turnout Close Race Raises Concern in Washington," *Washington Post Foreign Service*, November 5, 2001, A17.

16. See especially Conferencia Episcopal de Nicaragua, "Mensaje de los Obispos de Nicaragua sobre la Justicia y Paz con Ocasión de las Fiestas Patrias," *Documentos Conferencia Episcopal de Nicaragua*, September 3, 1998, www.tmx.com.ni/~cen.

Chapter 6

Violence and Personal Insecurity: The Alemán Administration's Authoritarian Response[*]

Elvira Cuadra

Conflict, even violent conflict, lies at the heart of politics. Nevertheless, political analyses of conflict often focus only on events involving established and important political forces. Where the conflict involves participants on the margins of the normal political order—the regular actors who pursue conventional aims using well-known and generally approved methods—it is not unusual to miss the conflict's political content and regard it as simple criminality. In countries that, like Nicaragua, are caught up in a maelstrom of rapid and radical change, however, it is precisely those new actors and their recourse to unconventional and contentious political action that must be examined to grasp fully the dynamics of the political process.

This chapter marks a first attempt at a systematic analysis of the role of violence in the Nicaraguan political system that has taken form over the last decade. It rests on the thesis that the means used to regulate and mediate conflicts in a democracy must be integral parts of a model of democratic governability. Yet it is precisely that model that is only just being developed in transitional democracies. Thus, where there are high levels of violence in a transitional system, it is necessary to resolve the conflicts in order to arrive at a model of democratic governability.

Without such resolution, the levels of conflict can easily surpass the capacity of the nascent political system to contain them, creating instability and, in the worst instances, leading to state failure. This leaves a fledgling democratic government three options. The first and least desirable is to resort to authoritarian methods to suppress the conflict, a decision which opens the way to restoring a

---

[*] translated by David Close

103

more broadly authoritarian political system. A second option is to have limited recourse to authoritarian practices to confront violent conflict, thereby leaving authoritarian traces on an otherwise democratic system.[1] The best result is for the political system to grow more democratic as it confronts the realities of violent conflict. Although it may well be that a system in fact needs to face and resolve the challenges posed by highly contentious political behavior to become more fully democratic, this is a daunting task. To understand how this process is unfolding, we must look at how the Nicaraguan state has responded to political violence arising from the claims of nontraditional actors.

Nicaragua's evolving constitutional democracy confronted elevated levels of political conflict for four reasons. First, there is little consensus among the country's political elites as to what Nicaraguan democracy should look like, thus producing conflicts over defining the very principles of the emerging democratic state. Next, because the state's ability to resolve conflicts within the political system has been limited by, among other things, a lack of material resources, this dissensus frequently expresses itself as violent confrontation. Third actors on the margins of the political system who seek political change increasingly find themselves excluded from the normal political process, leaving them few options besides open confrontation to express their demands. Finally, and critically, the established elites, those who effectively define the contours of the political system, have shown little interest in accommodating demands from outside their number.

A decade's inability to bring violent claims for political action within the state's regular institutional framework has left Nicaragua a significant democratic deficit. There is little political space for the articulation of alternative perspectives and regular political institutions have proven unable or unwilling to develop instruments other than open repression or covert coercion to manage unconventional political behavior. Though these conditions have prevailed since 1990, this chapter concentrates on the period of the Alemán administration. Not only has the era of the Chamorro administration already been examined,[2] but Dr. Alemán's government has produced its own way to treat bitter political conflicts. His response was in keeping with his approach to dealing with other issues confronting his administration—to resort to the least desirable option from the perspective of democratic governance. In keeping with the strategy of caudillismo, as discussed throughout this volume, public policy under the Alemán presidency was driven more by the extent to which it served the leader's interest than the general welfare.

The Chamorro Administration

When Violeta Chamorro assumed the presidency of Nicaragua in 1990 the country embarked on its second major political transition since 1979. Yet this second change of regime was perhaps even more complex than that brought by the Sandinista Revolution, because it came at the end of a decade of internal war.[3]

Moreover, as few in the country expected Chamorro to beat the Sandinistas, little thought had been given to what a transition from revolutionary Sandinismo would entail. As a result, the country was not well prepared to face the conflicts that grew from reordering the political system, returning ex-combatants to civilian life, dealing with claims for properties expropriated and redistributed by the revolutionaries, or absorbing the economic shocks that would come with the new government's embrace of a structural adjustment program (see figure 6.1). I treat each challenge in turn.

At a purely political level, the Chamorro administration had hoped to define the nature of the country's transition to constitutional democracy. These hopes were unfulfilled, as the new government was torn by internal struggles to define its course, as well as facing strong and active opposition from the FSLN and its allied organizations. As a result, at the administration's close it had not progressed far along the road toward democratic consolidation.

This is important, because the Chamorro government's continual adjustments to a changing political situation affected the evolution of further conflicts. For example, because the government was unable to provide adequately for demobilized soldiers, both ex-Sandinistas and former contras resorted again to arms. This, in turn, brought new armed conflict to rural Nicaragua, as the old enemies fought not just each other but national security forces as well.

Property conflicts were a special nightmare for President Chamorro's government. In rural areas these were often violent and linked to the question of postwar reconstruction, as clashes broke out when the government decided to distribute land to either group of ex-combatants. The first years of the 1990s produced land seizures, violent evictions, and massive invasions of lands on Nicaragua's agricultural frontier. In urban areas property conflicts more often took the form of litigation and demands for restitution of or compensation for properties confiscated by the Sandinista government. The most controversial cases involved Nicaraguans who had acquired American citizenship and received the support of the U.S. embassy. The scale of the conflicts generated by the property issue and the economic disruption that they caused were sufficiently great that international agencies, such as the UNDP and the Carter Center gave special attention to the question. Unfortunately, these processes moved slowly and the property question appears likely to bedevil Nicaragua for some time to come.

Conflicts arising from the application of economic austerity policies were mainly urban phenomena, led by organized labor. The unions demanded stable employment and better pay and benefits. The government, for its part, had to balance the budget by cutting social spending and laying off government employees as a condition for receiving low interest loans from multilateral lenders. As a result, poverty rates grew dramatically as jobs were lost and the country's already weakened social safety net suffered further damage. To make matters worse, corruption began to flourish within the public sector.

Political Conflicts 1990-1996

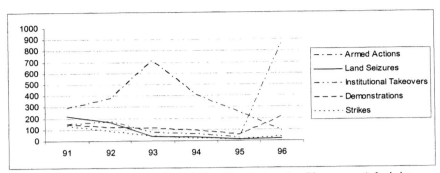

Figure 6.1: Five Forms of Political Conflict during the Chamorro Administration

Both urban and rural conflicts peaked in 1993-1994 (figure 6.1), as problems linked to pacification, property, and economic reform came to a head. In the northcentral part of Nicaragua ex-combatants continued using arms to press their claims. Land seizures continued unabated. Demonstrations and strikes protesting structural adjustment were common. Government's response to these challenges did not reflect a consciously chosen strategy, but rather was the product of conjunctural deals struck within the political elite.

Thus, the Chamorro administration never defined a policy for responding to and then treating the causes of violent conflict. It did not, that is, have a strategy for assuring domestic peace and public security. Depending on its relations with Sandinista opposition, the government's response swung between repression and accommodation. Further, the National Police saw its remit stretched far beyond its capacities, resulting in a failure to control political violence that made the forces of order appear incompetent.[4] In the end, President Chamorro left office with the country facing an unfinished transition, a host of unresolved social conflicts, and a state scarcely able to govern its nation.

The Alemán Administration

It was in this difficult context that Dr. Arnoldo Alemán was elected president of Nicaragua in 1996. The Liberal chieftain's arrival in office generated a series of expectations. These five were the most important. Alemán's leadership would be sufficiently strong to bring to a successful close the political transition begun in 1990.

- Completing the transition would open the way for democratic consolidation, a new social pact, and a new national project that would unite and inspire Nicaraguans.
- The new governing model would bring existing conflicts into the democratic system where they would be peacefully resolved.

- This model would also strengthen state institutions, leaving them better able to face challenges in the future.
- A consolidated democratic government would spawn an economic model responsive to the needs of the poorest.

Unfortunately, none of these hopes were realized, not least because they conflicted with the actual aims of the new administration. In fact, a preliminary assessment of the Alemán years shows that instead of consolidating democracy, the Liberal administration moved back toward authoritarianism. To see how this happened and to understand the consequences this implied for the democratic management of political conflicts we must examine four related themes:

- the changing political processes;
- the revised legal framework;
- the new role of social movements and civil society; the altered objectives of state economic management.

To begin with the political system, the most dramatic difference between incoming and outgoing administrations was that Alemán led a more unified party, one with clearly defined interests and a solid social base. The PLC, though an alliance of various Liberal factions, possessed a much clearer identity than had President Chamorro's UNO. Put simply, the PLC is a party, indeed it is one with hegemonic aspirations; the UNO was an electoral alliance, with few shared objectives beyond winning power. As a result, within the PLC there was less jockeying for position and struggling for power than in the prior administration. As well, where Chamorro had faced a bewildering array of minuscule parties, each pursuing a private agenda, politics in the Alemán administration quickly evolved into a two-party straight fight between the PLC and FSLN.

In keeping with one of the less attractive traditions of Nicaraguan politics, however, the Liberals and Sandinistas soon discovered certain shared interests and formed a pact to secure those aims. This pact, which is treated extensively in Katherine Hoyt's chapter, was mainly about creating a Liberal-Sandinista political duopoly that would exclude all other political forces. As the details of the deal are set out elsewhere, we need only note that although the pact brought the signatories the control of the political system they sought, it has not produced political stability. Rather, it has brought partisan conflicts into many parts of the political system, producing standoffs between the PLC and FSLN, fought out by their appointees to the Supreme Court, the Supreme Electoral Council, or the comptroller's office.

One point, though, that we must examine here concerns the effects of the pact on organized interests, social movements, and civil society. There we find, as Kampwirth and Deonandan note, that the disarticulation and co-optation of social movements that began early in the 1990s grew stronger during the Alemán administration, causing reverses that still affect both old and new movements. Combining this with the weakening of parties that the pact occasioned shifted to the media and a number of NGOs much of the responsibility for representing society to the state. The NGO sector has taken on the job of organizing and articulating to government the demands of various sectors of society. Despite their hard work and good intentions, however, this brought a fragmented pattern of representation that both falls short of that earlier provided by the movements and tends to make the groups represented "clients" of the NGO.

This, of course, is one of the aims of neoliberal state reform, which seeks to take responsibilities from government and transfer them to the third, or non-profit, sector. However, it makes the NGOs struggle fiercely for scarce resources, both among themselves and with government. To improve their chances of getting funding, some organizations collaborate closely with the state, a choice that puts them at the politicians' mercy. Further, faced with the emergence of a new political sector, a government, and even more political parties, can come to see the NGOs as competitors.

To deal with the NGOs the Alemán administration created a legal framework to regulate, some say hamper, their work. As a result, the organizations have lost vital legal privileges relating to their rights to manage financial donations received from abroad. More importantly, the government has scrutinized the operations of the NGOs in the most minute detail, hounding organizations it felt were its enemies with constant audits and threats of judicial action. It is in its active persecution of certain NGOs that the Alemán government showed its authoritarian colors especially clearly.

Because the mass media, at least those not directly linked to the administration,[5] assumed the role of the government's critic and the people's watchdog, faithfully reporting the administration's missteps, it was only natural that the government would turn on them. The weakness of the legislative opposition, which became its near absence once the pact was concocted in 1999, left the media to take on that role, even to the point of formulating policy proposals different from the administration's. This did not sit well with either the government or the FSLN, neither of which wanted to see the press become Nicaragua's alternate government. As Deonandan's chapter describes, the administration began forming a legal framework that would restrict the freedom of the press, as well as resorting to the familiar tactics of withholding government advertising from and refusing information to out-of-favor media.

A similar pattern appeared in the realm of economic policy,[6] as Close summarizes in the prologue where there were signs of the formation of economic groups linked to the administration through personal connections. The purchase by Alemán supporters of a bank (BANIC), is one example, though it subsequently failed. The fact, however, that such groups had been the organizational base of the economy during the last decades of Somocista rule was troubling. It may well be that the formation of such groups is a characteristic of patrimonial rule, though that is a question that has yet to be investigated. Nonetheless, it is interesting that the Sandinistas also have strong links to particular economic interests.

Another possible indicator of the appearance of an Alemanista economic group was heightened conflict with COSEP, the umbrella organization of Nicaraguan big business. Any government will seek to benefit is friends, e.g., those firms that have historically contributed generously to the party's coffers. However, if it turns out that the Alemán administration went beyond this in its clashes with COSEP, it will suggest that the government violated a basic rule of capitalist democracy by systematically tilting the playing field to benefit its friends and harm its enemies. As this same pattern marked the administration's relations with the media and civic organizations, we should not be surprised to find a similarly aggressive partisanship marking the government's dealings with economic interests.

Further, while sectors of the wealthy were prospering, ever fewer numbers of the poor could afford basic goods and services. As well, changing international economic conditions, notably a collapse in coffee prices toward the administration's end, aggravated an already difficult economic situation. Yet the progressive closure of political space by the Alemán government left both citizens' organizations and business groups outside the charmed circle without resources to press for changes. To be sure, the government did create two multisectoral consultative bodies, CONADES (National Development Council) and COMPES (Council for Economic and Social Planning); however neither was able to exercise real influence within government.

Political and Social Conflict During the Alemán Administration

It is in the context sketched above that the high levels of social conflict that marked President Alemán's term must be seen. These conflicts, which frequently took violent forms, can be divided into two groups, organic and inorganic as described below.[7] As shall be discussed later, regardless of the nature of the conflicts, that is the legitimacy (or lack thereof) of the goals, they were met with an authoritarian response from the state.

1.   Organic Social Violence: This refers to violent incidents arising from unresolved political conflicts and involving organized groups. The best examples are the rearmed groups that flourished in the early 1990s and the armed rural bands that appeared in the second half of the decade.

2.   Inorganic Social Violence: This category contains incidents of violence undertaken by individuals, mobs, or semiorganized groups that have no obvious political objective, although deteriorating social conditions may contribute to their appearance and frequency. Youth gangs, suicides, and violent crimes against persons and property are put here.

Forms and Characteristics of Violent Conflict

Organic social violence includes armed actions (such as those carried by armed groups in rural zones), as well as any form of social protest that results in confrontations between demonstrators and the police. Among these are demonstrations, land seizures, and occupations of public buildings. Since 1996, there has been an overall decline in the frequency of violent political conflicts (see figure 6.2).[8] Figure 2 shows two exceptions: an increase in land seizures in 1997, perhaps linked to Dr. Alemán's election,[9] and a dramatic jump in mass demonstrations and occupations of public institutions in 1998, reflecting high levels of discontent with government policy. These dropped dramatically the following year.

Political Conflicts 1997-2000

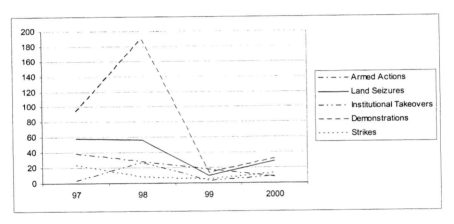

Figure 6.2: Five Forms of Political Conflict during the First Four Years of the Alemán Administration

In 2000 all forms of contentious political conflict, except armed actions, rose again. Although there is as yet no systematic analysis of these phenomena, a reasonable hypothesis is that the rebound was linked to heightened political conflict associated with municipal elections. Should data from 2001, when national elections were held, show a continuing rise in violent conflict, it will suggest a troubling correlation between general political activity and violent confrontation, hardly a recipe for consolidating democracy.

Turning now to consider nonpolitical or inorganic forms of social violence, figure 6.3 shows an upward trend during the first four years of the Alemán government. According to police statistics, the greatest rise occurred in crimes against property.[10] This has led authorities to link the rise in crime with increasing poverty, although there is still no systematic analysis of these data.[11]

Social Conflicts 1997-2000

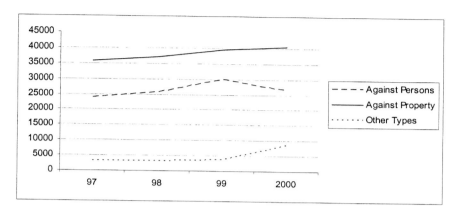

Figure 6.3: Forms of Social Conflict during the First Four Years of the Alemán Administration

While there has been a slight decline in crimes against persons (which covers everything from simple assault to premeditated murder), it is a rise in drug-related offenses that most merits attention. In the second half of the past decade police have intercepted significant quantities of narcotics being shipped to North America via Nicaragua. This prompted the authorities to fear that Nicaragua had become a new route for traffickers. The discovery of landing strips in the country's mountainous central region, along with the capture of a helicopter in the same area, made it seem that armed groups in Nicaragua were copying their Colombian counterparts and becoming narcoguerrillas. It now appears, though, that these were isolated incidents.

Finally, the growth of youth gangs and an alarming increase in suicides should also be considered. Although gang activity is far less significant in Nicaragua that it is in El Salvador, the most gang-plagued country in Central America, gangs are more numerous than ever before and have come to control whole neighborhoods in the nation's cities once night falls.[12] Suicides have also increased, from 204 to 211 between 1999 and 2000.[13] Again, neither phenomenon has received systematic study, but it is conceivable that both reflect a broader social crisis.

Interpreting the Evidence

Different beliefs about political violence prevail among different sectors of Nicaraguan society, but those of three actors—the Alemán government, the police, and civil society—have been most important. The government's view has been frankly authoritarian. It treated not just violence but all social conflict as threats to the "established social order" that had to be repressed. The government's view understandably permeated all state institutions, setting the standard by which social conflicts were judged.

Interestingly, the police, a national body in Nicaragua, does not have a single, dominant interpretation of social conflict and political violence. On the one hand, it recognizes the social and political origins of many of the conflicts it is called to resolve. On the other, it adopts President Alemán's line that those who participate in these conflicts are lawbreakers, a position likely shared by police everywhere. As a result, Nicaragua's police have responded differently to different kinds of conflicts.

Though we have presented civil society as a single actor, it must be noted that three views of political and social conflict are found there. The first adopts the authoritarian, law and order, position of the government. This perspective is most likely to be found among individuals directly affected by these conflicts and who thus support strong, repressive government action.[14]

Organizations that deal directly with the causes and consequences of social violence take a different view of the problem. They argue that social and political conflicts reflect deeper underlying problems. Therefore, they see the need to attack the roots of violent conflict with social programs and to resolve conflicts that do emerge with dialogue and negotiation, instead of always relying on force.

A third view of conflict is promoted by certain political leaders, academics, and public intellectuals. They see violent conflict as a natural outgrowth of "a culture of violence," which produces in turn a society composed of violent individuals. For them the solution is to develop a "culture of peace" through "civic education," that is educating people to behave civilly. Though this position is far more often proclaimed than actually examined to test its validity, it serves to justify many programs funded by international donors who want to help construct a more democratic Nicaragua.

In general, these views of civil society changed little throughout the 1990s. Indeed, it is rather more likely that they have been reinforced by official positions taken by both the Chamorro and Alemán administrations that viewed political and social conflicts as forms of criminality.[15] Nevertheless, the two governments reacted differently to contentious political conflict. In the case of President Alemán, the treatment accorded social conflict was not just brusque and authoritarian, but perfectly consistent with the political logic undergirding his entire administration.

Authoritarianism versus Civic Culture

Since 1996, it has been the perspective of the Alemán administration that has underlain the design and implementation of official responses to violent political conflict. This has meant relying on repression rather than negotiation and denying that violent social conflict can have a political base. To properly understand the implications of this it is necessary to look more specifically at the administration's policy on citizen security.[16]

Since the beginnings of Nicaragua's transition to constitutional democracy, opponents of the government have used direct action politics (demonstrations, confrontations, and strikes) as regular political instruments.[17] This has made the role of the police critical, as it is the police who are the most visible presence of the state in such situations and who find themselves engaged in violent confrontations with protestors.[18] Action of this sort can be considered contrary to democratic principles, which emphasize peaceful solutions to conflicts. However, whenever the goals of a protest have run counter to the interests of the elite, the chosen policy instrument has been police action, not dialogue. The FSLN's use of demonstration politics to secure its policy objectives in the early 1990s seems to have created a framework in which violent confrontation becomes an incidental backdrop to serious politics. Therefore, one deals not with the protestors, who are to be repressed, but with other members of the political elite, who are assumed to control the protesters.

The role of the security or anticrime policies in the broader political process should be to promote what Anthony Giddens[19] called "ontological security," a general sense of confidence and safety that generates a stable social and material environment. However, given the insecurity and instability that has pervaded Nicaraguan life since the early 1980s, it is easy to imagine that citizens see the state as incapable of providing any sort of safety. Further, as the last three Nicaraguan regimes—Somocista, Sandinista, and now Liberal constitutional—have relied heavily on the instruments of coercion to maintain order, citizens may even doubt that government can treat them in any but a violent manner.

The Alemán government showed no signs of breaking this mold, but rather added its own touches. More than any regime since the Somoza dictatorship, the government of President Alemán regularly used coercion and intimidation to gain partisan advantage. Although the Sandinista regime frequently resorted to force, especially in the middle 1980s, it could at least claim that it did so for legitimate national security reasons. As for the Chamorro administration, the first in the new constitutional democratic order, coercion was used to control open conflict and maintain order, but not as a regular governing instrument. Looking at any of the long series of protests and conflictive politics during the administration of President Alemán—armed band activities; student protests over university funding; strikes by doctors, health-care professionals, and transport workers; marches by the hungry; or the treatment of the media and NGOS suggests that the government could find only authoritarian responses.

Armed Bands

Centered in the Mining Triangle (Siuna, Rosita, and Bonanza) of northcentral Nicaragua, the armed bands that operated in the late 1990s were remnants of the much larger and more dangerous groups that destabilized the countryside during the Chamorro administration. President Alemán continued his predecessor's policy, which was based on ad hoc responses aimed at demobilizing the groups, because it worked. The government would use religious leaders as mediators to engage the band's leaders in discussions aimed at buying leaders' acquiescence and offering lesser material benefits to the followers, as a sort of consolation prize.[20] Before starting talks, however, military actions softened up the guerrillas to make them more amenable to negotiation. Left leaderless, the former fighters would try to reorganize, now bringing in criminals and poor peasants, as well as dissatisfied ex-Sandinista or Resistance soldiers.

In 1999, the National Police developed a plan for restoring security and reestablishing the state's presence in the former conflict zones. As this did not immediately bear fruit, the government authorized the formation of a special task force, integrating police and military units, prior to the 2001 electoral campaign, to defeat the armed groups. Both the government and security forces declared that there would be no negotiations, only surrender or death. This initiative appears to have been successful, killing the main armed leaders. There have, however, been reports of mistreatment of local civilian populations by the task force.

Demonstrations and Protest Activities

Strikes by health-care workers, work stoppages by bus and taxi drivers, and student protests over government funding of Nicaragua's universities posed great challenges for the Alemán administration in 1998 and 1999. Built around economic grievances, these protests were distinguished both by their capacity to mobilize supporters and by the elevated levels of violence that marked their confrontations with the police that left numerous casualties, even fatalities, among the protestors. The government's strategy in all these cases was to begin negotiations, using them as a way of buying time to organize a suitable police operation. To further delegitimate the protests, the administration painted the protesters as Sandinista stooges with purely partisan motives.[21]

The Media and the NGOs

The Alemán government's relations with the media and NGOs involved in development work and democracy promotion shows a different but still fundamentally authoritarian approach to politics. Instead of using physical coercion to control these groups, the administration used judicial and administrative instruments. The most notorious of these came to be called "fiscal terrorism," the use of repeated audits to harass opponents. As well, the administration promoted laws that restricted freedom of the press and expression. One of these created a College of Journalists, membership in which would be required to work as a reporter in any medium. As well, the government had resorted to one of the oldest tools for punishing political opponents: withholding government advertising from media adopting a critical or oppositional line.

In the case of the NGOs, the instruments are similar: fiscal harassment and administrative control through the office in the Ministry of the Interior responsible for NGOs.[22] In certain cases, like that of Dorothy Granados, more direct action was taken. Principally for questioning the administration's handling of relief funds flowing to Nicaragua after Hurricane Mitch in 1998 during a public meeting, Granados, a U.S. citizen who had long worked in the Nicaraguan health sector, found herself expelled from the country, without recourse to normal processes of law.

Natural Disasters and Hunger

The response of the president to claims for government help arising from a landslide on Casitas Peak during Hurricane Mitch in 1998, and a famine in the department of Matagalpa in 2001, offer further evidence of the extent to which the Alemán administration had come to view all criticism as disloyal and baseless. In the first case, the mayor of the nearest community had alerted Managua that a disaster was immanent, but Dr. Alemán personally dismissed the warning, because the mayor was a Sandinista. Three years later, driven by hunger, peasants from the department of Matagalpa marched on the capital and established a camp in a park opposite the presidential mansion. They were again dismissed by the president as Sandinista agents, a position from which even Vice President Enrique Bolaños quickly distanced himself. Eventually, a minimal "food for work" program was set up for them, but there was no attempt by the government to arrive at a policy of food security.

As with the more obvious forms of political action, the government's response to those seeking aid to avoid or attenuate crises reflected its authoritarian disposition. Unwilling to take claims for help at face value or acknowledge that the state might bear some responsibility for helping victims of disasters, the president lashed out, acting in ways that he apparently thought would make his unfeeling response legitimate. What is particularly telling about these cases is the personal involvement of President Alemán. That his behavior here parallels exactly the positions taken by his administration in the other cases analyzed leaves no doubt that the president's hand was behind those instances of authoritarian politics. Nicaragua was again in the hands of a caudillo, a man for whom personal satisfaction is the only criterion for judging the soundness of policy. Not only had democracy been sacrificed, but even the bases of institutionalized constitutional rule (polyarchy) that are democracy's prerequisites were placed in jeopardy.

The Contribution of Civil Society

This grim scenario does have a positive side, namely the effort that politically organized civil society has made to direct Nicaragua's pervasive social and political conflict into democratic channels. NGOs working in the area of social development and democracy promotion, and local groups involved in civic affairs have searched diligently for ways to mediate those conflicts and reduce their frequency and intensity. Thankfully, there are signs that the ordinary Nicaraguan citizen is indeed developing such democratic values as tolerance, respect for others' rights, and a repugnance for violent politics.[23] To the extent that the values become general throughout society, Nicaragua's chances to rebuild democracy are enhanced.

However, these efforts are fundamentally sectoral and local, hence limited in their effects. They are not, then, by themselves sufficient to counter the authoritarian discourse and practice that marked the Alemán administration and undid much of Nicaragua's new democracy. Moreover, because the work of the NGOs frequently focuses on the individual, building democracy one citizen at a time, there is a tendency to overlook the macrosocial component of conflict. If Nicaragua had a government disposed to view social and political conflict as something besides a novel form of criminality this would not matter. However, during the Alemán presidency this was not the case.

What is clear, however, is that in 2001 Nicaragua's citizens held views that were more democratic than were those of their governors. Certainly the behavior of President Alemán and his administration are clear evidence of this. Whether the events of that half decade have permanently weakened Nicaragua's democratic potential is a question that only time will answer.

Conclusion

Although the Alemán administration had strong authoritarian tendencies which revealed themselves with particular clarity in its handling of political conflict, it would be wrong to see it as simply a recreation of Nicaragua's authoritarian past. In fact, the administration developed a unique mix of attributes that set it apart.

First, it did share with past systems a traditional and conservative view of social conflict. As in the past, conflicts were seen as a direct threat to the government that had to be repressed and eliminated. There was no attempt to resolve the conflicts through negotiation, neither did the state seek to expand democratic space by treating the claims of protestors as at least potential matters for political attention.

Further, this perspective extended beyond the administration, *per se*, i.e., the executive and the Liberal leadership in the Assembly and the courts, to permeate the political system. The most striking result of this has been the progressive closure of Nicaragua's political system to those outside the current elite. Both the Sandinista and Liberal parts of the country's political elite appeared to share this view, which has parallels in the country's Somocista past.

Third, and closely related to the above, is how the country's political institutions and its system of conflict management treat cases of conflict. The state's reluctance to negotiate solutions even to specific conflicts indicates that its governing formula cannot and will not consider conflictive political behavior as indicative of a deeper malaise. Where dissent arises, whether from the press or protest movements, it can only be suppressed, because from the perspective of the nation's governors, its only purpose is to stir up discontent.

Finally, by closing off channels of protest at the same time that the political elite also restricts conventional routes of access to decision-making centers suggests that citizen quiescence and apathy is the long-term goal of Nicaragua's governors. Civil society, working mostly through NGOs, does try to create political space among citizens themselves. Although this is in keeping with neoliberal prescriptions, where civil society supplants the state, the Alemán administration viewed even these actions as threats. Unable to recognize an escape valve when it saw one, the government, and to a substantial extent its Sandinista opposition, chose instead to attack the NGOs.

Unless the administration of President Enrique Bolaños changes course radically, Nicaragua's best hope for democratic reconstruction will be a politically active civil society. But the actors who form this sector will have to move beyond the rather limited projects that now occupy them to articulate a broader social project if existing authoritarian patterns are to be undone and replaced by a functioning democracy. Academic studies can play an important role in this process, revealing the richness of Nicaragua's accumulated experience and pointing out where the experience of other countries can be of use.

Notes

1. For example, a state may elect to repress a violent political movement instead of adopting a strategy that combines heightened security measures with negotiations and conscious attempts to remove the roots of the conflict. Democratic rules would, however, continue to apply throughout the rest of society.

2. Among others, see David Dye, Judy Butler, Deena Abu-Lughod, and Jack Spence, *Contesting Everything, Winning Nothing: The Search for Consensus in Nicaragua, 1990-1995* (Hemisphere Initiatives, 1995); Elvira Cuadra, Andrés Pérez-Baltodano, and Angel Saldomando, *Orden social y gobernabilidad en Nicaragua, 1990-1996* (Managua: CRIES, 1998); and Angel Saldomando, *Nicaragua: con el futuro en juego* (Managua: CRIES, 1996).

3. The fact that Nicaragua's internal war of the 1980s involved a U.S.-sponsored military force, the contras—later renamed the Resistance—did not affect the postconflict reality facing Chamorro's government. There were soldiers to return to civilian life, the physical reconstruction of the nation to undertake, and the process of reconciliation to begin, just as if the war had been an entirely domestic affair.

4. This question is treated in depth in Elvira Cuadra, *La participación de la policia en conflictos de orden político*, Monografía de licenciatura (Managua: Universidad Centroamericana, 1995).

5. The administration decided in 1999 to open an official newspaper, *La Noticia*. It continues to function under the Bolaños government as the organ of the PLC (but primarily Dr. Alemán, while he was president [speaker] of the National Assembly).

6. The chapter by Dye and Close on the political economy of the Alemán years examines this and other matters of economic performance in more detail.

7. Angel Saldomando, *Violencia social en Centroamerica: Ensayos sobre gobernabilidad y seguridad ciudadana* (Managua: CRIES, 1998).

8. It can be argued that political conflict has been declining since 1994. However, a resurgence of all forms of violent political conflict, except the operation of armed bands, in 1996 disrupts that trend. It is probable that the spike of violence in 1996 was related to that year's bitterly fought electoral campaign.

9. It could be argued either that Alemán's election emboldened those who had lost property under the Sandinistas to reclaim it with force, or that his coming to power prompted the beneficiaries of land reform to take preemptive actions to protect their lands. In either case, the new president's apparent commitment to settle the claims of those who had lost land can be seen as at least a distal cause of the conflicts that developed.

10. Among crimes against property, breaking and entering and armed robbery grew most rapidly. Thus crimes using force were becoming more prevalent.

11. See, however, Saldomando, *Nicaragua: con el futuro en juego.*

12. Police statistics from 2000 showed 133 juvenile gangs with 2,576 members, most of them between 13 and 20. See Policía Nacional de Nicaragua, *Informe Annual 2000* (Managua: Policía Nacional, 2000).

13. Policía Nacional, *Informe Annual 2000.*

14. Sofia Montenegro, *Jovenes y cultura politica en Nicaragua: la generación de los 90* (Managua: Hispamer, 2002).

15. Cuadra et al., *Orden social.*

16. Nicaragua does not have a specific policy on citizen security, beyond that designed to ensure the maintenance of public order.

17. Saldomando, *Nicaragua: con el futuro en juego.*

18. Cuadra, *La participacion de la policia.*

19. Anthony Giddens, *Modernity and Self-Identity: Self and Society in the Late Modern Age* (Stanford, CA: Stanford University Press, 1991).

20. Elvira Cuadra and Angel Saldomando, "Pacificación, reinserción de excombatientes y consenso social," in Elvira Cuadra, Andrés Pérez-Baltodano, and Angel Saldomando, *Orden social y gobernabilidad en Nicaragua, 1990-1996* (Managua: CRIES, 1998).

21. The government's claims were baseless. Taking the health-care strike as our example shows the issue beginning when the Ministry of Health fired a number of union leaders. Matters grew worse when the ministry refused to obey a Supreme Court order to rehire the workers.

22. Nicaraguan nongovernmental organizations must register with the Ministry of the Interior (Gobernación), the department of government that is also responsible for internal security and law enforcement. One would expect that such organizations would be covered by a charitable organization's act, administered through whatever ministry looks after the companies' law, while NGOs with foreign links would be the responsibility of the ministry of external cooperation. Administering them through a state security ministry seems designed to intimidate.

23. For a fuller discussion see Montenegro, *Jovenes y cultura politica en Nicaragua.*

Chapter 7

Patrimonialism and Economic Policy in the Alemán Administration

David R. Dye and David Close

This chapter has two purposes: to describe and analyze the economic policies of president Alemán's administration, and to ask how Alemán's personal and political self-aggrandizement shaped those policies. To address these questions we briefly examine Nicaragua's economic history; the country's macroeconomic performance during the Alemán presidency; the government's general economic policy line; and how the administration addressed specific issues such as its relations with international donors and the banking crises in 2000-2001. At the close, we broach the question of how Alemán's economic management relates to the conscious undoing of democracy.

Perhaps the most striking characteristic of president Alemán's government was that it was leader-centered—Alemán's style of rule rested on ruthless personal domination both of an official party, the PLC, and throughout the government.[1] It was also given to confusing public property with the private possessions of its members. Regimes with these attributes are often labeled patrimonial or neopatrimonial.

Nicaraguans had firsthand experience with corrupt, patrimonial politics during the Somoza dictatorship. From 1936 to 1979, public well-being regularly finished a distant second to the dictator's desires, producing widespread hardship and preparing the ground for the Sandinista revolution. Although President Alemán did not reintroduce repressive Somocista politics, he and members of his administration are accused of having systematically enriched themselves at the public's expense. In the president's case, press reports indicate that a personal estate of $30,000 with which he began his political life as mayor of Mana-

119

gua in 1990 had grown to $250 million by the time he left the presidency in 2002.[2]

The case of Arnoldo Alemán suggests that patrimonial public management has economic and policy ramifications that go beyond corruption. Both in an economic and a political sense, Alemán aspired to build an empire—he wanted to turn himself into an economic force to be reckoned with, and desired to keep a large share of power after he left office. The scale of these aspirations guaranteed that the Big Man's deeds would have manifold impacts. Though our survey is indicative rather than exhaustive, we argue that the methods used by the caudillo to build and control his empire harmed both economic development and public welfare. Those methods weakened the coherence of and in some cases grossly impaired the implementation of public policy. Alemán's zeal in appropriating government-owned assets furthermore retarded and distorted privatizations, hindered competitiveness, and jeopardized foreign assistance. His desire to accumulate private assets also crowded out other investors, further hampering economic growth. Finally, the patrimonial leader's unrelenting drive for economic and political advantage contributed to the collapse of several banks.

Our initial premise about whether undoing democracy produces a specific form of political economy is simple—the general characteristics and political goals of any administration inevitably influence its conduct of economic policy. Thus, a government that is always on the alert for partisan advantages and ways for its leader to enrich himself will manage a nation's economy to secure those goals. This does not mean that such an administration automatically produces economic policy failures. It does, however, suggest that economic performance will be skewed, and that policy outcomes will be far from optimal when viewed either in growth or in public welfare terms.

Political repercussions inevitably follow. Even well-functioning democracies periodically produce corrupt politicians. There, however, the norms of accountability, transparency, and adherence to the rule of law work to detect and punish corrupt behavior. Therefore, such behavior does not become the rule. But in Nicaragua the rule of law is weak and the justice system fragile. This has encouraged rulers to attempt to continue in power indefinitely and grant themselves immunity from investigation and prosecution. As Nicaragua's experience suggests, these behaviors imperil democratic consolidation.

Nicaragua's Economic History

Nicaragua has never been rich. It has an open, natural resource-based economy that is embedded in a social structure marked by rigid class divisions and a political system that has usually been the instrument of the dominant classes. The nation's economy has been characterized for centuries by low productivity and, except for brief interludes, very little redistribution of what wealth has been produced.

Albeit with some diversification into maquiladoras and tourism, Nicaragua's economy remains built around natural resources today: 30 percent of its GDP comes from the primary sector, 28 percent from the secondary, and 42 percent from the tertiary, although many of these are informal sector workers.[3] It sells its produce—coffee, seafood, sugar, meat, and now sweatshop garments—in highly competitive and unstable markets, which limits the country's short-term development prospects.

Historically, much of Nicaragua's land was concentrated in large-scale holdings that relied on cheap, servile labor. Thus the revenues generated by the country's agricultural produce did not spread throughout society. Until the development of the cotton staple, around 1950, the Nicaraguan economy was also highly labor-intensive, using few sophisticated inputs and offering little opportunity for diversification. In addition, although there has always been some initial domestic processing of Nicaragua's raw materials, high value-added processing occurred in the developed countries that bought the products.

Nicaragua, then, stayed a model of underdevelopment. For many years there were only desultory attempts to change the system that kept the nation's citizens impoverished. The political elite was corrupt and self-serving, but even had it been painfully honest it would have encountered structural obstacles in the form of capital shortages, weak infrastructure, and a semiliterate population with few skills appropriate to a modern economy.

The Sandinista revolution offered the country a chance to break with its economic past. However, Sandinista economics were about building socialism and at least as concerned about producing egalitarian outcomes as modernizing the economy proper.[4] Worse, the Sandinista regime produced grave economic hardships, for its misnamed "mixed economy" lacked coherence and impeded capital accumulation.

Fighting a counterinsurgent war against U.S.-trained and equipped counter-revolutionaries further retarded economic progress. A decade's civil war brought death and destruction, along with enormous economic dislocation. Along with drawing young men into the military and gearing national production to defense, economic mismanagement spurred hyperinflation of some 33,000 percent in 1988. To try to control this inflation, the revolutionary government brought in a harsh austerity program. This choked whatever life was left from the economy, and by the end of the Sandinistas' tenure GDP per capita had fallen to 60 percent of its prerevolutionary level.

After defeating the Sandinistas in the 1990 elections, the government of Violeta Chamorro (1990-1996) faced a series of complex problems. Its first priorities were reducing inflation and restoring a fully capitalist economy. However, it also had to address claims for properties expropriated by the revolutionary government; manage the privatization of state holdings; and reach a workable structural adjustment program (SAP) with the World Bank and IMF.[5] Table 7.1 shows that this was a slow process.

Much of Chamorro's economic policy aimed to meet the conditions of its SAP. Structural adjustment is the generic name for policies devised in the 1980s by the United States, other major aid donors, and the principal multilateral lenders to address the dangers to the world economy posed by highly indebted Third World countries. The debtor states would receive soft loans from the multilaterals upon changing their economic policies to meet the lenders' conditions, which included reducing budget deficits, opening the country to foreign trade and investment, and making debt repayment a budgetary priority.

As would its successor, the Chamorro government had trouble meeting its creditors' stipulations. It missed deadlines for spending cuts, which meant not meeting targets for deficit reduction, and was unable to fulfill its structural reform objectives. Thus, in 1996 the IMF suspended disbursements to the country under the Enhanced Structural Adjustment Facility, a special SAP for low-income countries, signed with Nicaragua two years earlier.

A further complication affecting economic policy in the early nineties was the property issue. Not only did the Sandinistas predictably resist efforts to take land and homes away from people who had received them from the revolutionary regime,[6] a considerable faction of the president's own party, who wanted faster action, also opposed Chamorro. Indeed, the latter group staged a parliamentary revolt in a failed attempt to get their way. Eventually, in 1995, a settlement was reached and by 1996 Nicaragua was growing again. Yet it had proven unable to meet the conditions of its structural adjustment program, relied heavily on international aid, and faced a mammoth foreign debt. Further, the country's fall in the United Nation's Development Program Human Development Index rankings reflected real declines in citizen well-being.[7]

The Economics of the Alemán Administration

President Alemán inherited an economy that showed clear signs of reactivation. Further, at least a few of the big questions (for example, privatization and the property issue) that had so divided the country in the previous six years were moving toward negotiated solutions. Within this breathing space the new gov-

Table 7.1: Economic Indicators for the Chamorro Administration

Year	GDP ($US per capita)	Annual Inflation (percent)	Foreign Debt (percent GDP)	Budget Deficit (percent GDP)	HDI (Rank)
1991	424	865.6	619	8.1	85
1994	414	12.4	656	13.0	106
1996	422	12.1	317	14.6	117

NFPS = nonfinancial public sector.
(*Sources*: BCN, Indicadores Económicos; UN, Human Development in Nicaragua, 2000.)

ernment still had to address the problem of its SAP, as well as the issue of extreme foreign indebtedness. Changing donor priorities later required it to grapple with fighting poverty and make a pretense of improving the transparency of government operations. But though it showed better results by the end of the decade, Nicaragua was still off the pace in the drive to adjust to a new international economic order.

In terms of economic growth and managing inflation (table 7.2), the Alemán administration did not do badly. According to official figures, real GDP growth from 1997-2001 averaged 5 percent a year, while inflation fell to single digits, foreign and national investment grew substantially, and much public infrastructure was laid down.[8] In fact, as Alemán approached the end of his term Nicaragua was beginning to outperform its neighbors. However, these statistics do not show the president's indifference to improving economic competitiveness, his failure to make public administration more effective, his prickly relations with bilateral and multilateral lenders, or his footdragging over solving the property problem.[9] Such data also miss the administration's subpar results in the realm of human development, along with its tardiness in arriving at a workable poverty reduction strategy. Much less do they give any estimate of the effects of corruption and of the patrimonial management of public resources.

Table 7.2: Economic Indicators for the Alemán Administration

Year	GDP per capita	Year end inflation period	Foreign debt (percent GDP)	NFPS deficit (percent GDP)	HDI ranking
1997	421	7.3	305	7.3	127
1999	448	7.2	296	12.5	121
2001	486	4.8	252	16.1	116a

NPFS = nonfinancial public sector.
a) 2000.
(*Sources*: BCN, *Indicadores Económicos*; UN, Human Development in Nicaragua, 2000.)

Economic Policies for Substandard Growth

To the extent that the Alemán administration had a master plan for economic growth, it was based on opening Nicaragua's economy more quickly to foreign trade, attracting direct foreign investment (FDI), and using tax incentives to spur service exports in maquiladoras and tourism. In 1997, a tax reform law mandated a timetable for tariff reductions that would drop barriers against most imports from outside Central America to 10 percent by July 1999.[10] Given the low savings rate of a semiprostrate postwar economy, policymakers assumed that foreign capital was indispensable in practically all sectors. To do this meant making Nicaragua into an export platform.

Owing to war, political instability, and general economic weakness, Nicaragua's economic base underwent little expansion or modernization between 1978 and 1994. There was a surge of new activity in the first years of the Chamorro administration, as Nicaraguans returned home from the United States or other parts of Latin America. But it was only with Alemán's government that large-scale projects made their appearance. The most visible of these were hotels and shopping centers, which once built gave Managua an air like that of other Central American capitals. Complementing these projects, which were mainly foreign-financed, Asian and U.S. companies took advantage of very cheap labor and invested in garment industries in Managua's burgeoning free zones. Other foreigners put money into electricity generation, telecommunications, and agribusiness, or bought up Nicaragua's traditional industries once tariff reductions left these vulnerable to competition and takeover.

But though the ratio of investment to GDP shot up, overall policy was not shaped to promote export success. On the contrary, Alemán displayed a sovereign indifference to helping the economy compete in world markets— supposedly the ultimate goal of his policies. Absorbed in his private pursuits, he ignored a competitiveness agenda developed in 1999 by economists at the Instituto Centroamericano de Administración de Empresas (INCAE),[11] leaving the work of devising a competitiveness plan to then vice president Bolaños. Flagging external competitiveness became a more salient problem after 1998, when Nicaragua's terms of trade turned adverse, exports began to stagnate, and the trade gap turned into a chasm.

In the opinion of economists, inadequate diversification of the export base is one of Nicaragua's pressing economic problems,[12] and the Alemán administration did little to remedy it. This was not for lack of "incentives" to export goods and services. Alemán built on the Chamorro policy of using generous tax exemptions to spur development of maquilas, and later had the Assembly pass a similar set of tax privileges for investments in tourism. As foreign experts and the IMF favored a "neutral" incentives approach, i.e., no favor for particular sectors,[13] the government later changed course and offered a blanket subsidy to all exporters. In the end, none of this was enough. Though maquila plants and tourist projects sprouted at a rapid pace, overall export (dollar) value in the Alemán years grew at just 5.5 percent a year, and the bulk of the country's exports continued to come from traditional agricultural goods.

The reason was that export success is not primarily a matter of tax policies, but of policy management as a whole. At this level, the Alemán administration neither nurtured the development of business clusters, the approach being tried now,[14] nor did it see to maximizing the myriad conditions for competitiveness identified by INCAE economists. These experts emphasized the need to lower infrastructure costs across the board, overcome glaring deficits in education and technology, and strengthen institutions to permit the quick resolution of property, commercial, and investment disputes.[15] Progress in all three areas was poor, often for reasons related to Alemán's patrimonial use of his powers.

In the infrastructure realm, Nicaragua's failings became chronic in several areas. Though Alemán succeeded in inducing FDI in energy generation, his government signed injurious power purchase agreements that locked Nicaragua into long-term energy costs much higher than those of its Central American neighbors.[16] One of these, with a worthy international partner named Enron, was accompanied by suspicion of a high-figure bribe being extracted in the guise of an operating fee. Similarly, the government's questionable handling of the privatization of Enitel (the state telecoms company, detailed below) limited public investment in new phone lines through most of its term. In a country with just three telephones per hundred inhabitants, fixed phone lines grew by fewer than 10,000 per year. Those who could afford to meanwhile turned to Bell South for cellular service, paying a cost nearly double that in neighboring El Salvador. Many proved willing, and by 2001 cell phone lines outnumbered fixed lines by a small margin.[17]

In these cases Alemán's indifference to maximizing the yield of public policy had presumptive roots in his desire for self-enrichment. Another trait of patrimonial regimes, clientelistic power-wielding, came into play in the education sphere. Alemán appointed political stalwarts to important government posts, then rotated them capriciously to prevent any Liberal rival from emerging from his shadow. During his term, progress was made toward a master plan for educational reform with civil society input and consensus. But when the president sacked education minister José Antonio Alvarado in 1999—to impede him from using his post to become the caudillo's successor—implementation of the blueprint was sabotaged. Although secondary school enrollments crept up, the problem of an unskilled workforce went unattended as vocational and technical education continued to be neglected.[18] As a result, average labor productivity in the economy failed to rise—hardly a lure for foreign companies that wanted to do more than stitch garments.

Some sectoral policies suffered from both clientelistic practices and corruption. There were five agriculture ministers in five years. Agricultural policy was further vitiated by the feathering of partisan and personal nests. In 1997, Alemán clove off the Rural Development Institute (IDR) and placed it directly under the presidency. It first became the focus of intense suspicion for paving rural roads past the properties of PLC officials. Then, in the wake of Hurricane Mitch, the agency was charged with rebuilding the country's damaged cattle herd. According to an investigation by the state attorney's office, millions of dollars from the program went without public bidding to buy cows from an Alemán crony in Honduras that were then sold to supposed "beneficiaries" of the program at twice the purchase price. Many of the animals turned out to be underweight and reproductively defective.[19]

Alemán's languid resolution of property disputes, which continued to be a major impediment to investment, hindered economic growth still further. A year after Alemán took office, some 40 percent of all property confiscation and indemnity cases under official review had been definitively solved.[20] A widely heralded agreement with the FSLN in September 1997 granted the president powers to quicken the pace of property solutions by effectively forcing former owners to accept compensation in the form of government bonds.[21] However, as Alemán preferred to cater to his supporters among the confiscated, this power was little used, and by mid-2001 the percentage of cases regarded as "finished" was only 61 percent. Meanwhile, the government denied legal status to numerous cooperatives to which the Sandinistas had awarded titles shortly before leaving power. As reports surfaced of ever more extensive purchases of farmland by the president, it became apparent that Alemán had little interest in stabilizing land tenure for cooperative members when their title insecurity led them to sell him their land at bargain basement prices.[22]

The president's way of solving investment disputes was to use muscle against other investors. Having an interest in beachfront property for potential tourist development in the southern municipality of Tola, Alemán conspired to prevent anyone else from acquiring land in the area. When an Italian investor named Almerico Domenico attempted to buy twenty-acre property in the same zone, Alemán had him summarily deported early in 2001. He then proceeded to oust a second rival, a Nicaraguan who had sold the Italian his lot, of a much larger property contiguous with his own holdings in the area.[23] Similar tactics thwarted other investments in this and neighboring areas.

Inadequate Social Welfare Impacts

If economic growth was suboptimal under Alemán, so too were improvements in public welfare. Improvements undoubtedly occurred for some sectors. In one of the unheralded economic policy successes, changes in the crawling peg devaluation of the currency in 1999 helped keep inflation between 7 and 8 percent in the following years, boosting real wages for the formally employed population.[24] The average wage earner's salary, then, covered a larger portion of the cost of a basic market basket of goods at the end of Alemán's term than at the beginning. Open unemployment also fell steadily, from 16.4 percent of the economically active in 1996 to 10.7 percent in 2001. But with little progress in upgrading skill levels, underemployment remained high, at around 50 percent.

According to surveys designed by the World Bank, using the unmet basic needs indicator, the percentage of Nicaraguans living in poverty fell from 75.7 percent of the total population in 1993 to 72.6 percent in 1998, with a like decrease recorded in chronic malnutrition among children.[25] Unfortunately, the statistics are misleading. If poverty fell in percentage terms, the absolute numbers of poor Nicaraguans rose by nearly 200,000. More importantly, several studies have suggested that the percent reduction was predominantly the effect of overall economic growth—i.e., public policy consciously directed at reducing poverty had little to do with the outcome.[26] The reduction was also substandard; comparing Nicaragua's performance with others in Latin America, Dijkstra concluded that the real income gain achieved from 1993-1998 should have produced double the poverty decline actually recorded. Influenced by post-Mitch aid, trends for 1998-2001 showed a similar pattern although the poverty percentage fell somewhat more quickly.[27]

Other social indicators improved somewhat during the Alemán period, but did so largely because of increased foreign aid. From 1996 to 2000, central government spending on the social sectors, especially education and health, increased from 11 percent to 16 percent of GDP.[28] Most of the increase occurred after Hurricane Mitch. The process made social spending more aid-dependent, with two-thirds of public investment coming from foreign sources. More important, the impact of the increased expenditure was unexpectedly limited, particularly in the area of rural development. Among the reasons for this poor performance, experts identified the fragmentation of policymaking, pervasive inattention to the operating efficiency of government agencies, and (significantly) inability to evaluate whether funds were being well used.

Domestic policy's scant impact on poverty levels, and the reasons underlying that lack of impact, clearly reflected Alemán's patrimonial politics. Leaders intent on emptying the public purse rarely take an interest in providing more effective public services. Alemán's disinterest in administrative reform first torpedoed expansion of the tax base, a prerequisite for lasting improvements in governmental performance. As do other poor countries, Nicaragua relies heavily on sales and excise taxes for its government revenues. Early in his term, Alemán went to great lengths to secure a widely touted change, the Tax Justice Law, that supposedly closed loopholes and enlarged the base of taxpayers. But though the law was adopted in April 1997, its revenue effect had petered out by the end of 1998, and the ratio of tax income to GDP declined over the following three years. Instead of reforming his agency, tax czar Byron Jerez, Alemán's principal accomplice in corruption, preferred to spend his time exerting fiscal pressures against businessmen who criticized the government, while perpetrating multifarious frauds with tax credit checks.[29]

As the government received an aid bonanza after Hurricane Mitch, its failure to consolidate its revenue base proved not to be fatal. But the way in which aid money has been used in Nicaragua points to a number of additional problems spawned by the patrimonial management of government. Alemán's initial response to the disaster, which struck in late October 1998, was tardy and in some areas of the country improperly partisan, leading some donors to rethink their ties with the country. Meeting in Stockholm in May 1999, the Consultative Group of donor states voiced concern that the Nicaraguan government lacked the will and capacity to make significant changes in favor of democracy and transparency.[30] Despite these misgivings, they gave generously for reconstruction, and total foreign assistance in 1999, excluding aid from NGOs, topped $554m.[31]

By the time post-Mitch aid started to arrive, however, relations with a number of bilateral donors had become strained. In one highly public controversy, Alemán attempted in 1999 to allocate housing units built by a European Union-funded project to members of his personal staff, creating a minor diplomatic flap which forced him to back off. As some diplomats privately admitted, the episode reflected Alemán's calculation that the donors needed to aid him as much as he needed their assistance. The evidence regarding how post-Mitch aid was used is not all in. But anecdotes suggest a continuance of preexisting patterns: aid was spent to have a maximum political effect—rebuilding roads, schools, and health clinics, i.e., visible physical infrastructure—without guaranteeing the funds necessary to maintain the highways, staff the schools, or provide the clinics with medicines. This sort of spending may nourish political clienteles but it does not maximize help for those who most need it. Donor mistrust of the government compounded these problems. To keep the administration away from their resources, donors insisted on running their own projects, which led to inadequate coordination and duplication of efforts.

Even had the government been well intentioned, a deeper problem was apparent—its incapacity to adequately target aid money to have real poverty-fighting impact. A chronically weak bureaucracy, vitiated further by corruption, was the main culprit. Perhaps the clearest case of poor administration has been Nicaragua's health ministry. By 1997, with significant foreign help, a master plan for institutional reform had been formulated and salaries were raised without, however, spurring much improvement in performance. Although overall coverage expanded somewhat, management reforms designed to overcome the ministry's deficiencies and boost primary health care provision in rural areas soon lost steam.[32] A scandal that broke in 2001 over diversion of the ministry's medicines to the PLC election campaign, and the flight in 2002 of Alemán's health minister and her husband from the country to avoid corruption charges, suggest some of the reasons why.

Relations with the International Financial Organizations

Nicaragua is a small, marginal player in the world economy. In 2000, the country derived 25.7 percent of its national income from official development assistance.[33] The nation has run a current account deficit in its balance of payments every year since 1980; the estimated deficit for 2001 was $980 million,[34] roughly 39 percent of gross domestic product. This gap is closed each year by a combination of massive foreign aid, partly as loans that increase the foreign public debt; by large-scale family remittances from Nicaraguans in the United States and Costa Rica; and to a lesser extent by foreign direct investment. For Nicaragua, globalization involves depending heavily on the goodwill both of the international community and of Nicaragua's overseas diaspora.[35]

The goodwill of international donors is crucial in regard to forgiving debt. Although it was reduced dramatically in 1995-96, Nicaragua's external debt in 2001 still stood at $6.4 billion, two and a half times the GDP,[36] the highest in Central America as a percentage of gross domestic product. Foreign indebtedness thus remains a major obstacle to Nicaragua's economic development. The debt question also reminds us of the extent to which Nicaragua's economic policy is made within frameworks set by international lenders, principally multilaterals like the IMF, World Bank, and Inter-American Development Bank. Their prescription—small public sectors, balanced budgets, free trade, and now poverty reduction policies—now lies at the core of most poor nations' development plans.

When Nicaragua entered the ranks of countries seeking an SAP, the IFIs already had a decade's experience with those packages. The general tenor of policy prescriptions did not change in that time, although the multilaterals made adjustments that recognized the plight of very poor countries, notably making them eligible for concessional (soft) loans. The principal qualification for inclusion in a SAP is low per capita income, generally less than $900 annually. To date, Nicaragua has been involved in three IMF-sponsored programs: the Enhanced Structural Adjustment Facility (ESAF); the Heavily Indebted Poor Countries initiative (HIPC); and the Poverty Reduction and Growth Facility

(PRGF). PRGF is ESAF's successor; HIPC is a separate program that exists alongside the others. Nicaragua has found it difficult to meet the conditions of any of these programs, although it is slowly wending its way toward HIPC completion.

The first ESAF was signed in 1994 under the Chamorro administration. Though supposed to run until 1997, the IMF suspended it in October 1996, before Aleman's election, after the government repeatedly failed to meet conditions regarding fiscal savings, international reserves, and foreign debt payments. When he signed a new ESAF with the Fund in March 1998, Arnoldo Alemán inherited similar conditions. He meanwhile began a quest to have Nicaragua included in the IMF-World Bank program to reduce the debts of Highly Indebted Poor Countries (HIPC). Only very poor countries with very high external debts qualify for inclusion in the HIPC. But once qualified, a state can have up to 80 percent of its debt held by the Paris Club countries forgiven, and it is assumed that other creditors, including the multilateral organizations such as the World Bank and IDB, will follow suit.[37]

However, this happens only after a long process that includes a debtor country successfully following reform programs like the ESAF for three years. Although the Alemán administration fared somewhat better in implementing its ESAF than did Mrs. Chamorro, in the end it too came up sorely short of the mark, and for reasons that have directly to do with its politics.

Turning "Adjustment" to Advantage

Under the 1998 ESAF, privatization of Nicaragua's telephone company, Enitel, and other utilities took priority. The government's first try at selling off a 40 percent stake in Enitel ran aground in May 1999 after it was disclosed that it had negotiated an overpriced deal with a firm called Mastec for the installation of 100,000 new phone lines that Enitel's new owner would have to honor. At the time, Mastec was run by Jorge Mas Canosa, the powerful head of the Miami-based Cuban American Foundation and a key Alemán backer. Pressure from the IFIs forced Alemán to rescind the contract but the bid process meanwhile collapsed. A second tender fell apart in September 2000 when only a single bidder appeared and the government rejected its price. It was not until September 2001—as Alemán's term was nearing its end—that a controlling interest in Enitel was finally sold to a group of investors backed by Honduran magnate Miguel Facussé.[38]

Enitel is but one example of how the political and economic interests of the president and his coterie slowed the privatization of Nicaragua's public corporations, delaying needed investments and imposing costs on consumers. More than structural reform, however, it was management of the public finances that broke the IMF's confidence in Alemán. After the Mitch disaster struck, the Fund temporarily allowed the government to run astronomical budget deficits on the condition that expenditures were backed by foreign funds for reconstruction. But after 1999, the deficit was supposed to decline substantially. It did not.

The reason was Alemán's interest in winning municipal elections in November 2000 and a national election in November of the following year. Spending burgeoned first due to the bloated budgets of the Supreme Electoral Council, administered by an Alemán crony. Public sector wage increases and continued "high impact" social investments designed to impress voters inflated the budget still further. Though not unmanageable at 14.1 percent of GDP, the public sector deficit in 2000 was too much for the IMF, and the 1998 agreement was suspended in March 2001.[39] A temporary, six-month interim ("staff monitored") program was put in place in June.[40] But the targets in the replacement program proved even more illusory, and by the end of 2001 fiscal profligacy had produced a dramatic $170m drop in foreign reserves, which on the IMF's "net adjusted" basis ended the year near zero.

Failure to complete the 1998 ESAF was important not simply because it soured official relations with the IMF. It also set back Nicaragua's completion of the HIPC debt reduction process. In September 1999, President Alemán prematurely announced that Nicaragua had reached HIPC startup (called "decision point"), a claim from which he quickly had to backtrack. But under pressure from the G8 nations to get more underdeveloped countries moving into the HIPC, the IMF and World Bank admitted Nicaragua to decision point in December 2000, despite its flagging performance. The IFIs also agreed to shorten the time Nicaragua needed to reach "completion point" and reap the eventual benefits of debt reduction. Meanwhile, however, it would still have to implement reforms.

In October 1999 the ESAF was renamed the Poverty Reduction and Growth Facility (PRGF), and new goals and terms to be fulfilled were announced. A PRGF differs from its predecessor in three critical ways:[41]

- Targets and policies in PRGF-supported programs come from a country's own poverty reduction strategy outlined in its Poverty Reduction Strategy Paper (PRSP).
- Poverty reduction is integrated into broader macroeconomic policymaking and is at least a partial focus of all economic policy discussions with the IMF.
- PRGF-supported programs focus on governance, especially transparency and accountability.

Suddenly faced with new requirements, the Alemán administration dillydallied in negotiating a poverty reduction strategy with organized civil society. Although the consultation was not all that social groups desired, a product was nevertheless finished in July 2001. The IFIs judged the plan overall as satisfactory but noted a series of deficiencies that required further work, in particular reform of the social sector bureaucracies.[42] In addition, the strategy would have to be implemented in a fashion that constituted "acceptable performance" during one year before the Fund agreed to HIPC completion. In 2001, certain goals of the strategy began to be pursued. But after Nicaragua went off-track with the ESAF, progress toward PRSP targets was not counted toward HIPC. Thus, the one-year countdown only began once the Bolaños government finalized a new three-year PRGF with the Fund in December 2002, and completion point is unlikely to be reached before 2004.

With regard to transparency issues—a polite name for curtailing corruption—Alemán adopted cosmetic measures to allay immediate concerns and get into HIPC. But ensconced in pact-making with the FSLN, he did not respond substantively to donor concerns. The president even refused to meet with representatives of the IMF, other IFIs, and international aid donors early in 2000 to discuss their worries about transparency.[43] An issue of particular interest to donors was the government's footdragging on a promise to create a merit-based civil service. In 1999, this issue became salient as evidence increased that at least some government ministries were docking the pay of their employees to fund the PLC. In 2000, the Inter-American Development Bank reproached the Emergency Social Investment Fund (FISE) for making the same deduction, suspending funding until FISE workers received their full wages.

In summation, Alemán's handling of relations with the IFIs produced the same flawed results as other aspects of his policy management, and for the same self-serving reasons. Only certain goals were achieved, and these only came after the caudillo had extracted a price for reaching them. In the end, the president left his successor a poverty reduction plan with no money to fund it, as well as a seriously damaged relationship with the IMF, which was dismayed by the extent of his 2001 election-spending spree. In 2002, a new government began paying the price, as the Fund again pressured Nicaragua to undertake thorough tax reform, complete privatizations Alemán left undone, and take measures to strengthen Nicaragua's existing banks while devising a strategy to pay off debts left by banks that failed during Alemán's term.

Confronting Crises: Coffee and Banking

In addition to Hurricane Mitch, President Alemán's government confronted two other grave crises. One of these was the result of economic forces: falling coffee prices created a long-lasting state of emergency that has sown devastation through the country's coffee zone. The second crisis, a plague of bank failures, is principally the result of fraud and corruption. A part of the responsibility for the bank collapses is directly traceable to Arnoldo Alemán, while another part was nourished in the business and political ethos that his administration fostered. The two crises are interrelated, and we shall treat them together.

The cases reviewed so far illuminate Arnoldo Alemán's corruption and empire-building imposed indirect costs on the economy and populace. However, his machinations with regard to the banks went beyond this level of damage. In his furious drive for power and lucre, Alemán put the financial stability of his country in grave peril, signaling that there was no limit to the caudillo's disregard for the welfare of his fellow Nicaraguans, who have been directly saddled with the payment for their leader's folly.

Coffee Farming: The Price of Official Neglect

In the early 1990s, official policy aimed to rebuild Nicaragua's war-damaged coffee zones, and credits were made available for renewing plantations. But after growers embarked on costly expansion plans, the Chamorro government's difficulties led financing for the renovation program to be suspended, saddling many producers with large debts. Within the sector, relationships were also changing as new players appeared. By the mid-1990s, the Centeno Roque brothers had begun creating a small empire by taking out bank loans and using them to become large-scale growers as well as financiers for thousands of smaller producers in the northern coffee areas. By the late 1990s, the brothers' consortium, called Conagro (later Consagra), was by some accounts buying up and exporting a third of the country's coffee crop.

In 2000, world prices for Nicaragua's coffee crashed. Dramatically increased production from Vietnam, which became a coffee exporter in 1995, is usually identified as the culprit. By the middle of 2000, a crisis was brewing in Nicaragua's coffee sector as producers unable to pay their bank loans faced foreclosure. Since then, growers have progressively stopped maintaining their holdings, causing their productive potential to plummet. The economic crisis has also had a social side, as thousands of laid-off coffee workers have no means of subsistence.

The response of the Alemán administration was to dither. Small and large producers alike were put off with promises of foreign help for debt refinancing that never materialized. Though they refrained from massive foreclosures, banks offered no more than a case-by-case review of each debtor's situation, while falling prices made them reluctant to roll over many loans. The farmers soon turned to protest, and they were seconded by their workers who took to the roads to plea for food aid. The coffee crisis, both economic and social, was still unresolved when Alemán passed the reins on to Bolaños in January 2002.

The banking crisis, whose effects Bolaños has also inherited, bears direct relation to the coffee crisis. The two main failed banks—the Banco Intercontinental (Interbank), and the Banco Nicaraguense de Industria y Comercio (BANIC)—had loaned heavily to coffee growers both before and after Hurricane Mitch. Their collapses, in August 2000 and August 2001 respectively, deprived growers of new credits at a time when their plantations were becoming moribund from neglect.

The Financial Sector: Wrecking Banks for Political Gain

The collapse of Interbank and BANIC was the product of fraudulent practices, abetted by poor bank administration, and compounded by weak regulation by the superintendent of banks. The Interbank case is the more dramatic of the two, for it witnessed fraud that on the scale of Nicaragua's minuscule banking system can only be termed colossal. At the core of the operation, Interbank credit managers, with or without the connivance of the bank's directors and in gross violation of elementary prudential norms, directly lent the Centeno Roque brothers $85m, while an additional $115m disappeared into the hands of proxies.[44] Multiple forms of fraud were involved, as the brothers offered fake guarantees for many loans, including deeds to the properties of many of their small-scale clients who were unaware that their holdings had been mortgaged.

What the brothers Centeno did with all the money that they milked from Interbank (and several other banks in lesser amounts) is still unknown. Nor have their obscure political connections to high-ranking Sandinistas who stood behind Interbank been ferreted out.[45] Basic lineaments of the story nevertheless suggest that the brothers' political cover was extensive, and that the fate of their empire was bound up with the political pact between Alemán and Sandinista leader Daniel Ortega.

When the brothers could not pay up on certain loans, the bank superintendent was forced to intervene in August 2000. The day before the intervention was to start, president Alemán announced it was coming, deliberately touching off a run by depositors. His action forced the Nicaraguan Central Bank to step in and lend Interbank $83m to stave off immediate collapse. The superintendent soon decided the bank was unsalvageable and in October 2000 announced it would be liquidated. Although the Centenos and a host of Interbank officials were quickly brought up on charges, they were just as quickly acquitted, demonstrating that they enjoyed high-level political protection.

The liquidation of Interbank dealt a blow of unknown proportions to the patrimony of the Sandinista Front, whose funds were known to be hiding behind the bank's board of directors. Ortega soon took his vengeance on Alemán over the loss. In October, he charged that another bank, the Banco Nicaraguense (BANIC), was also in financial trouble, creating a fresh panic that cost the bank $60m in deposits and required another lifeline from the Central Bank, this time of some $22m, to prevent BANIC from disintegrating. At the root of Ortega's action were BANIC's connections to Arnoldo Alemán.

In 1997, BANIC was still state-owned. A social upstart, Alemán probably desired to gain control of BANIC in order to turn it into the nucleus of a personal economic group. It is now suspected that before the bank's partial privatization in early 1999, an Alemán crony named Donald Spencer milked BANIC of large sums of money through a series of fraudulent loan operations. After the bank was privatized, cronies of Spencer turned up as shareholders, and suspicion emerged that they had purchased their shares with monies loaned by the bank itself. Although wrongdoing could not be proven, BANIC's portfolio was widely believed to be riddled with holes. In this shaky financial condition, Daniel Ortega's torpedo started a slide into oblivion that culminated when the superintendent decided in August 2001 that the bank's situation was irremediable.[46]

As BANIC was another big coffee lender, its demise aggravated the problems of the coffee producers. It was also the last in a string of four significant banks to go broke in the space of a year (the other two were the Banco del Café and Banco Mercantil). As important as the impact on coffee finance was, it pales in comparison to the financial costs the nation suffered. In order to persuade other banks in the system to cover the failed banks' deposits, the government was forced to compensate them for a vast portfolio of suspect loans that would probably prove unrecoverable. It did this by issuing Central Bank monetary certificates ("Cenis"), whose face value exceeds $350m. The certificates now comprise part of Nicaragua's internal debt, and ordinary Nicaraguans will eventually pay for them in one form or another.

Patrimonialism, Corruption, and Public Policy

Corruption in patrimonial systems goes beyond the vending machine politics of money in/policy out found in consolidated democracies. Hence the study of corruption in patrimonial polities must seek out instances of behavior where rulers treat the national economy as their personal property. To the extent that the system is patrimonial, it will be proportionately kleptocratic. This was the case in Mobutu's Zaire and in Nicaragua under the Somozas, countries where the trappings of democracy were just that—mere trappings. However, Third World states undergoing "transitions to democracy" ought to be moving away from this manner of managing both politics and the public's wealth.

Theory aside, the sundry revelations of corruption that surfaced while he was in office, and the numerous investigations that have blossomed since the end of his term, argue squarely for classifying Arnoldo Alemán as a kleptocrat. Alemán's self-enrichment has been so variegated, and his economic dealings so extensive, as to suggest that he sought consciously to outdo the record even of the Somozas for a five-year stretch in power. The panoply of Alemán's illicit actions includes: (1) simple embezzlement, for example, using government credit cards to pay his personal expenses; (2) myriad and complex forms of peculation and subsequent laundering of funds; (3) kickbacks from businessmen and foreign investors; (4) attempts to control privatizations for personal gain; and (5) direct diversion of state resources to both private use (paving roads to his farm) or partisan use (medicines for the PLC). And the scale of the assets he sought to garner for himself and his cronies is awesome.[47]

We have argued here, however, that Alemán's voracious appetite had wider repercussions for the economy and public policy than the mere theft of public resources would indicate. In a system supposedly transiting toward democracy, Alemán's neopatrimonial style of politics resuscitated traditional clientelism in its most retrograde form. This clientelism, which operated both at the apex and the base of the pyramid of power, virtually dictated that public policy would be distorted as the caudillo sought to feather his multitude of nests and keep his party firmly entrenched in power. Due to Nicaragua's dependence on the IFIs, a basic macroeconomic coherence was maintained almost to the end. But other policy areas became seriously disconnected, discontinuous and inefficacious in promoting public welfare. We have presented evidence of this in the education, agriculture, and health fields; others could be cited.

Alemán's thirst for public assets complemented and deepened these distortions. When privatization plans agreed to with the IMF could not be shaped to satisfy the satrap's avarice, they were simply postponed while he and his coterie went on extracting what value they could from state assets. In the case of the banks, the president's striving to secure economic and political advantage went beyond policy distortion to outright sabotage, with potential systemic repercussions. Meanwhile, his penchant for accumulating private assets held up the solution of property disputes and hobbled investors who could have contributed to the country's prosperity. The overall results made Nicaragua grow more slowly than it should have and prevented the population from reaping all the benefits of its collective efforts. The effects will unfortunately extend into the future, for the country has lost valuable time in making inevitable adjustments to a rapidly changing international environment. For the average Nicaraguan, this means having to go on for at least several years more shouldering a foreign debt burden that should have been wiped off the books.

That statistically speaking the Alemán administration produced a decent economic record must not blind us to these realities. Riding to power as Nicaragua's postwar recovery was just getting under way, Alemán enjoyed golden opportunities to lay sound bases for Nicaragua's long-term growth and prosperity. Most of these he cast aside, along with the goodwill of international donors. In the end economic growth and investment fell well below their potential, and improvements in public welfare were only a fraction of what they should have been. The economic costs of patrimonialism may be difficult to quantify, but they are easily perceived.

Does the economic policy record of the Alemán administration reflect the practice of undoing democracy? Intimate threads connect the two. Maintaining his grasp on the public purse—the key motivation of every patrimonial ruler—required Alemán to create a ring of impunity around his actions. This he achieved through his pact with Sandinista caudillo Daniel Ortega in 2000, which as told in Chapter 2 subjected the institutions of accountability in the Nicaraguan state to the whims of two bosses determined to thwart any independent investigation into their actions well into the future. Once democratic development was undone, and Alemán concluded that power would not slip from his grasp, his drive to milk the public sector of everything he could before he had to leave office appeared to become uncontrollable, helping to generate the results we have just surveyed.

Patrimonial policymaking and implementation can produce results in flush times, in wealthy settings, or where the money wasted on the leader's self-aggrandizement and the machine's political preservation is not critical. But Nicaragua is neither wealthy nor is it enjoying good times. It has few resources that can be diverted from public goods and services and devoted to private or partisan objectives. A caudillo's government, like Arnoldo Alemán's, thus imposes an economic cost on the country. And when that government succeeds in strengthening the role of partisan calculation in public affairs, and rejigs the constitution to permanently weaken oversight structures, it can compromise the nation's economic well-being for years to come.

Notes

1. David Dye, et al., *Patchwork Democracy: Nicaraguan Politics Ten Years after the Fall* (Cambridge, MA: Hemisphere Initiatives, November 2000), 12-14.

2. *La Prensa* (*LP*), "Alemán, genio y figura ..." January 10, 2002.

3. Banco Central de Nicaragua (BCN), *Informe Annual* 2002, www.bcn.gpb.ni.

4. Phil Ryan, *The Fall and Rise of the Market in Sandinista Nicaragua* (Montreal: McGill-Queen's University Press, 1995).

5. The material in this section relies on David Close, *Nicaragua: The Chamorro Years* (Boulder, CO: Lynne Rienner, 1999), 117-45; 161-70.

6. The most contentious part of the property question was what to do with the luxurious properties taken over by top-ranking Sandinistas. The FSLN leadership argued that these homes could not be returned without prejudicing the claims of ordinary people to far more modest dwellings. However, the presence of leaders of the former revolutionary government in expensive houses made the *confiscados*, those who had lost property, more intransigent.

7. The United Nations Development Program (UNDP) began issuing its *Human Development Report* in 1990. We take the figures from the early 1990s as reflecting Sandinista social policy initiatives and rankings from later in the decade to show the effects of austerity politics.

8. Unless otherwise noted, all figures in this chapter are official statistics of the Banco Central de Nicaragua (BCN), taken or calculated from the Bank's *Informe Anual* or the monthly *Indicadores Económicos*. A compendium of statistics on the Alemán period may be found in the 2002 Nicaragua Country Profile of the London-based Economist Intelligence Unit.

9. Our emphasis here will be on the president's responsibility for policy shortcomings. We do not intend a blanket criticism of the government or its ministers. While several of these have recently been indicted on corruption charges, others now serve in the new government of president Enrique Bolaños.

10. For a discussion of the Tax Justice Law, see the 2nd Quarter 1997 Country Report of the Economist Intelligence Unit. The downward trend in customs tariffs was partially reversed in May 2001, when many tariffs increased to 15 percent in order to harmonize with other countries in Central America.

11. Instituto Centroamericano de Administración de Empresas (INCAE), "Agenda de Competitividad de Nicaragua para el Siglo XXI," June 1999, prepared by E. Montiel and T. Sandino. The plan, based on ideas of Harvard economist Michael Porter, is only going into effect in 2002.

12. This argument is made most forcefully by José Luis Medal, who notes that Nicaragua possesses the highest trade and current account gaps in Latin America in proportion to GDP. Cf. "Balance macroeconómico del período 1997-2000," *La Perensa*, December 29, 2000. With total GDP valued at some $2.5 billion, Nicaragua ran a 2001 fob-fob trade déficit of $1,036 million.

13. Mario D. Tello and William Tyler, *La promoción de exportaciones en Nicaragua, 1997-2010: Experiencias y alternativas* (Managua: MEDE-MIFIN, 1997).

14. A glimpse into the competitiveness policy of the Bolaños administration is provided in World Bank, *Republic of Nicaragua, Competitiveness Learning and Innovation Loan*, Report No. 21532-NI, December 2000, 2-9.

15. INCAE, 24-34.

16. According to a recent study of the Nicaraguan Chamber of Industries, electricity in Nicaragua cost an average of 11.1 U.S. cents a kilowatt hour in 2000 compared to 7.1 cents in Costa Rica.

17. According to the government regulator TELCOR, between 1996 and 2001 conventional phone lines in service increased only from 111,397 to 153,630; by comparison cell phones in service shot up from 5,100 to 154,526.

18. Once finished in 2000, the Plan Nacional de Educación emphasized the need to revamp secondary education to provide lateral exits into technical trades, among other foci. (See text at www.medc.gob.ni.) This plan is also going into effect in 2002.

19. *El Nuevo Diario*, "Las ranas por vaquillas IDR," July 2, 2002, provides a summary of the case.

20. These figures can be found on the Web site of the Ministerio de Hacienda y Crédito Público, www.hacienda.gob.ni under Intendencia de la Propiedad.

21. A basic analysis of the property agreement can be found in the Country Report of the Economist Intelligence Unit for the fourth quarter of 1997.

22. Of 1,834 cooperatives in this situation, only 88 had received legal ratification (solvencia) by mid-2001. A World Bank-funded project meanwhile made slow progress in providing titles to 40,000 individual smallholders. But due to the government's failure to clean up the property register, most titles issued could not be registered, and their recipients refused to invest in the properties. Cf. Deininger and Chamorro (2002: 15)

23. *El Nuevo Diario*, "Alemán deporta a italiano," February 2, 2001; "Lorente tragó la medicina amarga," February 3, 2001.

24. For the technical background on exchange rate policy, see Corbo (1999) and Reyes (1999).

25. Instituto Nacional de Estadísticas y Censos (INEC), Datos Comparativos de Pobreza EMNV 93-EMNV 98, Managua, November 1999. According to INEC's data, the portion of poor people measured this way fell from 76.7 percent in 1998 to 74.8 percent in 2001.

26. Geske Dijkstra, "Structural Adjustment and Poverty in Nicaragua," March 2000 (paper prepared for the 2000 meeting of the Latin American Studies Association, 23); World Bank, *Nicaragua Poverty Assessment: Challenges and Opportunities for Poverty Reduction*, Report No. 20488-NI , February 2001, 54 (see www.worldbank.org). The World Bank observed that the 1993-98 reduction occurred mostly in rural areas. The causal factors were primarily repopulation after the contra war and, for a time, favorable terms of international trade (e.g., for coffee).

27. Dijkstra, 22. There is a double explanation for how, in light of this poor performance, Nicaragua's HDI rankings improved. First, several countries (Honduras, Guatemala, Namibia, and Botswana) suffered declines in HDI that moved Nicaragua ahead of them. Second, in 1999 the UNDP changed how it calculated its income index. As a result, Nicaragua's score on that measure went from .28 in 1998 to .50 in 1999.

28. World Bank, *Nicaragua Public Expenditure Review: Improving the Poverty Focus of Public Spending*, Report No. 23095-NI, December 2001, 82.

29. Details are found in Chapter 9.

30. Carlos Chamorro, "Dialogo franco con los donantes," *Confidencial*, no. 30 (May 1999).

31. The five-year average from 1997-2001 was $496m; data provided by the Secretaría de Relaciones Económicas y Cooperación, Ministerio de Relaciones Exteriores, May 2002.

32. World Bank, 2001: 71.

33. OECD, 2000.

34. BCN, 2002: 133.

35. OECD, www.oecd.org/dac/dac/images/AidRecipient/nic.gif

36. BCN, 2002: 144.

37. IMF, *Factsheet Debt Relief under the Heavily Indebted Poor Countries (HIPC) Initiative*, (www.imf.org/external/np/exr/facts/hipc) give the 80 percent figure but one Paris Club publication, www.clubdeparis.org/en/presentation/presentation.php?BATCH= B04WP04 for 2002 suggests that 90 percent of debt held by creditors in that group could be forgiven.

38. Later evidence showed that Enitel figured in the Channel 6 fraud, details of which appear in Chapter 9.

39. IMF, 2001: 4-7.

40. For details, see Government of Nicaragua, "Memorandum de Políticas Económicas y Financieras," submitted to the IMF in August 2001, www.bcn.gob.ni.

41. IMF, *Factsheet—The IMF's Poverty Reduction and Growth Facility* (2001), www.imf.org/external/np/exr/facts/prgf.

42. IDA/IMF, 2001: 1.

43. Nicaragua News Service, "Alemán tells international community to mind its own business," January 31, 2000.

44. Figures are from Interbank interventor Rodolfo Delgado, *Confidencial*, no. 297, (July 7-13, 2002).

45. Rumors connected the Centenos to Alemán and to international drug traffickers.

46. For an analysis of BANIC's financial condition, see Banco Central de Nicaragua, "La Intervención del Banco Nicaragüense de Industria y Comercio," in *Boletín Económico*, July-September 2001. See www.bcn.gob.ni.

47. On August 7, 2002, as this chapter was nearing completion, the government formally accused Arnoldo Alemán, along with five members of his family and a host of associates, of money laundering. Chapter 9 presents more details.

Chapter 8

The External Debt of Nicaragua and the Alemán Liberal Administration: Images and Realities[*]

Salvador Marti Puig

This chapter considers three fundamental aspects of both the economic and foreign policies of the government of President Arnoldo Alemán: Nicaragua's foreign debt and its effects on the nation; relations between the Liberal government and the various multilateral lenders; and the government's implementation of the terms negotiated with the lenders and the manner in which it sold them to the Nicaraguan people. In examining these elements it has been necessary to consider the effects of Hurricane Mitch (1998) on Nicaragua's economic policy, the country's relations with the international community, and the renegotiation of the nation's external debt.

In evaluating the Alemán administration's handling of the debt issue and its impact on democracy this chapter draws on theories of governance to illuminate key themes. In particular, it will argue that rather than managing social conflict through effective public policies designed to promote social cohesion and good governance, the Alemán government instead opted for an approach that increased social inequality in the country and exacerbated the vulnerability of its citizenry.

External Debt: A Brake on Development

Almost every developing country has a substantial external debt.[1] To meet their debt payments, these countries have to take funds that should go to national development and give them to international creditors. Generally, these payments

---

[*] translated by David Close

represent between 30 and 40 percent of export earnings, but run to 45 percent in Latin America. Devoting so many resources to debt servicing reduces the capacity to import the capital goods, raw materials, and new technology desperately needed by poor countries if they are to modernize and move forward.

The external debt on which we shall be focusing is the money that poor countries owe banks, wealthy northern countries, and multilateral lenders. It is the result of years of loans to national governments and now often exceeds the borrower's capacity to repay. External debt continues to grow, although debtor countries have regularly met the service (interest plus some amortization of the principle) owing. The paradoxical result is that Third World debt in 1996, the last year for which there are complete data, is four times higher than in 1982, when the Third World debt crisis erupted (see table 8.1). In many cases this is the result of indebted countries having to take new loans to cover missed payments or simply to assist a flagging economy.

It is useful to distinguish between long-term ($1.376 trillion in 1996)[2] and short-term debt ($545 billion in 1996) which must be paid within twelve months and which constitutes 27.5 percent of total debt.[3] Long-term debt consists of three elements: bilateral, commercial, and multilateral debt. The first of these comes from loans made by wealthier states in the north to poorer states in the south and most often takes the form of export credits; it represents 44 percent of long-term, developing country debt and was valued at $601 billion in 1996. Commercial debt is contracted in financial markets, mainly with the largest international banks; in 1996 it amounted to $440 billion and accounted for 32 percent of long-term debt.[4] Multilateral debt results from loans granted by multilateral international financial institutions (IFI), such as the World Bank and IMF; it contributed 24 percent of the total and in 1996 was valued at $335 billion. Because the IFIs are often the only lenders willing to finance developing countries with high debt loads, multilateral debt has grown rapidly in recent years.

Finally, there is debt service, which includes both interest and amortization payments and which has risen ceaselessly. In spite of the rise in debt service, however, there has not been a significant reduction in total developing country debt. Between 1986 and 1996, the developing world paid debt service amounting to $1.834 trillion, equivalent to 92.4 percent of its total 1996 international debt.[5]

As table 8.2 shows, interest payments make up nearly half of debt servicing costs. Thus, payments made to service international debt are unable to keep overall debt from growing. High interest payments in fact make paying off accumulated external debt nothing but an illusion for developing countries. Therefore what looks to creditor countries like a simple obligation that the debtor must meet according to schedule appears to debtor countries as lost investments and more years of being unable to attend to people's basic needs.

Table 8.1: Evolution of the External Debt of Developing Countries

Year	1973	1980	1986	1990	1991	1.992	1993	1994	1995	1996
Total external debt	113	456	1.152	1.383	1.436	1.496	1.578	1.740	1.897	1.985

Source: Adapted from Oliveras, *Deute extern, deute etern?* 1999:4.

Table 8.2: Developing Country Debt Service

Year	1986	1990	1992	1995	1996
Debt Service	131	163	161	207	206
% of total debt	11.4	12.4	10.8	10.9	10.4
% as amortization	6.0	6.3	6.1	5.9	5.4
% as interest	5.4	6.1	4.7	5.0	5.0

Source: Adapted from Oliveras, 1999:5.
(Percentages of amortization and interest calculated on total debt.)

Even if debt is a normal and useful part of development strategy, it now contributes neither to growth nor to development, but rather impoverishes future generations. Instead of contributing to building a base for development, new debt is added to pay past debts so that debtor countries may have access to ordinary capital markets. In this sense, the loans coming from official multilateral sources contribute to unproductive debt. And if a country actually pays its debts it will have little left for productive ventures. Debtor nations have insufficient domestic savings and must borrow from abroad to fill the gap between their savings rate and their rate of investment. Thus, even if they want to, many nations are unable to meet their growing international financial obligations because current debts inhibit future growth.[6] The most extreme instances of this phenomenon are seen in those countries whose external debt is greater than their annual national income (see table 8.3). The paradigmatic case of extreme indebtedness is Nicaragua, whose debt is six times greater than its total yearly output. Another indicator of extreme indebtedness is having to meet debt service payments equal to more than 30 percent of total exports (table 8.4), a list which finds Nicaragua in the sixth-worst position.

Table 8.3: Developing Countries with External Debt Superior to GDP

Country	Foreign Debt ($USm)	Per capita debt ($US)	GDP per capita ($US)	Debt/GDP (%)
Nicaragua	9.287	2322	380	611
Mozambique	5.781	361	80	452
Congo (Brz)	6.032	2413	659	366
Guinea Bissau	894.000	894	253	354
Angola	11.482	1094	398	275
Ivory Coast	18.952	1425	566	252
Mauritania	2.467	1121	461	243
Tanzania	7.333	251	121	207
Zambia	6.853	867	454	191
Malawi	2.140	223	134	167
Sierra Leone	1.226	299	187	160
Nigeria	35.005	323	229	141
Jamaica	4.270	1779	1318	135
Syria	21.318	1545	1144	135
Mali	3.066	292	221	132
Vietnam	26.495	366	282	130
Jordan	7.994	1558	1237	126
Laos	2.165	461	369	125
Honduras	4.567	830	664	125
Cameroon	9.350	730	603	121
Gabon	4.492	492	3682	122
Togo	1.486	372	307	121
Burundi	1.157	196	178	110
Panama	7.180	2762	2790	101

Source: Adapted from Oliveras, 1999:5.

Table 8.4: Developing Countries with a Debt Service
Superior to 30 Percent of Total Exports

Country	Debt Service/Exports (%)
Zambia	174,4
Guinea Bissau	66,9
Sierra Leone	60,3
Haiti	45,2
Pakistan	35,3
Nicaragua	38,7
Algeria	38,7
Brazil	37,9
Mozambique	35,3
Argentina	34,7
Morocco	32,1
Honduras	31,0
Indonesia	30,9

Source: Adapted from Oliveras, 1999:8.

For years, but especially since the Jubilee 2000 and External Debt, Eternal Debt campaigns launched by international NGOs, critics have stressed the necessity of forgiving the debt to let debtor nations embark on the path of sustainable development. Faced with this claim, creditor governments respond that forgiving the debt would mean that they would have to carry a higher budget deficit, which would limit their capacity to extend official development assistance, while the IFIs argue that forgiving the debt would convert them into charitable institutions and would be unfair to countries that had paid their obligations. More importantly, there is general agreement among creditors that any serious reduction of international debts must be accompanied by a commitment on the part of the debtor countries to adopt economic policies that reduce their need to borrow. This requires increasing domestic savings, private and public, changing the tax system so that it is both fairer and generates more revenue, and, above all, by pursuing policies that lead to greater equity and sustainable development.

How International Financial Institutions View Abolishing Third-World Debt

Although international multilateral financial institutions have never seriously considered totally writing off the debt, there have been periodic attempts to reschedule Third World debt. These initiatives, which increased markedly in the wake of the Mexican debt crisis of 1982, are all parts of structural adjustment programs (SAP). Adopting an SAP requires a country to implement a series of market-friendly policies, such as stabilization and privatization, to better cope with their debt. However, SAPs also bring "collateral damage" in the form of reduced living standards for the poor.

Facing countries with ever worsening and seemingly insoluble debt problems, in 1996 the IMF and World Bank proposed a new mechanism to assist what would now be called Heavily Indebted Poor Countries (HIPC).[7] The initiative brought together for the first time all significant creditors and proposed forgiving up to 80 percent of the net present value (NPV) of the external debt of the poorest and most deeply indebted countries as a way to set them back on the road to development.[8] To qualify for HIPC, and it is the Fund and the Bank which decide if a state is eligible, states must meet certain criteria.[9] These include:

- show a high level of indebtedness and external vulnerability;
- have no sources of multilateral finance other than the International Development Association (IDA), the World Bank agency that grants credit on concessionary terms to very poor countries;
- have successfully implemented an SAP, thus have restructured their economies;
- demonstrate that traditional methods of debt reduction have been insufficient to arrive at a state of "sustainable indebtedness."

The object of the HIPC is thus to reduce debt to bearable or sustainable levels, not to eliminate it entirely.[10]

The HIPC Initiative consists of two, three-year steps (although the length of a step can be tailored to suit particular circumstances) and a completion point at which the Paris Club[11] negotiates a reduction of up to 80 percent of a country's external debt. In the first period a country, which has previously agreed to an IMF adjustment package and committed itself to making debt service payments, receives debt relief of up to 67 percent, as per the Naples Terms of 1994. The country then arrives at a decision point, when a debt sustainability analysis, or DSA, is done and the executive boards of the Fund and the Bank decide on a country's continued eligibility. In the second phase a qualifying country puts into effect a poverty reduction strategy, assisted by the IMF and IDA. There is the additional expectation that Paris Club creditors, and possibly others, will also participate. At the end of the second phase comes the completion point, when the recipient country must demonstrate that it has met its policy commitments and the IMF and IDA deliver the remaining debt relief package. The Paris Club creditors, along with other bilateral and commercial debt holders, then also apply their reductions, up to the maximum of 80 percent of the debt's NPV. If these steps are insufficient to bring a country's debt down to a sustainable level, the IFIs will undertake to do this by restructuring the state's multilateral debt.

No sooner was the HIPC proposed than criticisms began of its harsh terms and likely unworkability. As a result, the 1999 G8 Summit approved changes, known as HIPC II. The new program gives greater emphasis to growth and poverty reduction, and slowly replaces the SAPs with Poverty Reduction and Growth Programs (PRGP), which will be financed through the IMF's Poverty Reduction and Growth Facility. This differs from earlier plans by putting poverty reduction at the center and by stressing the need to bring all stakeholders together to design and implement the plan.

Despite these changes, criticisms persist, because HIPC II demands the application of adjustment programs and the payment of debt service during the life of the program. Critics argue that this leads to ignoring a population's basic needs, thus perpetuating conditions of poverty and hunger. Moreover, the initiative is available to only a handful of countries and any debt taken on during the program is excluded from coverage, thereby creating new debt.[12]

As a result, although the HIPC raised great expectations for solving the problem of unsustainable external debt, in practice it has not produced the desired results. International NGOs, such as Oxfam, Eurodad, and the Jubilee 2000 Coalition criticize the initiative for not enacting a policy of "flexibility" or using a case-by-case approach to eligibility, as had been discussed in the policy's elaboration, and for excluding indicators of human development from the definition of sustainable debt.[13]

Debt Negotiation and Governance

Like the SAPs before it, the HIPC has unmistakable political effects. Although ostensibly about only economic policy, the conditions that must be met to participate in one of these programs generally means redefining the state and its relations to society. At the very least, the cast of players with privileged access to government will change. However, the consequences can easily be more far reaching, extending to the very governability of a political system.

This is because politics is a process for achieving social cohesion by filtering and processing demands, regulating conflicts, and implementing public policies. Each policy represents a series of actions in a conflictive area of social life that seek to control conflict through the redistribution of costs and benefits, by means that include coercion. The aggregate result of any public policy reverberates through society, changing or reinforcing existing balances of power.

When the result is relative cohesion among groups and individuals within a society, one can speak of the *governability*[14] of a community. When political action cannot produce cohesion, the society becomes *ungovernable*. The ability to produce a governable society is both the objective and the acid test of any political system.

Ungovernability occurs when the political balancing mechanism malfunctions. When this happens, the state does not respond to demands in ways that are anticipated and acceptable. Unresolved conflicts accumulate and worsen, until the system either becomes gridlocked or simply fails. Governability thus depends on a political system's capacity to regulate collective conflicts with effective public policies.

We can evaluate the performance of a government by observing its actions in areas that generate significant conflicts or social tensions: distribution of wealth; level of unemployment; spending on social services; levels of political violence; the presence of women and minorities in political life, and so on. This evaluation is best done over time so that it may monitor changes and discern tendencies. Governability or ungovernability will be measured by how well policies respond to articulated social needs.

From Governability to Governance?

The debate on governability has been transformed with the arrival of a new concept that claims to offer a fresh perspective: governance. The literature generated by consultants and researchers working for various international organizations since the 1980s has pushed the concept of governance to the fore, achieving great influence over the design of policies recommended to developing countries.[15] Indeed, governance figures prominently in programs of political conditionality.

The concept is rooted in the perception that the capacity to satisfy social demands is not the sole preserve of government, but rather results from the efforts of numerous actors. Governance, which implies the conscious coordination of independent actors, stands apart from both coordination by the market (relying on the supposedly self-equilibrating tendencies of markets) and coordination by the state (through enforceable laws). Governance need not assume a central directing authority; in fact it speaks of the state "steering and not rowing." Further, governance sees government as just another member of a network of more or less equal partners who exchange resources. At its simplest and least controversial, governance reminds us that government is not the sole architect of well-being, above all not in a democracy.

Looking at the international sphere, we find evidence that reinforces the credentials of governance. The international order is literally anarchic, there being no true world government, yet there are international laws and regimes, as well as plurality of actors, state and nonstate, which shape the direction of international politics. Thus, the regulation of such global problems as the management of external debt of developing countries need not rest in governmental hands, but rather in the capacity for self-directed action of the multiplicity of actors engaged in the international economy.

Although governance reduces the public policy presence of the state it does not ignore political institutions. In fact, administrative mechanisms and questions of state capacity occupy much of the governance literature. However, they are not central. The function of the political system is less about direction than it is about coordination; less about issuing orders than getting other social actors into the policy process and forming partnerships between the private and public sectors. The state may be *primus* but it is very much *inter pares*.

This recasting of the role of political institutions and even of politics itself has consequences for democracy. If many of the decisions that affect society are no longer made by a democratically elected government but are officially the work of multiple actors working through multilateral institutions, from whom do citizens demand an accounting? Who takes responsibility? The actors involved, public and private, can resort to endless buck-passing and finger-pointing to avoid facing the consequences of bad policies.

But our bottom line requirement is that politics keep society reasonably cohesive. Democratic politics pursues this cohesion by fostering real equality of opportunity for ever greater numbers of citizens. It is not clear that a country can provide more freedom and more equality of more people be secured within the framework of institutional vulnerability that comes with high foreign debt. Revenues dedicated to debt repayment are not available for schools or pensions or hiring nurses. And the terms of SAPs, the HIPC's prerequisite, have made redistributive policies direct wealth toward the top of the social hierarchy rather than the bottom. Nicaragua's experience demonstrates some of these obstacles.

Nicaragua's External Debt

Nicaragua is both one of the world's most heavily indebted countries and one of the few that qualifies for inclusion in the HIPC Initiative.[16] Further, it is in this condition despite having had SAPs in force since the early 1990s.[17] After an initial period of stabilization that brought quintuple digit inflation under control, in 1994 the Chamorro administration set in motion ESAF I, an Enhanced Structural Adjustment Facility.[18] ESAF I had multiple aims. These included reducing Nicaragua's budget deficit and shrinking the public sector, stimulating foreign direct investment and encouraging domestic public investment using foreign resources, and strengthening the private banking sector by privatizing or closing state-run banks. Among the side effects of the plan were higher unemployment caused by cutting 285,000 public sector jobs, continual erosion of the purchasing power of wages due to steadily rising utility prices, and the failure of many small and medium firms following the lifting of tariffs. Further, the general budget cuts demanded by ESAF I contributed to a decline in overall demand and its emphasis on the financial sector saw investment flow to commercial activities rather than agriculture or manufacturing.[19]

None of these policies, however, brought Nicaragua's external debt within sustainable limits. In 1990, when the FSLN lost power, the country's debt stood at $12.987 billion, about seven times greater than one year's GDP. The debt fell during the Chamorro administration (1990-1996) as several countries forgave Nicaragua's debts to them: Russia ($3.1 billion), Mexico ($1.06 billion), and the Paris Club countries ($1.03 billion).[20] By the end of 1998, Nicaragua's foreign debt was $5.948 billion, widely dispersed among numerous creditors (tables 8.5 and 8.6).

Table 8.5: Nicaraguan External Debt at the End of 1998

	$USm	%
Multilateral Institutions	**1.895**	**31.9**
IMF	52	0.9
IDA/IBRD	504	8.5
IDB	830	14.0
CABEI*	447	7.5
IFAD**	21	0.4
OPEC Fund	28	0.5
Nordic Fund	13	0.2
Official Bilateral	**3.805**	**64.0**
Paris Club	1516	25.5
Russia	356	6.0
Germany	427	7.2
Other Official	2289	38.5
Costa Rica	491	8.3
Guatemala	455	7.7
Commercial	**248**	**4.2**
Total	**5.948**	**100**

Source: Adapted from IMF/IDA, Preliminary Document on the Initiative for Heavily Indebted Poor Countries, p. 35.
(Percentages may not equal 100 due to rounding.)
*: Central American Bank for Economic Integration.
**: International Fund for Agricultural Development.

Table 8.6: Holders of Nicaraguan Debt

Creditor	% of Debt
Paris Club	25.5
Multilateral Lenders	31.9
Central American Countries	16.3
Ex-Socialist Countries	11.1
Other Latin America	7.0
Other Countries	4.0
Commercial Debt	4.2
Others	1.0
Total	100.0

Source: Adapted from *Envío*,1998.

Even though the debt service Nicaragua paid fell throughout the decade from 309 percent of exports in 1993-1994, to 92 percent in 1996, and 45 percent in 1998, the payments were still far above the 20-25 percent level that the World Bank and IMF consider to be sustainable. And Nicaragua made enormous efforts to get as far as it did. For example, between 1990 and 1996, 34 percent of aid received by Nicaragua went to debt service, compared to only 22 percent to productive investments. Further, in 1996 the country spent more per capita on debt service ($47) than on health and education ($34). Thus in a country considered a bad risk for foreign investment due to its weak infrastructure, expensive credit, and extreme social and political instability, the government gave a higher priority to debt service than to investment in long-term national development. As a consequence, Nicaraguan indicators of social well-being now register at levels closer to those of other HIPC countries, the majority of which are in sub-Saharan Africa, than to the rest of Latin America (see table 8.7).

Because of the situation in which it found itself after 1997, Nicaragua began seeking incorporation in the HIPC to reduce its foreign debt. This was seen as the best option for the country's economic future, despite the government's past problems with implementing the ESAF and the social costs that continued austerity would bring. Although the Chamorro government failed to meet the conditions of ESAF I, the Alemán administration still set about negotiating ESAF II, which was concluded in March 1998. Although the negotiations went on for seven months, the administration accepted all the Fund's proposal without a word of protest. The most plausible explanation for this behavior is that President Alemán saw ESAF II as the royal road to HIPC.

Table 8.7: Comparative Indicators of Social Well-Being

Indicator	Nicaragua	Mean HIPC	Mean LA & C
GNP per capita, 1998 ($US)	410	388	3960
Infant Mortality/'000 births	57	97	31
Life expectancy	68	52	70
Population with potable water (%)	62	49	73
Illiteracy (%)	37	47	15
Female Illiteracy (%)	37	57	16

Source: Adapted from IMF/IDA, Preliminary Document on the Initiative for Heavily Indebted Poor Countries, p. 5.

The fundamental problem is that ESAF II, although designed to let poor countries manage their external debt and thus focus their energies on development, prescribes policies that place huge burdens on the poor. It hardly seems sensible to premise postmanageable debt growth on gutting social programs in the present, but that is what ESAF II proposed. Its central component was budgetary austerity, meaning spending cuts to get a balanced budget.[21] These were to be achieved through laying off 10,000 public sector workers; raising indirect taxes; closing the Banco Nacional de Desarrollo; privatizing three public utilities (phones, electricity, and water) as well as a publicly owned petroleum company; and adding 1.5 percent a month (18 percent yearly) to the price of electricity, water, and gasoline.

Knowing that ESAF II would harm large portions of Nicaraguan society, and thus be politically costly for the administration, President Alemán came before Nicaragua's National Assembly on January 10, 1998, to explain that the money raised from the new levies would go to fight poverty. He did not, however, go into detail about the nature of these antipoverty measures.

As a direct result, the Resident Representative of the United Nations Development Program (UNDP) in Nicaragua issued an analysis of the possible impact of ESAF II. The document argued that economic reactivation needed to go beyond the bottom line and include social objectives. Not only did the Alemán administration not use the UNDP report to pressure the IMF, it dismissed it angrily.

This of course brought the FSLN into full and open opposition, turning to mobilizational politics to combat what it called the devastating impact of the ESAF and the administration's policies that harmed ordinary Nicaraguans. The Sandinista caucus in the National Assembly agreed that no one was against reducing the debt, raising more revenue, or making government work better, but they certainly did oppose the way these objectives were being pursued. At the same time, key sectors of civil society began organizing to come up with a viable alternative to the ESAF. In 1998 they formed the Propositivo de Cabildeo e

Incidencia (Lobbying and Advocacy Group) to both lobby government and to propose alternatives to the IMF's policies. Further, the opposition criticized the lack of transparency surrounding the negotiations between the Fund and the Alemán administration.[22]

Although facing stiff opposition, the administration did not back down. Alemán's need to get a deal with the IMF and the fact that his government's economic performance would be monitored by the roughly forty members of Grupo Consulatativo de la Comunidad de Donantes (Consultative Group) left him little maneuvering room. To get to HIPC and the budgetary room that reduced debt payments would produce, Alemán had to take the country through ESAF II.

What the president did not tell the country, however, was that qualifying for HIPC would not eliminate Nicaragua's foreign debt. The program covers only 80 percent of the debt held by Paris Club countries, which in Nicaragua's case represents only 25.5 percent of the total (table 8.6). So, even successfully negotiating entrance to HIPC would cut Nicaragua's external debt by a little more than one-fifth. Yet admission to HIPC demands negotiating with all other creditors to convince them to forgive 80 percent of the debt Nicaragua owes them and by 1998 the Liberal government had not even contacted any of these other creditors. The most plausible explanation for this action is that any debt that has been negotiated becomes priority debt on which interest payments must be met. It appears that the Nicaraguan government sought to renegotiate its debt only with creditors who were likely to continue making loans to the country, allowing the remaining 74.5 percent of its debt to fall past due.[23]

Finally, it is also necessary to address the myth that Nicaragua is paying its debts from its own pocket, as roughly half the funds dedicated to debt retirement comes from donors.[24] Accordingly, qualifying for HIPC and having a portion of its debt forgiven could lead to Nicaragua receiving less foreign aid to help with its remaining debt. This would necessitate using more domestically generated revenue, thereby leaving development programs even worse off than they were.

Hurricane Mitch and the International Community: A Missed Opportunity?

All the Alemán administration's plans were scotched in October 1998 when Hurricane Mitch struck Nicaragua. Mitch flattened not just the country but all the optimistic projections about growth and even the possibility of implementing ESAF II. Government sources[25] estimated that Mitch destroyed 15 percent of the nation's agricultural output (especially basic food crops like corn and beans), 17 percent of its housing stock, 8,000 kilometers of roads and 3,800 meters of bridges, 90 health centers, and 343 schools. In total, 18.2 percent of the population suffered some damage from Mitch, whose financial cost was approximately

$1.5 billion. Three thousand people died and 1,200 were injured, with children accounting for over half the casualties.

Yet as so often happens, from tragedy grows hope. The world quickly responded with a show of solidarity as governments, NGOs, and international organizations offered assistance. On October 22 Austria forgave all Nicaragua's debts, roughly $40 million, and the United States forgave $13 million. France and Cuba later did the same, forgiving $70 million and $50 million, respectively. Spain offered a three-year moratorium on payments and promised new loans at very low rates. Overall, Nicaragua's total external debt fell to $6.075 billion after Mitch, and serious negotiations regarding HIPC were begun.

This gave the administration an unparalleled chance to get new resources at reduced prices and so rebuild the country and reactivate its economy. With this in mind, Nicaragua and the other Central American states went to Washington to meet with the Consultative Group (officially the Consultative Group for the Reconstruction and Transformation of Central America) and arrive at a plan to get immediate help. Managua proposed a reconstruction program valued at $1.52 billion (the estimated cost of hurricane-related damages and nearly equal to the year's GDP) that focused on transportation, energy, and housing.

The Washington meeting dealt with immediate concerns, damage assessment, and evaluating the effectiveness of emergency response policies, leaving the design of a comprehensive reconstruction strategy for future meetings that would be held in Stockholm (1999) and Madrid (2001). However, the message the international community—above all the top representatives of the IFIs—sent Nicaragua concerned the need for the country's political class to cease its squabbling and offer the nation good governance.[26] Further, the Group pushed the Liberal government to set up consultative committees including representatives of business and civil society to design a plan for national reconstruction.[27]

In response to this opportunity, Nicaragua's organized civil society, represented by 320 groups, established the Civil Coordinating Committee for Post-Emergency Reconstruction (Coordinadora Civil para al Emergencia y la Reconstruccion, CCER). The CCER's job was to propose a plan for national reconstruction that reflected the most deeply felt needs of the population and to assess the policies that the government actually applied. With these objectives in mind, the CCER sent representatives to Washington (and later to both Stockholm and Madrid) where they presented a document declaring that they wanted a different development model, one that was sustainable and that eliminated the grotesque extremes of wealth and poverty that existed in Nicaragua.[28]

The Stockholm meeting of the Consultative Group, Forum for the Reconstruction of Central America I, was extremely important. Members of the Consultative Group undertook to provide $9 billion in economic assistance, $3 billion of which would come from the Inter-American Development Bank (IADB) and $1.8 billion from the World Bank. Significantly, this aid could not be used for general economic purposes, much less for projects not related to the disaster.

Rather it was tied to a list of purposes, the Stockholm Declaration,[29] that included reducing environmental and social vulnerability; redressing inequality; meeting the needs of those harmed by the disaster and not the donors' political goals; increasing the transparency of government operations; decentralizing governmental functions and powers with the active participation of civil society; assuring respect for human rights; and reducing the external debt of the affected states.

Meeting in 2001 in Madrid, the Second Forum for the Reconstruction of Central America concentrated on macroeconomic conditions in Central America and the commercial interests of the donors. The spirit of solidarity reflected in the Stockholm Declaration had given way to international business as usual and the motives of the donor countries were shown to be rooted in compassionate charity but not a thirst for justice. Once the worst of the crisis had passed, the absence of political pressure on the donor states let them shift their focus to new crises, elsewhere in the world. Thus only two years after Stockholm, concern with social justice again became the sole preserve of a handful of NGOs.

The Reality of Aid and the Performance of the Alemán Liberal Government

Despite the international community's rhetoric, most of the promised aid was never sent. The Secretariat of External Cooperation of Nicaragua reported a year after the hurricane that the country had received less than half the aid it had expected and that the European Union had yet to send a cent. Spain is a particularly telling example. One of the most enthusiastic supporters of the project when it was a matter of issuing communiqués and reading speeches, Madrid only delivered 30 percent of its promised emergency aid and less than 4 percent of its commitment for reconstruction assistance in 1999.

Results were no better when it came to meeting the goals sketched in the Stockholm Declaration. Two years after the tragedy only 17 percent of Nicaraguans affected by Mitch reported having made investments or repairs that would alleviate future catastrophes. Meanwhile only 36 percent of the houses lost had been rebuilt. As for the objectives of transparency and good governance, the Alemán-Ortega Pact, struck in July 2000, took the country in the opposite direction, toward greater secrecy, opacity, and the progressive closure of political space and stifling of alternative policy initiatives.

Examining the government's management of the aid that it did receive also gives cause for concern. In the first place, the administration disbursed the aid slowly and maintained very tight control of the process.[30] This led to a situation that left municipalities nearly unable to act (and showed how meager their own resources were), had no role for civil society (which only worked through decentralized forms of cooperation), and saw the executive fail to coordinate its efforts with those of the military and the police. In the second place, there were many accusations of fraud, favoritism, and diversion of funds. One set of accusations was based on Alemán's practice of prioritizing the distribution of assistance to towns with Liberal mayors, leaving communities with Sandinista mayors waiting. A second set focused on the president's attempt to keep the NGOs out of the relief operation by keeping them from receiving material sent to them for distribution to the victims of the hurricane.[31] A final source of criticism was the administration's use of disaster relief aid to build infrastructure serving private enterprise while ignoring the needs of families, the majority of them campesinos in the interior of Nicaragua, devastated by the catastrophe. The clearest evidence of this misuse of funds is that among the "reconstruction projects" one finds the expansion of the Masaya-Managua highway to four lanes, a road not affected by the storm, as well as work on the similarly unaffected Managua-Leon road.[32]

However, the most shocking of the Alemán government's actions occurred in September 1999, when Nicaragua entertained high hopes of getting HIPC status and the president staged a huge fiesta to celebrate the anticipated arrival of economic good times. Hosted by Alemán and Cardinal Obando y Bravo, there was free food, music, and a huge balloon floating freely to symbolize Nicaragua's coming release from the bonds of debt! That is, they were celebrating Nicaragua being declared one of the world's poorest countries. In the midst of the pomp and self-congratulation, President Alemán declared that entering the HIPC would bring Nicaragua its second independence. And all this despite knowing that Nicaragua's acceptance as a candidate to enter the initiative presupposed enacting rigorous structural adjustment policies.

However, the party did not impress the Fund and the Bank, who delayed Nicaragua's entry to the HIPC due to a disagreement over the government's use of reconstruction funds. The entire HIPC timetable was affected. The completion point was also set back (even though Nicaragua reached the decision point in December 2000), in this case because of a dispute between the IMF and the government arising from the administration's failure for the third year running to fulfill its ESAF obligations.

Facing this situation, the Alemán administration could not negotiate a new three-year program with the multilateral lenders.[33] All Alemán could manage was an Interim Plan, covering the last six months of his term and setting new talks for early in 2001, when the next government will have taken office.[34] Thus debt relief for Nicaragua programmed for the concluding point of the HIPC depended on the rapidity and thoroughness with which the newly elected government can comply with the IMF's dictates. Alemán's celebration of Nicaragua's second independence was at best premature.

Thus, after nearly five years of Liberal government under President Arnoldo Alemán Nicaragua's foreign debt stood at $6,624,600,000 in May 2001. Debt restructuring with the Paris Club countries had made little progress.[35] This was what a government that had made reducing Nicaragua's foreign debt its raison d'être had accomplished. The results achieved are insubstantial to the point of being derisory. The administration lost its credibility and caused its people extra hardship because it gave greater emphasis to transferring the country's scarce resources to wealthier creditor nations in the north than to providing for its citizens' well-being.

Conclusion

Finally, in this section it is useful to sketch some tentative ideas about the most productive ways to come to grips with the phenomenon of Nicaragua's external debt and the paradoxes that emerge in its negotiation.

- To what extent is it possible to speak of "governance" (or what is the concept's relevance) as a solution to problems of external indebtedness when the debtor countries are in thrall to the policies of multilateral financial institutions? In such cases can "governance" be anything but a synonym for "administrative efficiency"?
- Will the HIPC be an instrument to manage the debt of countries that would otherwise have defaulted? Is it sensible for the IMF and World Bank to demands the great sacrifices needed to enter HIPC from impoverished governments whose debts are essentially irrelevant at an aggregate level?
- Can one imagine the appearance of political opportunity structures for the development of impoverished countries via the "enabling coalitions" formed by networks of NGOs (from both north and south), the official development agencies of donor countries, academics, and the anti-globalization movement?
- How should we conceive of the development of Nicaragua when its government applies economic policies elaborated outside the country and which focus the economy almost exclusively to debt repayment? During the Alemán administration, over half of government revenues went to debt service: How long can a government ignore its people's basic necessities in order to satisfy the conditions of the IFIs?
- Can we consider Hurricane Mitch and its catastrophic consequences as a metaphor for the record of the Alemán administration? Will inefficiency, cynicism, corruption, opportunism, and clientelism be terms by which the Liberal administration will be forever remembered?

Everything we have said points to the need for critical reflection about the reality that lies behind the concept of governance. First, it is necessary to signal the existence of a consensus among policymakers that the hierarchically organized state has passed its prime and is being replaced by a more horizontally based system in which organizational networks have been gathering force. As a result, there emerges a concept supposedly stripped of its ideological connotations that gives rise to an analysis of the "peaceful and consensual" exercise of political power.[36] Here we must indicate the risk that comes from assuming the withdrawal of the state as the arbiter of the common good, as well as of accepting the vision of a complacent civil society that has lost its capacity to criticize and to promote social change. This, in turn, spins off political practices built around: (1) lower political participation; (2) the primacy of the individual over the group; (3) the substitution of the market for the state and its associated political actors; (4) the preponderance of the technical over the political; and (5) a new hegemonic international order imposed through multilateral international institutions. Thus, it appears that over the past decade constitutional democracy built around social democratic citizens' rights has fallen prey to management. Accordingly, the "absent center" of the organizational web of governance, a weaker state, cannot automatically be taken as positive for democracy, since the disappearance of government equally implies the disappearance of the will to build an egalitarian social order and the increasing difficulty of achieving social justice.

Second, we must take note of the importance that the governance model affords the combination of economic "prerequisites," approved by the U.S. government, the IMF, World Bank, and World Trade Organization, that are used to judge the daily performance of Latin American governments. This "Washington Consensus" can be seen as the economic counterpart of governance. It forces states to clear the way for the market by deregulating, liberalizing, privatizing, making economic adjustments, and recognizing the primacy of global markets. The state's role becomes that of guaranteeing property rights and orchestrating a harmonious process of capital accumulation.[37] Thus, the collapse of the populist-nationalist state in Latin America has returned to the market the provision of many formerly public goods and services, leaving the state a merely residual redistributive role.[38]

My third and final observation is that one must not forget that one of the great problems of the global governance model is presenting as global that which is not. The state in Latin America, above all in Nicaragua, is very different from what it is in Europe or North America. While in developed countries the state can claim to manage the interests of capital in ways compatible with those of all citizens, the Latin American state still signifies patrimonialism; the conflation of public and private realms; law that is not universal but particular; no effective checks and balances; a bureaucracy that cannot be considered a public service; manipulation of the media, extremely limited redistribution of wealth; cronyism; and corruption. However, curing this misuse of the state should not automatically suggest reducing government's role to some irreducible minimum, but rather of reinventing both the state and democracy in Latin America. And democracy must not be limited to a sense of legitimate origins in elections, but must include "operational" legitimacy, gained through respecting legal and constitutional norms, as well as assuring that the basic needs of all citizens are met.

To conclude this chapter I want to stress that the negotiations of Nicaragua's foreign debt between the Alemán government and the IFIs took place in a rarified atmosphere where citizens' needs and nonfinancial national development objectives did not matter. This was possible for three reasons:

1. the general lack of transparency surrounding Nicaraguan government operations, but especially in the allocation of resources;
2. Alemán, his administration, and the country's political class evaded their responsibilities to Nicaraguans by recourse to a populist discourse that emphasized the need for external conditionality;
3. the discourse accompanying the concept of governance allowed the administration to evade its responsibilities in ways that made opposition from civil society more difficult.

Overall, the president's approach to debt reduction negotiations was in character with the caudillo's style that marked his administration. Democracy was sacrificed not just to expediency, but to an expediency based on short-term partisan and personal goals. Thus it is hardly surprising that Alemán failed to secure Nicaragua's entry to the HIPC Initiative.

Notes

1. Background information regarding the HIPC and debt issues generally may be found on these Web sites: www.worldbank.org/hipc; www.onerworld.org; www.oxfam.org; www.debtwatch.org; www.debtchannel.org; www.socwatch.org.uy; www.jubileeplus.org; www.unsolmon.org.

2. All figures are in U.S. dollars unless otherwise noted.

3. Short-term debt has grown considerably: in 1986 it represented only 18.2 percent of the total debt. It owes its growth to the increasing inability of states to make payments as they fall due. Although there are not reliable data regarding the short-term debt, it is believed that it is evenly divided between commercial and export credits.

4. Commercial debt has been increasingly transferred from banks to financial markets, facilitating the commercialization of external debt in secondary markets. By 1995 the value of debt bonds stood at $133 billion, 38 percent of the total commercial debt.

5. A. Oliveres, *Deute extern, deute etern?* (Barcelona: Justícia i Pau, Col. Quaderns per a la Solidaritat, #1, 1999).

6. J. Atienza, *La Deuda Externa y los Pueblos del Sur* (Madrid: Manos Unidas, 2000); P. Talavera, *Crisis económica y condonación de la Deuda Externa en los países periféricos* (paper presented to the Jornadas Internacionales sobre la Deuda Externa, Barcelona, 2000).

7. There is still little literature treating the HIPC, however, the *Canadian Journal of Development Studies* published a special issue on developing country debt in 2001. The

issue contains seven articles, one of which (Castro-Monge 2001) presents a case study of Nicaragua. Unfortunately, this came to light too late to be included in this study.

8. Under the Naples terms, the prior benchmark agreed to by creditor states in 1994, countries with a GDP per capita of no more than $500/year or a debt with a net present value (NPV) not less than 350 percent of exports, could see the NPV of its debt cut by up to 67 percent.

9. Thirty-six states, most of them from sub-Saharan Africa, could qualify for HIPC. At the moment, nineteen are covered by the initiative (Benin, Bolivia, Burkina Faso, Cameroon, Gambia, Guinea-Bissau, Guyana, Honduras, Malawi, Mali, Mauritania, Mozambique, Nicaragua, Niger, São Tomé and Príncipe, Senegal, Tanzania, Uganda, and Zambia), receiving an estimated $131 billion in assistance. This represents a 47 percent reduction of NPV debt beyond that offered by earlier debt reduction schemes.

10. External Debt is sustainable when the ratio of the present value of the debt to export earnings is less than 250 percent and when debt service amounts to less than 25 percent of exports.

11. The Paris Club is the name applied to practices developed since 1956 by creditor countries to deal with international debt payment problems. For more information visit its Web site: www.clubdeparis.org.

12. D. García-Olivé and P. Talavera, *La reacción social ante el tratamiento de la deuda* (Barcelona: Mímeo, 2000).

13. A. Oliveres, *Deute externe*, 1999; P. Talavera, "Crisis economica," 1999, *Intermón, La realidad de la ayuda 1999/2000* (Barcelona: Intermón, 2000); XCADE, *La consulta social per l'abolició del deute extern a Catalunya* (Barcelona: Mediterrània, 2001).

14. This is somewhat different than, though closely related to, the concept of governability that evolved in the 1970s, associated with the work of Samuel Huntington, Anthony King, and Richard Rose.

15. One issue of the *International Social Science Journal*, no. 50 (1998) is dedicated to the concept of governance and provides a useful introduction to the concept.

16. Nicaragua was to have reached the decision point for entering the HIPC in 2000.

17. This does not include the austerity program adopted by the Sandinista government in 1989, the Stabilization Plan. Although the Plan had all the hallmarks of an SAP it was not established according to IMF guidelines and so austerity did not bring access to cheap credit.

18. The ESAF is an IMF program that was developed in the 1980s to provide concessional financing to very poor countries with long-term balance of payments problems.

19. PNUD-Nicaragua, *El desarrollo humano en Nicaragua, 2000: Equidad para superar la vulnerabilidad* (Managua: PNUD 2000).

20. It should be noted that several countries which forgave Nicaragua's debts to them (including Russia, the Czech Republic, Mexico, Colombia, Venezuela, and Argentina) no longer make loans to the country.

21. The Liberals inherited a 14.3 percent deficit which they cut to 8.5 percent within a year. The ESAF's goal was to reduce the deficit to 4 percent by 2000.

22. There were also extremely high levels of political unrest in 1998, which witnessed protests by students and the rural poor, as well as a five-month doctors' strike.

23. "Nicaragua: Hora de oportunidades y de oportunismos," *Envío*, 201 (1998): 3-15.

24. In 1998, the government of Nicaragua planned to pay $208.8 million in debt service: $121.5 million toward amortization and $87.9 million in interest. The government received $106.9 million in aid, $30 million of which were cash donations for debt service and to cover balance of payments deficits. The remainder was to finance projects and so free resources for the government to apply toward the external debt. See, *Envio 6*, 12-13.

25. The data are from the Central Bank, as reported in *Envio 6*.

26. In a parallel development, meetings between Alemán and Ortega began. The leaders held long talks on both November 20 and 23, 1998, after which Ortega announced his party's support for the Liberals' reconstruction plans, including gaining access to HIPC. This may be seen as the prelude to the Pact.

27. As carried out by the Liberal government, the consultative committee over-represented big business and invited NGO representatives as individuals, not in their official capacities.

28. Coordinadora Civil para al Emergencia y la Reconstrucción (CCER), 1998.

29. Consultative Group for the Reconstruction and Transformation of Central America, *The Stockholm Declaration*, www.ccic.ca/archives/devpol/1999/ apg7_stockholm _declaration.htm.

30. Arnoldo Alemán delayed declaring a national state of emergency and ordering a massive evacuation. "No, he said, that sort of mobilization is something the Sandinistas would do. As a result, many UN aid operations were not even started ...Who was going to take the Nicaraguan drama seriously if its own president didn't?" For details see, A. Bendaña, 1999, "El huracán estructural de Nicaragua," *NACLA Report*, verisón electrónica en español: www.nacla.org/espanol/septoct99/deuda.htm. It was October 30, fully four days after the flooding started, that the National Emergency Committee was established and began planning to deal with the crisis.

31. In the days immediately following the disaster many containers of donated material were held in customs, because the government demanded the payment of duties from 40 to 100 percent of their declared value. It was several days after Mitch hit when the shipments were finally released.

32. There was not even much progress on the debt front. Between 1998 and 2000, the Nicaraguan government continued dedicating 22 percent of its expenditure budget to debt service while the Paris Club creditors limited themselves to granting a moratorium on payments. See, D. Vukelich, "La devastación de la deuda," *NACLA Report*, verisón electrónica en español: www.nacla.org/espanol/septoct99/deuda.html.

33. The IMF broke off negotiations for a variety of reasons. Among them were the government's handling of the financial crisis growing out of the scandals associated with the failures of Interbank and BANCAFE; changes to the 2001 budget; the use of IADB funds destined for the Emergency Social Expenditure Fund (FISE) to pay workers who contributed to the Liberals' campaign fund; an $80,000 loan from the Central Bank to the government, which was expressly prohibited under the ESAF; a debt moratorium for coffee growers and the crisis in BANIC (Banco Nicaraguense de Comercio), which eventually failed, resulting from uncollected loans to coffee growers; and, finally, a budget deficit that grew from 11 percent of GDP in 1998 to 15 percent in 2000, when the ESAF set an 8 percent limit.

34. The Interim Plan had no financial assistance from the IMF but it did not affect the IADB or the World Bank. Indeed, it was after the Interim Plan was signed that the

IADB made a $25 million loan which it had withheld for several months. The loan went to the Central Bank to cover balance of payments shortfalls and was conditional on the privatization of the electric company in bidding open only to prequalified firms and on the guarantee of a stable economic environment. The conditions also included a stipulation made by the IMF in earlier negotiations with the Nicaraguan government: the sale or closure of BANIC.

35. Nicaragua has only restructured bilateral debts, partially or totally, with the Republic of China, Mexico, the Czech Republic, the Slovak Republic, Peru, and North Korea. It still has outstanding bilateral debts of nearly $2.2 billion to renegotiate with sixteen countries. Of this latter group Costa Rica, Guatemala, Honduras, Brazil, Bulgaria, Iran, and Libya are owed the most.

36. J. Rosenau and E. Czempiel, eds., *Governance without Government: Order and Change in World Politics* (Cambridge: Cambridge University Press, 1992).

37. J. C. Monedero, *La trampa de la gobernanza: Nuevas formas de participacion politica* (Madrid: Mimeo, 2002).

38. R. Goma and Q. Brugue, "La administracionpublica y sus clientes: ¿Moda organizativa u opcion ideologica?" *Gestion y Analisis de Politicas Publicas*, 1 (1994).

Chapter 9

President Bolaños Runs a Reverse, or How Arnoldo Alemán Wound Up in Prison

David Close

On August 7, 2002, President Enrique Bolaños announced to the nation that his administration had charged Arnoldo Alemán, and thirteen other persons, including several members of the president's family, with fraud, embezzlement, criminal conspiracy, and money laundering. The sum involved, approximately $100m, is roughly 0.8 percent of the national GDP and would cover a year's education spending in Nicaragua. To give sense of the magnitude of the amount, a U.S. president charged with graft of comparable dimensions would have to make away with $74 billion. The Liberals replied that they would defend Arnoldo to the end, that their fingers would fall off before they would press the button to vote against their chief, and that people in power everywhere steal from the state.[1]

Constitutionally precluded from a second consecutive term as president, Arnoldo Alemán nevertheless wanted to keep his patrimonial system intact. To do so he planned to use the seat in the National Assembly the Pact automatically gives ex-presidents. Bolaños, however, wanted Nicaragua to have a government that ran more economically and curbed corruption. Since their objectives were incompatible, one of the two leaders would have to lose, and in the early going the betting was that the loser would be Bolaños. Eight months into his term, though, the momentum had shifted.

No one would have predicted that Enrique Bolaños would begin an anti-corruption campaign and try to organize an anti-Alemán movement. After all, he was Alemán's vice president, until resigning in 1995 to run for the presidency. Moreover, Don Enrique, as he is generally known, had headed the very feeble anticorruption agency established by Alemán to meet donor pressures. Most of all, Bolaños was known as a crusty conservative[2] who first made his political mark as an anti-Sandinista leader in the eighties whom Washington thought too divisive to carry the colors against the FSLN in 1990. Yet before 2002 ended, Don Enrique had Arnoldo Alemán under house arrest, and before 2003 was out ex-president Alemán had entered prison to begin a twenty-year sentence for fraud and money laundering.[3]

These developments are significant enough to merit a brief chapter. At a minimum, Bolaños offers a very different leadership style, one far less given to micromanagement of party and public affairs, personal enrichment, and bombast. At best, his administration could give Nicaragua a chance to wipe out the worst excesses of patrimonial electoral caudillismo and return the country to the path of constitutional democracy. This is a very tall order, perhaps too much for Bolaños to achieve. The president has, however, shown that the system built by the Pact is not invincible and that it may well be possible to remove not just Arnoldo Alemán but also the system he created from Nicaraguan public life.

This chapter starts by looking at the system that Arnoldo Alemán put in place to guarantee his continued dominance of Nicaraguan politics from outside the presidency and suggests why he has been balked. It then turns to Bolaños's surprising anticorruption campaign. A concluding section speculates about the president's motives in challenging his former boss and considers how Bolaños's actions might affect the course of Nicaraguan politics.

Circumventing the President: Alemán's Plan to Rule from the National Assembly

Although Arnoldo Alemán had to leave office, he had no intention of surrendering power. Although he failed to get immediate presidential reelection included in the Pact, he did win a free National Assembly seat for the past-president. The problem was how to convert this perk into real power. During the Chamorro presidency, the Assembly had been a significant factor in Nicaraguan politics,[4] but Alemán had brought the legislature to heel. True, the Sandinistas still boycotted sessions and used all the tools the chamber's regulations allowed them to oppose the president's agenda, but momentum had shifted and now favored the executive. Alemán had regained control of the budget, setting aside 20 percent of the total for the discretionary use of the president and the head of the central bank, and the Pact itself so strengthened the executive's hand that the Assembly's capacity to initiate legislation and authority to oversee the operations of government were greatly circumscribed.

Nevertheless, the National Assembly retained some power. Nicaragua's president has limited decree powers,[5] so most government business needs legislative approval. As well, the legislature has an active committee system, capable of tying up legislation or amending bills beyond recognition. Further, the body has a tradition of strong, active speakers that dates from the first, appointed, Sandinista assembly, the Council of State. The president of the National Assembly, the speaker's formal title, does more than preside over plenary sessions. Although there is little published analysis of the Nicaraguan parliament's workings,[6] it appears that the speaker negotiates and controls the agenda of the house, has substantial influence over appointments to committees and the Assembly's presidium, and can, if he or she wishes, become a significant public figure.[7]

All of this suggests that Nicaragua's National Assembly can be a useful oppositional instrument. Interbranch conflicts are routine in democracies with division of powers constitutions. During Dr. Alemán's presidency, however, the National Assembly worked in far closer concert with the executive than at any time since the FSLN lost power. And as the Liberals controlled both the Assembly and the presidency after the 2001 elections, the usual sources of legislative-executive conflict would be minimized. Or would they?

Alemán's plan apparently was to retain as much control over Nicaragua's public affairs as possible. The best way to do that, given that he could not run for immediate reelection, was to have a loyalist become president, while Alemán actually ran the country from the National Assembly. To implement the plan, the then-president's first choice as PLC standard-bearer was Ivan Escobar Fornos, a distinguished constitutional lawyer, onetime president of the National Assembly, and unquestioning Alemán supporter. However, Escobar seemed too close to Alemán to have a credible claim to independence. The Liberals also looked at Eduardo Montealegre, who is young, wealthy, attractive, and talented, but found him too unpredictable. The party finally decided on Bolaños, despite Don Enrique's independence and somewhat lackluster political skills.[8] In fact, it is conceivable that Bolaños's weaknesses as a campaigner and lack of interest in the nitty-gritty of partisan politics guaranteed his selection. This would leave the critical issues of party organization and patronage in Alemán's hands and give him a plausible claim that he, not Bolaños, was actually responsible for a PLC triumph. It apparently did not occur to Alemán that Bolaños would have his own ambitions or that the president of the republic would be able to trump the president of the legislature.

To make sure that he would keep his face before the public until the next election, draw a public salary,[9] maintain control of the PLC, and be well placed to return as chief executive should anything happen to President Bolaños, Alemán needed more than just a legislative seat: he needed to be speaker of the Assembly. However, the Assembly elected its officers before Nicaragua's new president was sworn in, when Alemán would still be chief executive and forbidden to sit in the legislature. The problem was solved when a PLC placeman, Oscar Moncada, won the Assembly's presidency in a race that saw the FSLN boycott the election rather than vote for either Moncada or Jaime Cuadra, the leader of the Azul y Blanco (Blue and White, colors of the Nicaraguan flag) caucus, a Liberal splinter loyal to Bolaños. As soon as Alemán took his seat in the Assembly his placeman resigned and Alemán was elected. The system Alemán was putting in place aimed to keep the loyalty of his caucus, garner voter

support, and keep President Bolaños from exercising the full powers of his office. To secure the first objective Dr. Alemán proposed raising deputies' salaries.[10] This was a familiar tactic, because in his term as president, Alemán dou-
bled the salaries of a long list of public officials. The money supposedly came
from party coffers, but evidence later emerged indicating that these were state
funds, laundered through a foundation (the FDN, Nicaraguan Democratic Foundation) that Alemán and his closest allies controlled.[11] This is unadorned boss
politics, but with a twist, because it put Bolaños in a very tight spot. Had the bill
actually got through to the president's desk he would likely have found it too
expensive and vetoed it. This would have heightened Alemán's reputation
among his caucus as the defender of their interests, reinforcing their loyalty to
the party leader.

To woo voters, Alemán proposed an education credit.[12] Piloted through the
house by former Central Bank president and Alemán loyalist, Noel Ramírez, the
measure called for poor families to receive a payment equivalent to 20 percent
of their yearly wages for each child in school, up to 100 percent.[13] Where the
deputies' salary proposal was boss politics, this was unvarnished populism.
Again, had the bill gone ahead it would have left Bolaños the option of vetoing
it and looking like an ogre or signing it and falling so far afoul of the IMF that
Nicaragua would never get the debt relief the country so badly needed. In either
case, Alemán would have had a handy club to use on his fellow Liberal.

All Alemán's legislative maneuvers had a dual logic. The first of these was
to keep his name and face before the public. Being an electoral caudillo demands having a stage on which to perform, as well as bounty to dispense. It is
not a job for an éminence grise, managing events behind the scenes. A leader
has to be seen leading. But this cannot take place in a vacuum; there has to be an
objective.

That objective, the other part of Alemán's legislative logic, was regaining
the presidency. Throughout the latter half of his term rumors were constantly
circulating about how he would retain the presidency. The adoption of the Pact
was followed by musings about a constitutional convention to draft a new
document that permitted consecutive presidential terms. When nothing came of
this, speculation turned to how Alemán might weaken Bolaños's campaign to
guarantee a feeble mandate that would make the new president dependent on
congressional goodwill. Once Don Enrique won office convincingly, attention
shifted to the National Assembly, where the battle between the two men could
be presented as normal legislative-executive conflict. Controlling the legislature
became especially valuable to Alemán after charges were brought against him in
March 2002. Blocking Bolaños's initiatives would make Nicaragua seem ungovernable and perhaps give Alemán the leverage to escape prosecution for alleged corruption.

Bolaños's political agenda was built around two themes: economic policy,
including relations with lenders and donors, and ethics and corruption. Near the

top of his list was a probity law. The National Assembly directorate, which sets the legislature's agenda and was at the time presided over by Alemán, had different views. Thus the bill took four months to make it onto the floor of the chamber, at which point Alemán himself proposed amending the measure to exclude assets held by an official's spouse or children from disclosure requirements. A number of European ambassadors indicated their countries' discomfort with that provision, implying the possibility of suspended financial assistance and the amendment was quickly withdrawn.[14] Despite this setback, Alemán had shown that he could use his control over the legislative order paper to obstruct Bolaños. In itself, this is not unusual: legislatures squabble with presidents and speakers use their powers to advance their own priorities. What sets this case apart is the combination of Mr. Alemán's apparent desire to make himself Nicaragua's unofficial prime minister and the probity bill's objectives, which could threaten him and his closest associates.

Obstructionism arises again in the National Assembly's handling of the budget. Legislatures in democracies with U.S.-style division of powers constitutions are supposed to criticize, amend, and sometimes defeat the spending and taxing proposals of the executive. In Nicaragua, however, policymakers are severely constrained by the conditions of the country's structural adjustment program. Therefore, room for deal-making is limited and it is impossible to change the grand lines of the budget without imperiling the soft loans and debt relief offered by the IMF, World Bank, or Inter-American Development Bank. The administration had to suspect that the FSLN, the principal opposition party and chief critic of neoliberal economics, would oppose its budget but the president should have been able to count on the PLC's support. This did not happen and it took a communiqué issued by the diplomatic corps in Nicaragua to move the PLC to back the administration's economic plan.

However, the PLC did not give up. First, it cut the budget of the presidency so deeply that the office of the chief executive was struggling to pay its light bill. It then put President Bolaños on the spot by rejecting a budget provision that would have taxed items included in the basic food basket, long subsidized to protect the poor.[15] Either Bolaños would have to veto this popular measure or see talks with the IMF scuttled.

When the National Assembly occasionally proved insufficient to Alemán's needs, he used the party against the chief executive. Although Bolaños headed the PLC ticket, the party is Alemán's. Thus in May 2002, with Alemán charged with various counts of corrupt practices and several of his top lieutenants either in jail (Byron Jerez, ex-director of Nicaragua's revenue agency) or having fled the country to avoid prosecution (Esteban Duquestrada, former minister of finance, and David Robleto, who held several portfolios in Alemán's cabinet), the party was mobilized to protect Arnoldo Alemán. The PLC scheduled a march in Masaya, Bolaños's hometown, to protest the president's handling of national affairs. A combination of serious flooding in much of the country and opposition from the residents of Masaya caused the march to be canceled,[16] but the PLC had plainly declared war on the president elected on its ticket.

The administration's response was to start a parallel PLC, the so-called Bolañistas. Vice President Jose Rizo was the main organizer and a man with a strong interest in seeing Alemán gone from Nicaragua's political stage: with Alemán out Rizo became the presumptive heir to the PLC's 2006 presidential nomination. Clearly Alemán did not expect President Bolaños to act so vigorously. Neither did he foresee how much power he would lose once out of the presidency. Alemán failed to put a placeman in the presidency and was paying the price.

The Anticorruption Campaign

Although Bolaños has a reputation for personal probity, his association with the Alemán administration and his unthreatening performance at the helm of that government's ethics body (the Comité Nacional de Integridad) cast doubt on his potential as an anticorruption crusader. Furthermore, Alemán's presence as speaker of the National Assembly seemed likely to block any plans Bolaños had to fulfill his campaign pledges to clean up government. Yet, within four months of his inauguration several central figures from the last administration were either in jail or had fled the country to avoid prosecution and Alemán himself had been charged with several counts of malfeasance.

Three cases have emerged. One concerns the *checazo* (check scam), most closely associated with Byron Jerez, who directed Nicaragua's revenue agency (DGI, Dirección General de Ingresos) during much of the Alemán administration. However, it touches Alemán, his family, and Alemán-appointed chiefs of several state institutions. This case is ironic because one set of charges of fraud against Jerez were dismissed in 1999, in a judgment that left many Nicaraguans suspecting the investigating magistrate had been suborned. New charges, based on different cases, were brought in 2002 and led to Jerez's jailing.

The second set of charges come from a curious deal which was supposed to let Mexican media giant, TV Azteca, supply Nicaragua's public television station, Channel 6, with programming and equipment for two years. The unstated quid pro quo was apparently that Azteca would get preferential treatment in bidding on new telecommunications frequencies. Although $1.3 million were diverted from various Nicaraguan state enterprises to finance the deal, the Mexican firm claimed never to have heard of it. Alemán and several key ministers, some of whom fled the country to avoid prosecution, are implicated and have been charged. Those now holding elected office, even when the position is ex officio as with Alemán, had to be stripped of their parliamentary immunity before prosecution could proceed.

Finally and most crucially, there are several investigations that touch Alemán, or his immediate family, directly. The most important of these are grouped into the *huaca*, an Inca word meaning buried treasure that was applied to a booty of some $100 million that the president had moved from Nicaraguan government coffers to his private accounts in Panama. It was on the outcome of this last group of cases that the future of Alemán's electoral caudillismo rested.

The Jerez File[17]

Like many Nicaraguans, Byron Jerez spent the 1980s in Miami. But instead of returning in the early 1990s, after the Sandinistas lost power, Jerez stayed in Florida to become the purchasing agent for the city of Managua, whose mayor was Arnoldo Alemán. After Alemán became president, Jerez joined him in Managua, becoming director of the DGI, as well as treasurer of the PLC. Jerez thus was Alemán's money man and presumably his most trusted lieutenant. Forced to leave the government in 2000 following charges of corruption, of which he was exonerated, Jerez returned to private life in Managua. In 2002 a new investigation into his stewardship began and evidence was discovered justifying new charges. Jerez was arrested as he and his family were apparently preparing to leave the country, arraigned, and jailed awaiting trial.

What brought Jerez to this pass was a case known as the *checazo*, built around the misappropriation of government checks. To this was later added the *camionetazo*, which involved pickup trucks. He is also charged with diverting disaster relief money from Hurricane Mitch to build a terrace at his summer home. Jerez seems to have pursued his illegal activities vigorously, because $11 million of his overseas assets have been frozen at the request of Nicaraguan courts.[18] Finally, his case leads to Arnoldo Alemán, both because money that was diverted went to a firm controlled by the ex-president's family and because the two men were principal signing officers for the Nicaraguan Democratic Foundation (FDN), which is suspected of being used for money laundering.

The *checazo* was a three-sided fraud. A state agency headed by Jorge Solís Farias, first the oil company, Petronic, then the phone company, Enitel, sent checks to the DGI, ostensibly as tax payments, or to shell companies owned by Jerez, supposedly to pay for goods or services. These checks were diverted, taken to Multicambios, a private foreign exchange agency, converted into U.S. dollars, and deposited either in Nicaraguan banks or abroad. One check is of particular importance, because it went to BANIC, a now failed Nicaraguan bank with Liberal party ties, to pay debts accrued by GENINSA, a holding company looking after Alemán family interests.[19] In short, Jerez and, apparently, Alemán got the heads in state agencies to steal public funds, and send those funds to Jerez, who appropriated the money either to his personal use or to accounts linked to President Alemán.

Most contemporary studies of corruption focus on bribery, especially of the legislature.[20] They emphasize how the private sector can suborn the state. What occurred in Alemán's Nicaragua was open fraud and embezzlement. His administration came to approximate a kleptocracy, a regime of thieves.

Almost as interesting as the *checazo* is the *camionetazo*. The details were simple enough.[21] Two Managua car dealers bought fifty-one pickups, valued at $2 million, in the United States, imported them duty-free, and paid no sales tax on them, yielding a 45 percent saving. The dealers then sold the cars to individuals or organizations for DGI credit notes, which are credits for quarterly tax bills used by the DGI to make purchases. These notes cannot legally be used by third parties, as was done here. Although only fifty-one cases of illegal sales were found, the DGI issued an average of seventy credit notes monthly, suggesting that other frauds may exist.

On April 24, 2002, Mr. Jerez was arrested, evidently as he was about to leave the country. Evidence of this intention was the fact that he had visited Panama the week before and, more convincingly, that when arrested he had with him $100,840, ten credit cards, two checkbooks, a .38 revolver, a .32 automatic, and an Uzi! Jerez was arraigned and committed to prison to await trail. He has appealed his detention.

Channel 6

Ostensibly, this is about a deal to upgrade Nicaragua's last government-owned TV station, Channel 6. The contract was a fraudulent, sweetheart deal. However, there is more to the Channel 6 story. Not only does it involve ex-president Alemán and former Mexican ambassador to Nicaragua, Ricardo Galán, as well as a host of Aleman administrations officials, but it also appears to have been a device to divert public funds to finance a shell corporation's participation in a fixed bidding process for a new cellular phone frequency.

Although the involvement of Galán, Alejandro López Toledo, another Mexican who was part of the rigged bidding, and Alemán administration officials is incontrovertible, the case against Alemán himself rested on circumstantial evidence.[22] Nevertheless, this was the first major case of corruption to point directly at the former president. Although there was no smoking gun, judge Gertrudis Arias found the evidence strong enough to start proceedings against Alemán. In response, the former chief executive invoked parliamentary immunity to avoid answering the charges.

The affair began in March 2001 when PCS de Mexico, which claimed to represent Azteca Holding, the parent of Mexican media giant TV Azteca, entered a bid for a new cell phone frequency in Nicaragua. PCS's bid, $8 million, with a projected $28.75 million in work to follow, was selected over a competitor's bid of $7.15 million, with $42.1 million in later work. Behind PCS were Ricardo Galán and Alejandro López Toledo. Galán was not only Mexico's former ambassador to Nicaragua but also an advisor to President Alemán and the chief lobbyist for PCS. López Toledo, besides being a principal in PCS, was also a member of the committee reviewing the bids for the frequency and the chair of that body's technical subcommittee. In his capacity as a member of the committee receiving bids, López Toledo was apparently instrumental in changing its evaluative criteria to favor PCS.[23]

Although it won the bidding, PCS did not pay its $8 million right away. It rather sought and received a special deal from Alemán's finance minister, Esteban Duquestrada, which gave the firm an easy payment plan. Apparently, this was necessary because PCS could not come up with the money, a small sum for the representative of a firm as large as Azteca Holding. Prosecutors would later deduce that PCS was a shell set up to win the frequency cheaply (some alleged that the frequency should have brought $25 million) with the aim of selling it for more later on. As Azteca denies ever hearing of the bid, let alone authorizing PCS to act for it, the prosecution's assumption seems well founded.

Channel 6 enters the picture as a conduit for sending $1.3 million in state funds to PCS. What made this possible was a contract the TV station had with Servicios Integrales Casco, S.A. Channel 6 was to rent programming and equipment from TV Azteca that Casco was to deliver and install. Unsurprisingly, TV Azteca has never received any payment and has declared the Casco contract a fraud.

This is how the system worked: Channel 6 would indicate that it needed money for some plausible purpose, perhaps buying publicity. The Office of the President would then order a state agency—the international airport authority (EAAI), the tourism institute (INTUR), the post office and communications department (TELCOR), the phone company (ENITEL), and the finance department itself, were all involved—to send a check. The check would then be taken, often by the station's general manager, Sidney Pratt, to Casco's lawyer, Mayra Medina, or to another front company, Sinfra (Servicios de Infraestructura), linked to López Toledo. The payments always coincided with the due dates for PCS's payments on its bid.[24]

The Channel 6 case has elements of fraud (rigged bids) and more typically patrimonial corruption (diverting public funds to private ends). Although Alemán denied responsibility in this matter, Martha McCoy, former press secretary in the office of the president and later charged in this case, claimed that only Alemán had the authority to order government agencies to make financial transfers to the TV station.[25] Several of those implicated have been indicted, while others have fled Nicaragua. The two Mexicans returned to their country, whose government has denied a request for their extradition.

Investigating Alemán

The charges leveled against the ex-president are many and varied. Some are routine:[26] misreporting the extent of his wealth and using public funds to pay for improvements to his private property. Others are more serious: money laundering and embezzlement. The gravest accusations stem from the alleged misappropriation of roughly $100 million of public funds.

Among the instances of routine corruption attributed to Dr. Alemán are the construction of a helicopter pad at both his and his sister's country residences, and paving a highway to his rural estate, El Chile. The road project has stirred particular interest, because it is an exact copy of something done by the Somozas. In fact, a series of articles by the Sandinista social analyst Orlando Núñez noted a number of striking parallels between the style and substance of Alemán and those of the Somozas.[27] If Alemán set out to make himself Nicaragua's elected caudillo he could have picked no better model.

A colorful example of Alemán's patrimonial approach to the management of public monies comes from the *tarjetazo*, or credit card scam. Between 1997 and 2001, he ran up charges of $1.8 million on the Central Bank of Nicaragua's American Express card. Among the charges on the statement are travel for family members, a $22,000 rug purchase in Egypt, stops at Versace and Luis Vuitton, not to mention Alemán's engagement party and honeymoon expenses.[28] The receipts were usually signed by Alemán's principal secretary, Alfredo Fernández. There is no indication that Alemán reimbursed the government.[29] Further investigation did, however, reveal that Noel Ramírez incurred over $300,000 in American Express bills while president of the Central Bank under Alemán; again, there is no evidence of repayment.

More critical to both Alemán and Nicaragua's current government is the *huaca*. Charged in this matter, besides Alemán himself, were his sister, daughter, brother and sister-in-law, and their son. Charges were also laid against Byron Jerez and his wife and daughter; Jorge Solís Farias, the onetime head of Petronic and Enitel; former finance minister Esteban Duquestrada; Alfredo Fernández, Alemán's principal secretary; and Ligia Segovia and Auxiliadora López, both assistants of Jerez. The prosecutor of this case, Ivan Lara Palacios, underlined the role of the Nicaraguan Democratic Foundation (FDN), incorporated in Panama, in laying out his charges.

The original FDN was established by the PLC in the early 1990s to raise money among Nicaraguans in Miami. The Panamanian version, however, appears to be a distinct entity as the party's current treasurer, Gilberto Wong, who succeeded Mr. Jerez in the job, claimed to know nothing of its existence.[30] The FDN-Panama is a nonprofit, private corporation formed by Arnoldo Alemán, Byron Jerez, and Maria Dolores Alemán Cardenal, Alemán's daughter. Money from shell corporations linked to Jerez or the Channel 6 affair flowed into the FDN's Panamanian accounts, then flowed out again to individuals and corporations associated with the ex-president. The Panamanian special investigator for drug-related crimes has indicated that his agency has tracked $31 million passing through accounts in his country registered to those charged.[31]

Finally, the activities of former finance minister Duquestrada merit mention. Between October 1999 and January 2000, a total of $6,965,000 was transferred from the Nicaraguan treasury to an account in Panama registered to the General Treasury of the Republic of Nicaragua. The prosecutor interpreted Duquestrada's actions in this way:

> What reason could the ex-Finance Minister have for opening an account in Panama for the Nicaraguan Treasury? Put differently, what was his objective in opening and maintaining accounts of the Finance Department in a Panamanian bank? It was part of the strategy of *"the Fraud of the Century"* perpetrated against the Nicaraguan State and its people![32]

Alemán's Response

Although he proclaimed his innocence at regular intervals, Alemán's first line of defense was to stonewall. He knew that as long as he controlled a majority of votes in the National Assembly he retained his parliamentary immunity and is safe. But the caudillo and his troops also took the offensive implicating Bolaños and other members of the administration in the corruption scandal. At issue here was campaign financing in 2001 for PLC candidates from the Panama-based FDN, which violated the electoral law. The plan may have been to annul the 2001 elections, necessitating a new round for which Alemán would have been eligible. However, Bolaños made public his books, which showed that he had received no money from the FDN.[33] The public's view on the matter was made clear in a late August poll in which 81 percent of Nicaraguans approved the president's actions, while 84 percent wanted Alemán stripped of his immunity from prosecution and brought to trial.[34]

Alemán suffered a serious blow on September 19, 2002 when he lost control of the National Assembly. A month earlier, in the backwash of the revelations about the *huaca*, Alemán had recessed the legislature for three weeks to give him and the PLC time to mount a defense.[35] To strip the former chief executive of his parliamentary immunity and send him to trial, his opponents needed a simple majority of all members of the Assembly, forty-seven of ninety-two members. The FSLN had thirty-eight deputies and the Azul y Blancos, the Bolaños loyalists, had eight. As long as the numbers stayed like that, Alemán was safe. The first sign of serious trouble came on September 19 when the so-called New Majority found the extra vote it needed to dismiss Alemán as speaker[36] and name a committee to consider a judicial request that Alemán be delivered for trial on charges of embezzlement.

While the committee took evidence during October, rumors of Alemán's possible exile circulated and the PLC tried to use its power as the largest party in the house to get its leader cleared. Even when the committee recommended on October 10 that Alemán lose parliamentary immunity, the Liberals did not give up. They resorted to a number of stratagems to delay the vote, such as boycotting sittings to break the quorum,[37] but on December 12, 2002, a majority of Assembly votes swung against Alemán, stripping him of his parliamentary immunity. He was rapidly charged, tried, and placed under house arrest.

The Sandinistas' Role

The FSLN was not a passive bystander to these proceedings. Besides its understandable delight at seeing Alemán and the PLC squirm, the party has its own interests to consider. At the heart of the Sandinistas' calculations lies Daniel Ortega's assessment of how Bolaños's anticorruption campaign affects his chances for another term as president. There are also concerns within the FSLN that this campaign could hit them.

The Pact allotted the Sandinistas a number of appointments to the country's courts and independent administrative agencies. In 2002 one of the six Sandinista-affiliated supreme court justices controlled the office that assigns cases to courts of first instance. It was thus not by chance that the judicial processes against Alemán and officials of his administration moved along smartly. While decisions rendered there might yet be reversed in appellate courts with Liberal judges, presenting concrete proof of the rumors of corruption that circulated during Alemán's term in office harmed him and the PLC.

Still, there were signs that the Sandinistas would not take this struggle against Alemán and institutionalized corruption to the end. Key Sandinista leaders, Tomás Borge and Bayardo Arce, indicated their doubts about the *huaca*.[38] Their hesitance may have reflected a fear of prosecution on similar charges. However, Daniel Ortega and his advisors apparently decided that a weakened Alemán-led PLC was the FSLN's ticket back to power. Were all to work out to their advantage, the Sandinistas could attack the PLC for corruption, misgovernment, and gridlocking the political process at the same time as they assailed Bolaños for following a neoliberal agenda harmful to the poor. It, though, would be a risky enterprise. The Bush administration detests the Sandinistas and would not happily accept their return to power. Moreover, were the FSLN to do anything that could be construed as helping Alemán avoid prosecution, they would suffer the electors' wrath.

An Interim Assessment

To attempt more than a summation and commentary at this juncture would be foolhardy and misleading, as there are still so many unknowns. We do not know if President Bolaños will be able to consolidate his gains from his anticorruption initiative and apply it to other fields. Neither can we tell if the wave of anticorruption sentiment in Nicaragua will become a part of the nation's political culture. More importantly, we do not know if the institutional and economic crises that have been simmering since Bolaños took office in January 2002 will finally boil over. Nevertheless, some things are clear. By beginning his anti-corruption initiative and pressing ahead with it, Enrique Bolaños took a significant step toward undermining the Pact. If a determined president with no more than ordinary political skills can so upset the projections of Nicaragua's wiliest politicians, it is clear that what worked when there were no restraints on a ruler's (or his party's) use of power becomes ineffective when even a minimal level of constitutional restraint exists. Further, the intensive coverage of the corruption issue has put probity and transparency on the public's agenda, perhaps creating a constituency for ongoing reforms.

Turning these possibilities into realities requires that the president and his advisors be able to link Nicaragua's current poverty to the corruption that pervades its political and economic elites. If honesty is seen as the only path to well-being the costs ordinary people paid while Alemán and Bolaños struggled for supremacy might be borne more easily. Help from the international community, especially Washington, will be needed, however, to assist Nicaragua back on to the path of constitutional democracy.

Implications for Nicaragua's Undone Democracy

In the introduction to this collection we observed that "(d)emocracy still exists in Nicaragua, but it will not thrive unless the system built by the Pact fails to work." Can that system be undone, the way constitutional democracy was? In the first months of President Bolaños's administration the attention of his government and all of Nicaragua was concentrated on Arnoldo Alemán and a handful of his relatives and political friends. But will putting Alemán, Jerez, and company in jail restore Nicaragua's undone democracy?

Much careful planning went into the Pact. That deal was not struck haphazardly but was rather designed to secure concrete objectives of Alemán and the PLC, as well as of Ortega and the FSLN. We have argued that the Pact sets the institutional framework for electoral caudillismo, boss politics shaped to fit the conditions of contemporary Nicaragua. Removing Alemán from the picture weakens that system by taking away its most skilled operator, but need not destroy it.

The core problem is that the pacted political system is constitutionally entrenched. Although Nicaragua's constitution is relatively easy to amend,[39] there may not be enough support to repeal the Pact's provisions, even without Alemán physically there to lead the PLC. Both the PLC and the FSLN believe in quotas of power that are exercised directly by political parties, while neither appears to believe that state institutions can be politically neutral. Even were President Bolaños to gain control of the PLC machine, he would still have the Sandinistas to deal with, and they have shown no sign of changing their stance on the question of partisan control or executive-centered government.

Although imprisoned in August 2003, there is still a chance that Alemán could be freed by a superior court packed with placemen.[40] That would certainly end Bolaños's campaign against corruption and could so weaken the president that he might be unable to rule. Nicaragua's democratic hopes would then receive a significant setback. Indeed, they already have been, because the pursuit of Alemán and his associates so occupied government throughout 2002 that little else got done and what was completed was finished well behind schedule. As a result, although President Bolaños began his quest for probity with public opinion solidly behind him, by 2003 Nicaraguans were changing their minds about their president.[41]

This does not mean that Bolaños's anticorruption campaign must fail, or that it made no difference that Alemán was indicted. Knowing that large-scale malfeasance will be detected, investigated, and prosecuted can serve as a powerful deterrent. For the process to move as far as it has required that the courts and comptroller set aside partisan loyalties, at least in this one matter. Though perhaps small in themselves, these actions extend the rule of law and mark a return to the path of building a state that serves the public interest instead of private ones. They may even serve as warnings to the still partisan parts of government that Nicaraguans are coming to demand honest rule.

In the excitement caused by Bolaños's anticorruption offensive it is easy to lose sight of what may prove to be his administration's most telling blow against electoral caudillismo. Personal rule demands full control of the state. That is the only way to assure access to resources and maintain a monopoly over the country's political agenda. Yet, as Arnoldo Alemán found out to his chagrin, the system left by the Pact can strip a boss of much of his power when the presidency falls into untrustworthy hands.

A president with a modicum of independence and a willingness to confront the legislature, even where that can mean gridlock, can thwart the ambitions of a caudillo who planned to govern from a free seat in the National Assembly. This suggests that competitive elections and a party structure or state of public opinion that makes it hard for a boss to impose a placeman and be sure of victory reduces the utility of that free seat. As an electoral caudillo cannot afford to strengthen the legislature, for fear of what might happen when he returns to the presidency, the only alternative is unlimited presidential reelection. Simply by challenging Alemán's pretensions to power, Bolaños took a small but vital first step toward giving Nicaragua another chance at constitutional democracy. Only time will tell if it succeeds.

Notes

1. *La Prensa*, "Mas de mil millones robados," August 8, 2002.

2. Bolaños was a lifelong Conservative. He was on the ticket with Alemán to reassure the traditional business elite, grouped in COSEP (Private Enterprise Council), which Bolaños once headed, that their interests would be looked after. In the end, Alemán rode roughshod over COSEP, just as he did everyone else. Interestingly, Alemán gives Bo-

laños's Conservative credentials as the key reason for picking him to head the PLC ticket in 2001. See Fabian Medina, "Reportaje Especial: Jaque al Rey," *La Prensa* August 12, 2002.

3. Details of the decision are found in *La Prensa*, "20 años para Alemán," December 8, 2003.

4. David Close "Nicaragua: The Legislature as Seedbed of Conflict," in *Legislatures and the New Democracies in Latin America,* ed. David Close (Boulder, CO: Lynne Rienner, 1995), 49-70.

5. This was the one aspect of executive authority that the Pact did not restore.

6. In part, this was because the president of the National Assembly during the Alemán years was reluctant to have his institution studied. In 1998, for example, my request to examine the recorded votes from the previous Congress, the one that passed the 1995 constitutional amendments, was refused by Dr. Escobar Fornos, the speaker, on the grounds that the machinery used to record the votes had been paid for by the U.S. government; hence nothing could be done without the written approval of the American embassy.

7. During the Chamorro administration, several presidents of the National Assembly took prominent roles in national politics. Under the Alemán government, however, the speaker had a much lower profile and seemed to act more as the chief executive's house leader.

8. Oliver Bodan and Lourdes Arroliga, "Encerrona PLC amarrada," *Confidencial,* January 7-13, 2001.

9. Alemán actually drew three public salaries: one in the National Assembly, another as a member of the Central American Parliament in Guatemala, and a third in the form of a former president's pension. Both parliamentary seats are ex officio, granted to immediate past presidents.

10. *Nicaragua News Service (NNS)*, "Alemán claims Assembly members not getting 'a dignified wage,' " February 4-10, 2002.

11. *El Nuevo Diario*, "Robe para el PLC," and "FDN jamas fue del PLC," August 9, 2002.

12. *Nicaragua News Service*, "Education ploy 'playing to the crowd,' " January 14-20, 2002.

13. Published accounts of the bill do not make clear if the salary was to be that of the principal breadwinner or a combined family wage.

14. *Central America Report*, "The delicate topic of corruption and international aid," July 19, 2002, pp. 1-2.

15. *La Prensa*, "Murio el 'canastazo,' " August 15-16, 2002.

16. *El Nuevo Diario*, "Masaya 'ardiendo,' " May 27, 2002.

17. Except where otherwise indicated, material relating to the various cases of corruption comes from the online editions of *La Prensa*, www-ni.laprensa.com.ni and *El Nuevo Diario*, www.elnuevodiario.com.ni. Both newspapers have full free archives for this period available at their Web sites.

18. *La Prensa*, "Procuraduria General de la Republica abre otra investigacion contra Aleman," July 23, 2002.

19. *El Nuevo Diario*, "Alemán atrapado!" June 29, 2002.

20. Gabriella R. Montinola, and Robert W. Jackman, 2002, "Sources of Corruption: A Cross-Country Study," *British Journal of Political Science* 31:147-170.

21. *Confidencial*, "Otras causas para Jerez," May 11, 2002, www.confidencial.com. ni.

22. Once charges relating to the *huaca* became public the case against Dr. Alemán, in relation to Channel 6, grew stronger.

23. *Confidencial*, "2do. 'round': conexion mexicana," March 24, 2002.

24. *La Prensa*, "Negocion de US$15 millones," April 10, 2002.

25. *El Nuevo Diario*, "Recomienda que Alemán no participle en discusiones," April 13, 2002.

26. It is routine in the sense that a resident of a part of the United States or Canada where pork-barrel politics is the norm would find Alemán's behavior objectionable but not exceptional.

27. *El Nuevo Diario*, "Segunda y definitive derrota del somocismo," August 25-26, 2002.

28. *La Prensa*, "Criminal derroche," 20 June 2002, "Amor a 'tarjetazos'," June 21, 2002; ND, "Alemán derrochaba mientras el pueblo moria de hambre," June 21, 2002.

29. Alemán did argue that the expenses were necessary parts of job as head of state and that the purchases at luxury shops were to buy gifts for other leaders. This line of defense disappeared quickly, however.

30. *El Nuevo Diario*, " 'FDN jamas fue del PLC,' " August 9, 2002. Wong later admitted that he had in fact received FDN monies to finance the PLC's 2001 election campaign, though he maintained that he did not know where the funds actually originated. See, *La Prensa*, "Gilberto Wong senala al PLC," August 24, 2002.

31. *La Prensa*, "Panama confirme lavado," August 10, 2002.

32. *La Prensa*, "Mas de mil millones robados," August 8, 2002; emphasis in original.

33. *La Prensa*, "Bolañistas presentan cuentas de cheque FDN," August 9, 2002.

34. *La Prensa*, "Mayoria aprueba carcel para Alemán," August 6, 2002.

35. *La Prensa*, "Alemán cierra la Asamblea Nacional," August 13, 2002.

36. *El Nuevo Diario*, "Cayo Alemán," September 20, 2002. In fact, the entire seven-member *junta directiva* (presidium) of the Assembly was dismissed, save for one Sandinista deputy.

37. *La Prensa*, "Arnolidstas no pudieron evitar el desafuero," December 13, 2002.

38. *El Nuevo Diario*, "Cuan seguros son los votos del FSLN?" August 23, 2002.

39. The Nicaraguan Constitution can be amended by a majority of 60 percent of the National Assembly in two consecutive legislatures (Articles 192 and 194).

40. Discussions regarding the elections of Supreme Court magistrates in May 2003 repeatedly raised the possibility that support for Alemán's release from custody was the PLC's condition for backing candidates for Nicaragua's top judicial positions.

41. Compare the poll results in *La Prensa* February 18, 2002, and those of a year later, 18 February 2003.

Chapter 10

The Caudillo is Dead: Long Live the Caudillo

Kalowatie Deonandan

It was with much eagerness and enthusiasm that scholars and policymakers alike embraced the so-called "third wave" of democratization that swept across much of Southern Europe, East and South Asia, the former Soviet Union, and Latin America, from the late 1970s to the 1990s.[1] Defining this wave was the move from authoritarian or military rule to a more liberal democratic form of governance. What has become increasingly obvious however is that in many of these societies considered part of this transition, including Nicaragua, the democratic wave is being overwhelmed by an antidemocratic tsunami of corruption, clientelism, neopatrimonialism, and hyperpresidentialism.

This antidemocratic eruption has spawned voluminous studies on the precise nature of these new "democracies" and the dynamics accounting for the failure to consolidate, or at least to make significant advances toward the democratic ideal. This study falls within the latter parameters as it attempts to explain how the democracy project was derailed in Nicaragua under Arnoldo Alemán. What is interesting about this case (as with others) is that the counterdemocratic assault on the country's nascent democratic institutions has been the result of a deliberate campaign carried out by the leader in conjunction with other actors from the political and economic elites. Agency in other words has been critical in this process of democratic decomposition, though this is not to deny the importance of structure.

In summarizing the studies on third wave transitions, Thomas Carothers, in a much-critiqued article, cites five core assumptions, undergirding the literature: (1) that "any country moving *away* from dictatorial rule can be considered in transition *toward* democracy"; (2) "that democratization unfolds in a set sequence of stages"; (3) that elections are a "foundation stone" for democracy; (4) that the "structural features" of a country such as its "economic level [or] political history" will not be major determinants in the democratization process; and

(5) that the transition is "being built on coherent functioning states."[2] The "third wave" paradigm however does not offer an explanation for those countries which Carothers classified as being in the "grey zone."[3] These are countries which exhibit some facets of the democratic model, such as a multiparty system, regular elections, an independent civil society, and a free press, but which suffer from "serious democratic deficits" manifested in such malaise as apathy among the citizenry, exploitation of state institutions by government officials, and failure by elected representatives to represent the interests of citizens.[4] Though critics have charged Carothers with simplifying or misrepresenting the transitology literature, his summary nevertheless carries enough substance to serve as a good benchmark by which to evaluate Nicaragua's transition under Alemán. In the concluding section of this chapter his claims will be assessed as they apply to Nicaragua.

All contributors to this study subscribe to the belief that Nicaragua's "democratic deficit" expanded during the Alemán presidency. Before discussing their conclusions, it should be pointed out that while contemporary Nicaragua is generally classified as part of the "third wave," it can legitimately be argued that it does not fit neatly into this categorization which, as noted above, is marked by the transition from authoritarianism to a liberal democracy. Prior to its adoption of this latter model, Nicaragua had moved from an authoritarian regime under the Somozas to a revolutionary interregnum (1979-90) under the leadership of the Sandinista National Liberation Front (FSLN). The essence of this revolutionary vision was the construction of a socialist democracy emphasizing wealth redistribution and greater social welfare, principles generally inconsistent with those of the liberal variant which stresses the legal and constitutional mechanisms of democracy, rather than outcomes. The objective here however, is to evaluate the form and substance of Nicaraguan democracy under Alemán based on the liberal democratic criteria. Nevertheless, it is important to keep this revolutionary history in mind as it formed part of the nation's structural features which influenced Alemán's rule and motivated his antidemocratic drive (and in the end is likely to prove an important force in helping to reverse it).

The rest of this chapter is organized into three sections. The first is a review of the theoretical concepts which guided the studies in this volume. It revisits our working assumptions about the meaning of liberal democracy and caudillismo. The second integrates the various chapters by examining caudillismo à la Alemán and the forces which contributed to his imposing this form of rule in Nicaragua. The final section assesses the future of Nicaraguan democracy within the framework of Thomas Carothers's claims regarding the third wave transition literature.

Liberal Democracy, Caudillismo, and Its Components

Liberal democracy for purposes of this analysis is understood to encompass not only formal institutions and procedures, such as free and fair elections, the rule of law, political and civil rights, transparency and accountability in governance, but also substantive criteria such as economic and social well-being. Though critics may counter that this last requirement is irrelevant or incompatible with assessments of liberal democracy which privileges the political and the procedural, the position advocated here is that for the basic foundations of democracy to be constructed, for fundamental democratic criteria such as genuine citizen participation to be met, economic injustices and inequalities must be addressed—a point that analysts such as Diamond and Linz concede when they acknowledged that a healthy democracy is dependent on economic growth and popular well-being.[5] Paul Cammack expands on this stating: "Far from it being the case that social and economic advancement can be considered separable from and additional to the consolidation of political democracy, the realization of citizenship which is essential if *political* democracy is to be reality itself requires substantial *social* and *economic* reform."[6]

Over a decade of "democratic transition" in Nicaragua, however, has left the country with little to boast about. It currently ranks as the second poorest in Central America with the majority of the population living below the poverty line. Furthermore, it is emerging from five years of political rule by the Alemán regime which was marked by rampant corruption and an all-out campaign to undermine the nation's democratic institutions.

Alemán's assault on democracy was multifaceted, following a strategy of caudillismo, a form of rule dominant in an earlier period of Latin American history but which continues to manifest itself in the present, in varying degrees. During the Alemán period, it was not only present, but was the defining characteristic of his administration. Caudillismo, as Close explains elsewhere in this volume, is defined by boss politics, whereby the motivations of governance are not to strengthen state institutions to better serve the citizenry, but rather to mobilize them into service for the personal aggrandizement of the leader and his cronies. Under such a system, the political modus operandi involves strategies of populism, verticalism, clientelism, and neopatrimonialism. (While old-style caudillos could incorporate military force into this strategic mix, this option is precluded for the electoral caudillo, who must therefore rely on the manipulation of state instruments, and to do so *within* a liberal democratic framework.) The various articles throughout this book have demonstrated how these various facets of caudillismo manifested themselves in practical terms during the Alemán presidency, and the extent to which they served to strengthen the executive at the expense of other institutions of government and importantly, to the detriment of Nicaraguan democracy.

Populism, an "ism" whose meaning and relevance is often challenged, nevertheless has applicability in the Nicaraguan context. For purposes here it is accepted that in its classical conceptualization it entails, as Alan Knight suggests, a from of rule marked by appeal to the people, charismatic leadership, a reformist agenda, and a multiclass alliance, to name a few.[7] Though it is difficult to argue that Alemán's regime embodied the qualities of classical populism, there were however populist dimensions to his rule, in particular, in his political *style* of leadership.[8] As Kampwirth explains in her chapter on the campaign against NGOs, his strategy was to articulate an appeal to the populace by portraying himself as a man of the people and by setting up a dichotomous framework of the "us" (the people, the marginalized, the poor) versus "them" (the established elites, the privileged classes, or the political opponent). The "them" could also refer to the outsider or the foreigner. In the case of NGOs, this was made simple as many were of external origins, and it was particularly this latter group which bore the brunt of his attack.

His populism, however, was only in form not in substance. Motivating his strategy was the desire to enhance his personal power, secure his political future (that is, ensure popular support for a future run at the presidency), and assuage the frustrations of Nicaraguans, the majority of whom were suffering from deepening poverty and marginalization as a result of the harsh austerity policies. So despite the fact that the economic conditions in reality excluded "the people" from the benefits of citizenship as Dye and Close demonstrate, the appeal to populism gave the illusion of inclusion, and hence of regime legitimacy. Alemán's style of populism, then, was tailored to the age of market liberalization; it was designed to facilitate the implantation of structural adjustment programs by placing the blame for economic woes elsewhere and simultaneously reinforce the power of the leader by weakening civil society groups or other organized political entities which might seek to hold him accountable.

Verticalism, another feature of Alemán's caudillismo, is understood to refer to an uneven distribution of power in society whereby one group, those in command of state resources, exert dominance and control over societal groups, with the latter having little or no means by which to compel the state to respond to its demands.[9] In a poor country such as Nicaragua, where the majority of the populace is poor, the exploitation of strategies of verticalism is made easy. The marginalized, by their very status, lack the resources to make demands on the state. At the same time, the necessity of focusing on daily survival absorbs a great deal of their time and energy, thus further limiting the resources and the opportunities they have for confronting the state. Even when the regime does face challenge from below, it is able to silence its opponents by manipulating the powers at its disposal. Alemán's harassment of NGOs, his assault on labor rights, and his attacks on the various media outlets are but some examples of this.

Clientelism connotes relationships of a patron-client type whereby the patron (the leader) confers favors in the form of goods or services, in return for the client's (societal groups or individuals) political loyalty and support. Such arbitrary methods of distributing public goods to private interests, as Foweraker and Landman argue, erode the rule of law, and thus undermine the foundations of democracy.[10] While clientelistic ties are primarily vertical in nature, that is between actors with different degrees of power as described above, they can also be horizontal, meaning that they refer to relationships where the power distribution is more equal, as between the political and economic elites. Clientelism under Alemán was predominantly of the latter sort whereby public and private elites colluded for personal gain at the expense of the public interest. Prominent scandals such as those involving the country's major banks, the Nicaraguan Bank of Industry and Commerce (BANIC) and the Intercontinental Bank (Interbank) provide insights into the extent of this collusion and the resulting damage they inflicted on the Nicaraguan economy and polity.

Neopatrimonialism pertains to forms of rule under which the leader appropriates state property for his personal use. In other words, as Theobald argues, the boundary between public and private goods, central to the concept of modern public administration, is almost nonexistent.[11] Blatant examples in the case of Alemán involve his use of public institutions as his private agencies such as his putting the Ministry of Transportation to work building roads leading to his private properties. Not surprisingly a neopatrimonial system of governance is also beset with rampant corruption[12] and borders on becoming a blatant kleptocracy. The prologue in this volume paints a vivid picture of the extent of the assault on the public coffers that took place under Alemán.

Caudillismo in Practice

The Role of Elites

While the foregoing section presented the understanding shared by the authors of this volume of what constitutes caudillismo in theory, here the objective is to examine the concrete strategies and policies utilized by the regime to roll back democracy, thus illustrating the practical bases for classifying this regime as one operating on caudillistic principles.

Precluded by domestic constitutional regulations from unilaterally reorganizing the constitutional framework to impose one-party dominance over the state, and constrained by pressures from international donors who demand that the formal institutions and processes of democracy be respected (before international purse strings would be loosened), Alemán's approach was then to exploit electoral democracy, to redefine the constitutional limits through elite bargaining. More concretely, as Hoyt explains in her chapter, he colluded through *El Pacto* with the leading political opposition, the FSLN (which together with Alemán's Constitutional Liberal Party [PLC] command over 90 percent of the votes), to distribute the spoils of power. One of the most dangerous (to democracy, that is) aspects of the agreement was its strengthening of executive authority and its concomitant reduction in the powers of other institutions designed to ensure accountability in governance. State bodies such as the Supreme Electoral Council, the Supreme Court, and the Office of the Comptroller General, all critical to keeping abuse of presidential authority in check, were reorganized to reduce their impact on the executive and were staffed with Alemán appointees.

Potential oversight from other political institutions such as political parties was also restricted. As noted above, the Pact was forged with the leading political opposition, the FSLN, and this brought into question the latter's legitimacy as a genuine force. Furthermore, it restricted political competition by imposing stringent new requirements for new political parties, thus ensuring that it was the parties of the pact-makers which held sway over the political scene. Additionally, the pact-makers, caudillos both, tried to ensure (though current events prove them unsuccessful) that their interests would be secured long after they were gone from office (for example by ensuring themselves a seat in the National Assembly and immunity from any kind of accountability or prosecution for alleged crimes committed while in office). While building democracy demands strengthening institutional capacity, Alemán's strategy was aimed in the opposite direction—building the state institutions to serve his private interests.

Some studies of pacted transitions have suggested that these could be productive in the cause of democratic development. The compromises inherent in such agreements, suggests Huntington, establish the preconditions for stability and thus enhance the likelihood of democracy's consolidation.[13] By the beginning of the nineties, however, such claims were being challenged as studies on elite-led democratization revealed that these were designed more to safeguard elite interest and to entrench clientelistic ties.[14] As David Becker writes, political alliances, or "pacts" have been the strategy adopted by elites to place their interests "at least temporarily beyond the bounds of democratic contestation."[15] The Alemán-Ortega Pact certainly was of this ilk. Not surprisingly, rather than moving Nicaragua toward democratic consolidation, the results were more in line with O'Donnell's model of delegative democracy, whereby horizontal accountability of the executive to the other branches of government is lacking, or weak, despite the presence of all the formal trappings of a democratic state.[16] The result of such forms of governance, explains Diamond, is that: "Voters are mobilized by clientelistic ties and populist, personalistic (rather than programmatic) appeals; parties and independent interest groups are weak and fragmented. Instead of producing an effective means of ongoing representation of popular interests, elections delegate sweeping and largely unaccountable authority to whoever wins the presidential election."[17]

With such political power at their command, individual leaders, such as Alemán, are therefore able to exploit the system for personal gain and impose a return to authoritarian forms of governance under the auspices of democracy. Given Daniel Ortega's role in fortifying Alemán's grasp on power, it can be legitimately argued that the FSLN and its leader were important "allies" contributing to Alemán's undoing of democracy despite having significant political and ideological differences with him.

While the Pact is illustrative of the collaboration with one faction of the elite, the political elite, other factions of this stratum were also critical to Alemán's hold on power and to his campaign against democracy. Among them were the Roman Catholic Church and its leader Cardinal Obando y Bravo—

guardians of the regime's ideological legitimacy. As Pérez-Baltodano tells us, the cardinal provided the justification for the antidemocratic rollback, a role in which he was much experienced given his support for the U.S.-led contra war against the FSLN throughout the 1980s. In a strongly Catholic country, where clerical leaders, and in particular the cardinal, enjoy a great deal of credibility and authority, the nation's Episcopal Conference (consisting of the cardinal and the bishops) provided the moral basis for Alemán's rule. Under conditions of neoliberalism, when the offerings of genuine economic benefits to the people are contracting significantly, divine legitimacy bestowed on the ruling order can be a boon to leaders as it serves to contain pressures from below. When such leaders deliberately seek to limit the gains dispersed in order to personally profit from public resources, divine sanction becomes even more critical to subdue the discontented populace.

According to Pérez-Baltodano, the Church's defense of Alemán included branding his critics as envious and irresponsible and even accusing them of deliberately orchestrating a smear to discredit him. Against the charges of gross misconduct by the regime, the Church retaliated that the corruption is rooted not in the ruling order, but in society where there is a general decline in moral values. In other words, it is not Alemán who is corrupt, but Nicaraguan society. As a cure for this sickness within the social order, the Church prescribed a classic remedy—a deeper commitment to spiritual values. The solution in essence is a personal one, and historically the clergy's nostrum for all social ills. To facilitate success, the Church encouraged beliefs in magic and miracles by publicizing reports of virgin apparitions and of miracles being performed throughout the country.

This inward and supernatural focus has the advantage of freeing Alemán from being accountable to any temporal force, such as the electorate. It points citizens away from participation in governance and from looking to temporal authority to address the political and social ills of the nation. Yet, essential to the functioning of an effective democracy is citizen participation, which is different from representation. It is only by the former that the genuine essence of democracy, "rule by the people," can be realized. When members of the polity refuse to exercise the rights of citizenship, due to a lack of trust in the system or its leaders, or due to a belief that justice will be theirs in the hereafter and not in the temporal realm, or due to a deliberate campaign of dissuasion by the regime, at just such a time when such involvement by civil sectors is critical, the quality of that democracy is then open to question.

The Church's support and defense of the regime, in classic clientelistic politics, did not come without a price. In return for their loyalty, the bishops gained a powerful ally for their conservative position on critical issues such as abortion, rape, and education, and matters pertaining to the family in general. Their success was evident in the rollback of many of the advances women had made under the leadership of the revolutionary FSLN prior to the 1990s, in the attack mounted by the regime against many NGOs and other organizations working with women and children, and of course, in the regime's definition of what constitutes the family. Institutional confirmation of the alliance between church and state and of the power of religious authority in public policy can be seen in the absorption of the Nicaraguan Women's Institute by the Ministry of the Family which had as its objective the defense of the family, traditionally defined, and the return of women to more traditional roles within the private sphere.

While the Church cloaked Alemán with the aura of moral legitimacy in his undoing of democracy, other players, specifically the international financial institutions (IFIs) such as the IMF and World Bank provided him with the opportunities and rationale, albeit inadvertently, for his actions. While in theory these organizations provide the stimulus for the implementation of the liberal democratic model (by emphasizing the need for free and fair elections and a liberalized economy), and even though they have adopted measures to check corruption and have called for the strengthening of civil society, they have, in fact, helped to create the conditions for the undoing of democracy. As Grugel sums up:

> Democratization became a global movements [*sic*] at the same time as the new global political economy of marketization and liberalization emerged. This points ... to the salience of the transnational context for understanding democratization.... It is important, however, not to assume that globalization is inevitably a positive force for democratization.... In fact, the evidence ... points to the ambiguous role of globalization and liberalization in democratization.[18]

This ambiguity is manifest in the discrepancy between the rhetoric of the advocates of globalization and democracy and the impact of their structural adjustment policies (SAPs). Rather than advancing democracy or development, SAPs, which generally call for greater liberalization, have more often proven a boon to elites who are able to exploit the process for personal advantage. State managers, for example, are able to capitalize on the privatization drive by selling off public institutions to corporate friends or family members in return for kickbacks. The plethora of corruption scandals which marked the Alemán administration, and in almost all of which the president was a central player or a major beneficiary, certainly proves that corruption can resist pressures from the IFIs. Globalization and its accompanying economic models promoted by international credit institutions facilitated and strengthened the neopatrimonial state.

Furthermore, because the success of the IFIs' neoliberal prescriptions demand a stable political environment for the much-desired macroeconomic growth to occur, the conditions become ripe for a leader so inclined to adopt repressive tactics to control social unrest under the guise of imposing order. For under conditions of dire poverty and deprivation, the imposition of SAPs can only aggravate an already volatile social situation due to its deleterious economic impact on those in the lower strata. When these factors are brought together in an environment such as Nicaragua's, where popular mobilization is well established given the nation's recent revolutionary history, a leader disinclined toward the democratic route is more than likely to resort to repression as a form of social control. As Cuadra confirms in her chapter on conflict and violence during Alemán's reign, there was a marked increase in social upheavals of all kinds and the state's response was to classify them all, regardless of the legitimacy of their objectives, as illegal and thus subject to police powers. Alemán's caudillismo then, and his undoing of democracy, is in part a result of the processes of economic globalization promoted by IFIs.

The Economy, Society, and Democratic Decomposition

Where the above discussion refers to the role of allies, explicit and implicit, in facilitating Alemán's rollback of Nicaraguan democracy, it must be kept in mind that the actual victims of this assault were the people. Economic data provided by Dye and Close tell the tale of the burdens and hardships faced by the majority while the leader saw his personal wealth expand exponentially. Although the literature on "third wave" transitions does not accord primacy to economic development in the process of democratic consolidation (though some authors acknowledge its relevance),[19] the Nicaraguan example tells us that such neglect ignores a critical dimension of consolidation. Just as citizen participation is an important yardstick for measuring the health of a democracy, so too is their standard of living and the extent to which they share in the nation's wealth. As Alfred Montero asserts, "no democracy can be considered consolidated until the quality of democracy is assured."[20]

The nature of Nicaragua's economy, that is its underdeveloped status, is a structural fact and as such, this imposes limits on the types of economic developmental strategies which can be pursued. Nevertheless, it does not preclude the state from *attempting* to implement public policies which serve the general interest, to resolve competing societal demands in a manner conducive to democratic rule. As Cuadra and Marti argue, one of the major litmus tests of a democratic political system is its ability to build a governable community out of opposing groups. Achieving this goal entails not exclusion but inclusion, whereby competing groups are brought into the policy-making process in such a way that their demands could be accommodated through negotiations and compromises, or at least the conflict resolved in a manner more conducive to social cohesion than to social disruption. Alemán's approach, however, was to eliminate rather than accommodate opposition. In their respective chapters, different authors highlight different strategies or combination of strategies employed against regime critics. Cuadra emphasizes the police powers; Kampwirth focuses on populist manipulations; and, in addition to the preceding, Deonandan referred to the legal tactics. In sum, they argue that Alemán's method of governing had more in common with the earlier authoritarian rule of the Somozas than with the contemporary emphasis on democracy.

With respect to opposition groups, be they unions, NGOs, women's organizations, or the media, the underlying objective of the Alemán administration was to limit the space available to these groups to project their demands onto the state, or to hold it accountable. It was aided in this by the fact that because the constituency of most of these organizations is drawn from underclasses in society (the media of course is an exception), these groups are equipped with few resources with which to challenge the regime. The weak are thus made weaker by a regime committed to enhancing the power of the leader, rather than the strength of the polity.

The Third Wave Reexamined

This seems an appropriate moment to return to a discussion of Carothers's summary of the transition literature. If one looks at the empirical evidence of Nicaragua under Alemán, it becomes obvious that his cynicism regarding third wave assumptions is well founded.

Firstly, it cannot be taken for granted that in adopting the mantle of institutions and procedures consonant with the liberal democratic model, that a state is moving irrevocably toward democratic consolidation. What such an assumption does not take into consideration is human agency and motives. Nicaragua demonstrates that democratic trappings were facades for the deliberate decomposition of democracy, and ironically the assault on democracy was carried out by the manipulation of the very institutions designed to promote and ensure democracy's well-being, such as the party system, the legislature, and the judiciary. As Michael McFaul elaborates: "Inert, invisible structures do not make democracies or dictatorships. People do. Structural factors such as economic development, cultural influences, and historical institutional arrangements influence the formation of actors' preferences and power, but ultimately these forces have causal significance only if translated into human action."[21]

Secondly, the notion that democracy unfolds in a sequence of stages or phases also does not stand the test in the Nicaraguan example. The end goal or result of these stages, the argument states, is democratic consolidation; if not there is stagnation and reversal. What the Nicaraguan case illustrates is that the path to democracy is one of advances and retreats. Under Alemán, there was general adherence to the formal rules of the democratic process, however, in light of the various corruption scandals, the theft from public coffers, and the abuse of office, it is obvious that there needs to be a distinction between formal and substantive democracy, and that the latter can be lacking while the former is present or is even being strengthened. At the same time, it cannot be concluded that because of the many deliberate strategies to undo democracy that Alemán had set Nicaragua on an irrevocable path of democratic rollback. Currently, under the new leader Enrique Bolaños, many attempts are being made to reverse the decomposition process which had been set in motion by Alemán.

Thirdly, and related to the above, the claim that electoral politics provides the "foundation stone" for democracy is also challenged in the Nicaragua context. While elections might be a necessary precondition, it does not ensure the quality of democracy. Alemán's caudillismo was instituted within the confines of electoralism. Electoral politics provided the veil of legitimacy for the manipulation and exploitation by elites of the state and the society. Motivated by electoral prerequisites, competing political actors, specifically the leaders of two dominant parties, the PLC and the FSLN, sought to protect their stake in the system by collusion, as exemplified by the Pact, to subordinate democracy to their personal agendas. In other words, the existence of formal rules and institutions of democracy does not preclude state managers from acting undemocratically, or as O'Donnell explained, it "does not preclude the possibility that the games played 'inside' the democratic institutions are different from the ones dictated by their formal rules."[22] (This is certainly not a shocking revelation given that the older, more established democracies have themselves been plagued with scandals within the various branches of government. Even if one looks at the current war on terrorism, there is abundant evidence of some of the fundamental precepts of democracy being violated in the name of national security.)

Of course, it is the genuinely free and fair elections that also brought to power a new president who is now in a position to undo some of the damage of the Alemán regime, though he faces an uphill battle given that not all elements of his government, including members of his own political party, are in agreement with this agenda. Nevertheless, his commitment to building democracy as opposed to exploiting it for personal gain will go a long way toward restoring popular confidence in the system—an important factor in the consolidation equation.

Fourthly, the assumption that the "structural features" of a state such as its economy or history do not impinge on the success or failure of democracy, is also not substantiated in the Nicaraguan context. The country's level of economic development very much influenced the decomposition process. As an underdeveloped and indebted nation, it is at the mercy of the policy prescriptions of the international credit institutions which propose remedies favorable to macroeconomic growth than to the development of a healthy polity. This approach, as was noted earlier, undermines democracy as it has the unwitting effect of providing opportunities which can be exploited by unscrupulous leaders for personal profit (in addition to being generally favorable to elite interests). It also creates the conditions for the implantation of caudillo rule. Demands for reduction in state spending, rollbacks in progressive legislations to attract investors, and guarantees of political stability to ensure market success in a poor country usually carry with them harsh consequences for vulnerable groups such as workers, small producers, students, women, and the poor, among others. The results in Nicaragua, as Deonandan shows in her chapter, were frequent protests, demonstrations, and strikes, the majority of which were met with some form of repression. Leaders such as Alemán who are inclined toward an anti-democratic response can find justification for their repressive tactics in the IFIs' demands for political stability. They can also defend their strengthening of the executive branch under the pretext that a strong leadership is required to contain the social upheavals.

Despite the structural weaknesses of the Nicaraguan economy, its limits on democracy were determined by its articulation with the political will or agency of the ruling regime. The Alemán administration chose to adopt undemocratic responses to social problems stemming from the structural fragility of the economy and from the policies of the IFIs. There is no necessary linear relationship between a country's underdeveloped status and its competence to install a democracy, as early modernization theorists might have us believe.

Equally significant as the structural parameters is the country's political history. Groups detrimentally affected by the so-called democratic transition are likely to explore means inside the democratic framework of recapturing their losses. David Becker observes that new democracies "must contend with strata and interest groups ... [such as] elements of the business sector, parts of the political or administrative elite ... that supported a previous authoritarian regime and still wield enough power to make democratic governance difficult or impossible, *if they choose to do so* [emphasis added]."[23] Becker's statement captures two important elements of the Alemán regime. The first is its connections to the previous corrupt rule of Anastasio Somoza. Many current supporters of the PLC are old Somocista defenders who would like to recoup wealth seized by the FSLN when it took power. Many would also like to get revenge on the FSLN by undermining its social support base (generally defined to include groups such as labor, students, NGOs, and generally those in the lower stratum), and to punish the latter for its revolutionary allegiances. Retaliating against the targeted groups within a democratic framework might involve marginalizing them in public policy, using forms of legal harassment to intimidate them or invoking police powers to suppress their demands—all theoretically legitimate powers at the government's disposal. The nation's political history then very much comes into play in the struggle to build democracy in the present.

Another aspect of Nicaragua's political history relevant to its prospects for democracy relates to the extensive social mobilization during its revolutionary period. Given this legacy, it should be expected that Nicaraguans would be highly organized and active at the grass roots, and that they would have greater expectations of the state (as a result of their experiences with socialism). Controlling this activism, especially to impose neoliberal strategies which require the retreat of the state from many areas of social welfare, demands a powerful executive, one willing to be ruthless despite the human crisis created by its policies. Conditions were ripe for a caudillo to take (or perhaps re-take) the helm.

Finally, Nicaragua has had a political history of caudillismo and hyper-presidentialism almost from the nation's inception (with arguably a couple of exceptions such as the Conservative era of the nineteenth century) and this bears some import on the potential for democratic consolidation. A glance at only recent history (since the fall of Somoza) gives a sense of the extent to which executive power has overshadowed other important institutions, especially the legislature. Sandinista president, Daniel Ortega, who led the revolution against dictatorship himself, resorted to authoritarian tactics. As Anderson and Dodd remind us, he ensured the subordination of the Assembly to the executive even though the former had become an elected body in 1984, silenced opposition by closing for a time the opposition newspaper *La Prensa,* imprisoned some of his political opponents (including Alemán), confiscated the properties of the wealthy, and even dealt harshly with the peasantry by directing state purchasing agents to confiscate their crops.[24] Similarly, they note that although the Chamorro administration was not beset by charges of abuse of power, it too displayed tendencies of hyperexecutivism. Particularly powerful in the administration was Antonio Lacayo, son-in-law and key advisor to President Chamorro. She bestowed on him a great deal of authority by appointing him prime minister, a position she especially created for him, and "[a]s her term wore on, he gathered even greater power into his own unelected hands, standing in for the president at press conferences and doing most of the talking even when she was present."[25] He, along with the president even tried to resist the legislature's constitutional reform limiting executive succession (by banning blood relatives from ascending to the presidency). Arnoldo Alemán is not an anomaly in this history, but very much in keeping with it.

This legacy of hyperexecutivism has had two important effects on the nation's democratic prospects. One is that candidates to the office of the presidency and those who have occupied it have a preconceived notion of the nature of the power of that office, of the degree of "political maneuverability" that is available to them. If their predecessors have been able to manipulate or expand presidential powers, then it could be argued that this is the conduct accepted or even expected of the officeholder. Second and relatedly, this legacy also affects the expectations of the citizenry. They have come to see this as part of the normal (not out of the ordinary), though distasteful feature of their country's government, regardless of its moment in history. Indeed, perhaps they too even expect it. The historical trend of hyperpresidentialism and the expectations (or lack thereof) which accompany it also contributes to the undoing of democracy as the expectations of the leader are not very high.

This history of caudillismo as well as the underdeveloped nature of the country's economy combine to bestow on the nation institutions of governance which are themselves weak in terms of their level of democratic development. Each preceding caudillo has had little interest in fortifying anything that might one day check his power; the interest has been to shape them to serve personal ambitions. Weak governing institutions not only facilitate the rise of caudillos, but they also become easy targets for manipulation by such strongmen wishing to avoid accountability.

In the end, despite Alemán's attempt to undo democracy in Nicaragua, and notwithstanding his many successes in this venture, it should not be assumed that Nicaraguan democracy has been permanently stymied. Current trends at the time of writing imply the contrary. Just as the process of undoing democracy has been a deliberate one, so too will be its reconstruction. It will require human agency, will and determination. The new President Enrique Bolaños's strategy to fight corruption by holding Alemán and members of his family and his administration accountable is one attempt to reverse the decomposition process. His vigorous anticorruption campaign is much lauded and very closely observed, with the anticipation of success given that the venture has the support of both international actors (IMF, World Bank, and other countries in the region) and by a spectrum of national players (civil society, the FSLN, anti-Alemán factions of the PLC, and other political parties).

Furthermore, while the Nicaraguan people may not be surprised by the abuse of power by their leaders, and while they may even come to expect it, they have also been willing to take steps to confront them either directly or through their state institutions (despite the frailty of the latter). Ortega, for example, has been kept out of the executive seat for three consecutive elections; Lacayo was stymied in his bid for the office by the ruling of the Supreme Electoral Council, and Alemán had to answer to the courts. "This kind of public involvement in checking delegative power is a promising sign that citizens feel a strong stake in democratization," according to Anderson and Dodd.[26]

Despite this prognosis of hope, caution is merited. For on the one hand, while executive accountability is being promoted and democracy strengthened, at the same time President Bolaños is deepening his commitment to the neoliberal program by pursuing deeper regional integration through his commitments to the Central American Free Trade Agreement (CAFTA), between the United States and Central American countries. Already he is facing strong criticisms from societal groups opposed to the deal and who have charged that the negotiations are lacking in transparency and that the administration is restricting input from the civil sectors. Opponents fear that the agreement's demand for greater market reforms will further erode labor standards (especially for those in the free trade zones) and its call for the extension of privatization in public services will devastate the poor. They are also concerned that Bolaños will be a too cooperative player in the international market (especially given the endorsement his presidential candidacy received from the U.S. administration). They point to the fact that he has remained silent in the face of increasing demands from the IFIs for greater efforts at privatization (for example of the hydroelectric power) before Nicaragua can receive HIPC debt forgiveness.

There is the very real possibility that this agreement will exacerbate old challenges to democratic consolidation as well as introduce new ones as increased market liberalization can only deepen the economic hardships for the population. Already 46 percent of those polled in a media survey claim that their economic conditions worsened under Bolaños.[27] This does not augur well for political stability as it can result in greater social unrest, thus exacerbating the cycle of unrest from below and repression from above. In such a scenario, democracy falls between the cracks.

Finally, the future of Nicaraguan democracy is also challenged by the problems within two leading political parties, the PLC and the FSLN—the internal strife, the lack of unity, and the absence of democratic decision making are some of the challenges they face. Effective political parties are essential to the development of constructive public policies and to keeping checks on the government. The PLC has been hampered by its internal division over the Alemán issue, with one faction supportive of Bolaños and his anticorruption campaign, and the other loyal to Alemán. While Bolaños may be winning this internal struggle in the short term, it is the long-term results that matter to ensure that a return to the politics and policies of the Somocista era are not a reality.

The FSLN meanwhile is divided too, between those who support the Ortega leadership and those who do not. Under Ortega, there is a decided lack of democratic governance within the Party—as can be seen from the fact that he has been the Party's leader and its presidential candidate for over twenty years. Leading FSLN members who have been critical of him, his political strategies and his stranglehold on the party leadership have been ousted from the organization, ensuring that he is surrounded only by loyalists. Given that he has been thrice rejected by the voters, this can only imply that there is popular dissatisfaction with him, something he seems unwilling to acknowledge. His lock on the leadership then can only obstruct the Party's ability to appeal to voters. "If the FSLN cannot break his grip, it may find itself sidelined in national elections, crippling genuine democratic contestation within Nicaragua."[28]

Notes

1. Samuel Huntington, *The Third Wave: Democratization in the Late Twentieth Century* (Norman: University of Oklahoma Press, 1991).

2. Thomas Carothers, "The End of the Transition Paradigm," *Journal of Democracy* 13, no.1 (January 2002): 6.

3. Carothers, "The End of the Transition Paradigm," 6.

4. Carothers, "The End of the Transition Paradigm," 9.

5. Larry Diamond and Juan J. Linz, "Introduction: Politics, Society and Democracy in Latin America," in *Democracy in Developing Countries 4: Latin America*, ed. Larry Diamond, Juan J. Linz, and Seymour Martin Lipset (Boulder, CO: Lynne Rienner, 1988), 46.

6. Paul Cammack, "Democratization and Citizenship in Latin America," in *Democracy and Democratization*, ed. Geraint Parry and Michael Moran (London and New York: Routledge, 1994), 189.

7. Admittedly populism is a much-contested term, but for purposes of simplicity, these are assumed to be some of the characteristics of classic populism.

8. Alan Knight, "Populism and Neo-populism in Latin America, especially Mexico," *Journal of Latin American Studies* 30, no. 2 (May 1998): 226.

9. Blanca Heredia, "Clientelism in flux: Democratization and Interest Intermediation in Contemporary Mexico" (paper presented at the 20th International Congress of the Latin American Studies Association, Guadalajara, Mexico, April 1997) quoted in María Pilar García-Guadilla, "Democracy, Decentralization, and Clientelism" (translated by Carlos Pérez), *Latin American Perspectives* Issue 126, 29, no. 5 (September 2002): 93.

10. Joe Foweraker and Todd Landman, *Citizenship Rights and Social Movements: A Comparative and Statistical Analysis* (Oxford: Oxford University Press, 1997), 16.

11. Robin Theobald, "So What Really is the Problem with Corruption" *Third World Quarterly* 20, no. 3 (June 1999): 492.

12. See Theobald, "So What Really is the Problem with Corruption" 491-502.

13. See for example Huntington, *The Third Wave,* 164.

14. See F. Hagopian, "Democracy by Undemocratic Means?: Elites, Political Pacts and Regime Transition in Brazil," *Comparative Political Studies* 23, no. 2 (July 1990): 147-170.

15. David G. Becker, "Latin America: Beyond 'Democratic Consolidation,' " *Journal of Democracy* 10, no. 2 (April 1999):139.

16. Guillermo O'Donnell, "Delegative Democracy," *Journal of Democracy* 5, no. 1 (January 1994): 55-69.

17. Larry Diamond, *Developing Democracy: Toward Consolidation* (Baltimore and London: Johns Hopkins University Press, 1999), 34-35.

18. Jean Grugel, *Democratization: A Critical Introduction* (New York: Palgrave, 2002), 65.

19. P. Schmitter and T. L. Karl, "What Democracy is ... and Is Not," in Larry Diamond and Marc Plattner, eds., *The Global Resurgence of Democracy* (Baltimore: Johns Hopkins University Press, 1993),

20. Alfred P. Montero, "Review Essay: Assessing the Third Wave Democracies," *Journal of Interamerican Studies and World Affairs* 40, no. 2 (Summer 1998): 121.

21. Michael McFaul, "The Fourth Wave of Democracy and Dictatorship: Noncooperative Transitions in the Postcommunist World," *World Politics* 54, no. 2 (January 2002): 214.

22. Guillermo O'Donnell, "Illusions About Consolidation," *Journal of Democracy* 7, no. 2 (April 1996): 41.

23. Becker, "Latin America," 138.

24. Leslie Anderson and Lawrence C. Dodd, "Nicaragua Votes: The Elections of 2001," *Journal of Democracy* 13, no. 3 (July 2002): 89-90.

25. Anderson and Dodd, "Nicaragua Votes," 89.

26. Anderson and Dodd, "Nicaragua Votes," 89.

27. Infopress Central America, "Bolaños Loses his Charm," *Central America Report* 30, no. 13 (4 April 2003): 2.

28. Anderson and Dodd, "Nicaragua Votes," 90.

Works Cited

Alemán, Arnoldo. *Así Piensa Arnoldo.* 1996. www.nfdd.org/Book/Socied.htm (July 7, 2001).

Alvarez Montalván, Emilio. *Cultura Política Nicaragüense.* Managua: Hispamer, 2000.

Anderson, Leslie and Lawrence C. Dodd. "Nicaragua Votes: The Elections of 2001." *Journal of Democracy* 13, no. 3 (July 2002): 80-94.

Arróliga, Lourdes. "¿Aborto terapéutico a debate hasta en próxima legislatura? Mayor distanciamiento entre clero y movimiento pro mujeres." *Confidencial,* no. 239 (May 2001): 6-12.

_____ . "Alemán ordena intervenir cooperativa y ONG suiza." *Confidencial,* no. 221 (December 2000):10-16.

Atienza, J. *La Deuda Externa y los Pueblos del Sur.* Madrid: Manos Unidos, 2000.

Babb, Florence. *After the Revolution: Mapping Gender and Cultural Politics in Sandinista Nicaragua.* Austin: University of Texas Press, 2001.

Banco Central de Nicaragua. *Informe Anual 2001.* Managua, 2002. www.bcn.gob.ni (August 3, 2002).

_____ . "La Intervención del Banco Nicaragüense de Industria y Comercio." *Boletín Económico* (July-September 2001). www.bcn.gob.ni (December 9, 2002).

Banco Mundial. *Informe sobre el desarrollo mundial de 1995.* Washington, DC: Banco Mundial 1995.

Banco Mundial–Fundo Mundial International. *A Framework for Action to Resolve Debt Problems of the HIPC.* Washington: World Bank-IMF, 1996.

Barricada Internacional. "Up to the ears in corruption: Accusations abound in Managua." *Barricada Internacional* 13, no. 358 (February 1993):6.

Bayer Richard, Patricia and John A. Booth. "Civil Society and Democratic Transition." Pp. 233-254 in *Repression, Resistance and Democratic Transition in Central America*, edited by Thomas Walker and Ariel C. Harmony. Wilmington, DE: Scholarly Resources Inc., 2000.

Becker, David G. "Latin America: Beyond 'Democratic Consolidation.' " *Journal of Democracy* 10, no. 2 (April 1999): 138-151.

Bendaña, A. "El huracán estructural de Nicaragua." *NACLA Report*. 1999. www.nacla.org/espanol/septoct99/deuda.html (August 13, 2001).

Blandon, Maria Teresa. "The Coalición Nacional de Mujeres: An Alliance of Left-Wing Women, Right-Wing Women and Radical Feminists in Nicaragua." Pp. 111-131 in *Radical Feminists in Latin America: Left and Right*, edited by Victoria Gonzalez and Karen Kampwirth. University Park: Pennsylvania State University Press, 2001.

Bodán, Oliver. "En el filo de la navaja." *Confidencial*, no. 179 (February 13-19, 2000) www.confidencial.com.ni (January 15, 2002).

La Boletina. *La Boletita*, 30-47 (April 1997-August 2001). boletina.puntos.org.ni/index (September 1, 1999-August 31, 2002).

Botey, J. *Apuntes sobre la deuda externa en América Latina, Centroamérica y Nicaragua*. Mímeo, Casa de Nicaragua de Barcelona, 2000.

Burbano de Lara, Felipe. "A modo de introducción: el impertinente populismo." Pp. 9-24 in *El fantasma del populismo: Aproximación a un tema [siempre] actual*, edited by Felipe Burbano de Lara. Caracas, Venezuela: Editorial Nueva Sociedad, 1998.

Cammack, Paul. "Democratization and Citizenship in Latin America." Pp. 174-195 in *Democracy and Democratization,* edited by Geraint Parry and Michael Moran. London and New York: Routledge, 1994.

Cañada, E. "El papel de las ONG en la reconstrucción de Nicaragua: Un balance autocrítico." *Mientras Tanto*, no. 80 (2001): 37-43.

CAPRI (Centro de Apoyo a Programas y Proyectos). *Directorio ONG de Nicaragua, 1999-2000*. Managua: Centro de Capacitación Profesional Nicaragüense Alemán, 1999.

Carothers, Thomas. "The End of the Transition Paradigm." *Journal of Democracy* 13, no. 1 (January 2002): 5-21.

Caster, Mark. "The Return of Somocismo? The Rise of Arnoldo Alemán." *NACLA Report on the Americas* 30, no. 2 (September-October 1996): 6-9.

Castro-Monge, Ligia Mariá. "Nicaragua and the HIPC Initiative: The Tortuous Road to Debt Relief." *Canadian Journal of Development Studies* 22:2 (August 2001): 417-453.

CCER (Coordinadora Civil para la Emergencia y la Reconstrución). *Visión de País* (January 2001): 1-12.

_____. "Convirtiendo la Tragedia del 'Mitch' en una Oportunidad para el Desarrollo Humano y Sostenible de Nicaragua." 1998. www.ccernic.org/documentos/wash_s.doc (June 5, 2001).

CELAM (Consejo Episcopal Latinoamericano), "Declaración Etica contra la Corrupción", Santiago de Chile, May 22, 1997. www.tmx.com.ni/~cen/ (March 4, 2002).

CENIDH (Centro Nicaragüense de Derechos Humanos). "Consideraciones del CENIDH sobre el proyecto de reforma parcial a la constitution política acordado por el PLC y la dirigencia del FSLN." TMs [photocopy].

Chamorro, Carlos. "Diálogo franco con los donantes." *Confidencial*, no. 144 (30 May-5 June 1999). www.confidencial.com.ni (July 27, 2002).

_____."Pacto está 'cocinado.' " *Confidencial*, no. 154 (August 8-14, 1999). www.confidencial.com.ni (November 24, 2001).

_____. "La Iglesia, el Poder y los Medios." *Confidencial,* no. 160 (September 19-25, 1999). www.confidencial.com.ni (January 7, 2002).

_____. "Opinión dividida sobre 'bondades' del pacto." *Confidencial* (October 10-16, 1999). www.confidencial.com.ni (August 17, 2001).

Chinchilla, Norma Stoltz. "Feminism, Revolution, and Democratic Transitions in Nicaragua." In *The Women's Movement in Latin America*, ed. Jane Jaquette. Boulder, CO: Westview Press, 1994.

Close, David. *Nicaragua: The Chamorro Years.* Boulder, CO: Lynne Rienner, 1999.

_____. "Arnoldo Aleman: Forward to the Past." *Nicaragua Monitor* (April 1996): 6.

Commission on Human Rights. 2001. "Department of State Human Rights Reports for 2000," U.S. Department of State, February. www.humanrights-usa.net/reprots/nicaragua.html (March 6, 2002)

Conferencia Episcopal de Nicaragua. *Documentos: Conferencia Episcopal de Nicaragua* (various) (August 1974-May 2002). www.tmx.com.ni/~cen (August 15-September 29, 2002).

Conniff, Michael. "Introduction." pp. 1-21 in *Populism in Latin America*, edited by Michael Conniff. Tuscaloosa: University of Alabama Press, 1999.

Consultative Group for the Reconstruction and Transformation of Central America, *Stockholm Declaration*. 1999. www.ccic.ca/archives/devpol/1999/apg7_stockholm_declaration.htm (August 1, 2001).

Coordinadora Nicaragüense de ONGs Que Trabajan Con La Niñez. "Pronunciamiento de la Coordinadora de Organismo No Gubermentales Que Trabajan Con La Niñez y La Adolescencia Sobre Los Niños y Niñas Que Trabajan Y/O Viven En La Calle." Paid advertisement in *Barricada*, 31 January 1997 www.barricada.com.ni (June 16, 2001).

Corbo, Vittorio. "Informe sobre la Situación Económica de Nicaragua." *International Monetary Fund*, July 1999. www.bcn.gob.ni (August 3, 2002).

Cuadra, Elvira. *La Participación de la Policía en Conflictos de Orden Político.* Managua: Universidad Centroamericana, 1995.

Cuadra, Elvira, Anders Perez Baltodano, and Angel Saldomando. *Orden Social y Gobernabilidad en Nicaragua, 1990-1996.* Managua: CRIES, 1998.

Cuadra, Elvira and Angel Saldomando. "Pacificación, Reinserción de Excombatientes y Consenso Social." In Elvira Cuadra, Andres Pérez Baltodano, and Angel Saldomando, *Orden Social y Gobernabilidad en Nicaragua, 1990-1996*. Managua: CRIES, 1998.

Cuadra, Scarlet. "Tintes políticos en la polémica sobre el aborto en Nicaragua: Unidos, la Iglesia y el presidente Alemán." *Proceso*, no. 1246 (September 17, 2000): 1-6. www.proceso.com.mx (June 19, 2001).

Darce, Denis and Ana Quirós Víquez. "La historia de las ONG's en Nicaragua y su relación con los gobiernos en los años 70s a nuestros días, 2000." Unpublished manuscript.

Deininger, Klaus and Juan Sebastián Chamorro. "Investment and Income Effects of Land Regularization: The Case of Nicaragua." *World Bank Policy Research Working Paper* 2752. January 2002. www.worldbank.org (August 4, 2002).

Delgado, Rodolfo. "Recuperamos $US 14.3 millones del Interbank. Entrevista con Rodolfo Delgado." *Confidencial*, no. 297 (July 7-13, 2002). www.confidencial.com.ni (November 14, 2002).

Diamond, Larry. *Developing Democracy: Toward Consolidation*. Baltimore and London: Johns Hopkins University Press, 1999.

Diamond, Larry and Juan J. Linz. "Introduction: Politics, Society and Democracy in Latin America." Pp. 1-58 in *Democracy in Developing Countries, Vol. 4: Latin America*, edited by Larry Diamond, Juan J. Linz, and Seymour Martin. Boulder, CO: Lynne Rienner, 1989.

Diamond, Larry, Juan J. Linz and Seymour Martin Lipset, eds. *Democracy in Developing Countries, Vol. 4: Latin America*. Boulder, CO: Lynne Rienner, 1989.

Diamond, Larry and Marc Plattner, eds. *The Global Resurgence of Democracy*. Baltimore: Johns Hopkins University Press, 1993.

Diggins, John Patrick. *The Promise of Pragmatism: Modernism and the Crisis of Knowledge and Authority*. Chicago: University of Chicago Press, 1994.

Dijkstra, Geske. "Structural Adjustment and Poverty in Nicaragua." Paper presented at the Congress of the Latin American Studies Association, Miami, FL, March 2000.

Dirección Nacional del Frente Sandinista. "Comunicado de la Dirección Nacional del Frente Sandinista." Managua: np., September 24, 1999.

Dye, David R. et al. *Patchwork Democracy: Nicaraguan Politics Ten Years after the Fall*. Washington: WOLA/Hemisphere Initiatives, 2000.

Dye, David, Judy Butler, Deena Abu-Lughod, and Jack Spence. *Contesting Everything, Winning Nothing: The Search for Consensus in Nicaragua, 1990-1995*. Washington: WOLA/Hemisphere Initiatives, 1995.

The Economist. "Curious Chance." *The Economist*. June 3, 2000. www.economist.com/ (January 7, 2002).

Economist Intelligence Unit. *Nicaragua: Country Profile 2002*. London, 2002. www.eiu.com (May 14, 2002).

_____. *Nicaragua: Country Report for the fourth quarter of 1997*. www.eiu.com (Febrary 12, 2002).

_____. *Country Report for the 2nd Quarter of 1997*. www.eiu.com (February 12, 2002).

Envío. (November 1996-May 2001). www.uca.ni/publicaciones/envio/ (September 1999-March 2003).

Ewig, Christina. "The Strengths and Limits of the NGO Women's Movement Model: Shaping Nicaragua's Democratic Institutions." *Latin American Research Review* 34, no. 3 (1999): 75-102.

Fairfield, Tasha. "Twenty Years After the Revolution: Nicaragua's Frente Sandinista de Liberación Nacional in the Opposition." Paper presented at the 23rd meeting of the Latin American Studies Association, Washington, DC, September 2001.

Fiallos, Mariano. "Ley Electoral partidizó CSE y cerró participación: Entrevista con Mariano Fiallos." *Confidencial*, no. 220 (December 3-9, 2000). www.confidencial.com.ni (August 21, 2002).

Foley, Michael and Bob Edwards. "The Paradox of Civil Society." *Journal of Democracy* 7, no. 3 (July 1996): 38-52.

Foweraker, Joe and Todd Landman. *Citizenship Rights and Social Movements: A Comparative and Statistical Analysis.* Oxford: Oxford University Press, 1997.

Galston, William A. "Civil Society and the 'Art of Association.' " *Journal of Democracy* 11, no. 1 (January 2000): 64-70.

García, Freddy E. "Gran desalojo: Policía inicia barrida en semáforos." *Barricada* 18, no. 6217 (January 31, 1997): 1.

García-Olivé, D. and P. Talavera. *La reacción social ante el tratamiento de la deuda.* Barcelona: Mímeo, 2000.

Garriga, A. M. *Preguntes i respostes entorn del deute extern.* Barcelona: Justícia i Pau, Col. Quaderns per a la Solidaritat, 1999.

Garvin, Glenn. "American Aid Worker Expelled by Nicaragua." *Miami Herald*, 9 November 1998. www.rosehulman.edu/~delacova/nicaragua/expelled.htm (June 13, 2001).

Giddens, Anthony. *Modernity and Self-Identity: Self and Society in the Late Modern Age.* Stanford, CA: Stanford University Press, 1991.

Gonzalez, Bayardo. "Forum for Discussion: The Y2Pact." *Nicaragua Monitor*, January-February 2000, 2-3.

Gonzalez, David. "Nicaragua's Trade Zone: Battleground for Unions." *New York Times*, 16 September 2000. www.nytimes.com/ (December 4, 2000).

González, Victoria. "The Devil Took Her: Sex and the Nicaraguan Nation, 1855-1979." Paper presented at the 22d meeting of the Latin American Studies Association, Miami, FL, March 2000.

Gould, Jeffrey. *To Lead as Equals: Rural Protest and Political Consciousness in Chinandega, Nicaragua, 1912-1979.* Chapel Hill: University of North Carolina Press, 1990.

Government of Nicaragua. "Memorandum de Políticas Económicas y Financieras." Submitted to the IMF in August 2001. www.bcn.gob.ni (August 6, 2002).

Grugel, Jean. *Democratization: A Critical Introduction.* New York: Palgrave, 2002.

Hagopian, F. "Democracy by Undemocratic Means?: Elites, Political Pacts and Regime Transitions in Brazil." *Comparative Political Studies* 23, no. 2 (July 1990): 147-170.

Heredia, Blanca. "Clientelism in flux: Democratization and Interest Intermediation in Contemporary Mexico." Paper presented at the 20th International Congress of the Latin American Studies Association, Guadalajara, Mexico, April 1997, quoted in María Pilar García-Guadilla, "Democracy, Decentralization, and Clientelism" (translated by Carlos Pérez), *Latin American Perspectives*, Issue 126, 29, no. 5 (September 2002): 90-109.

Hoyt, Katherine. *The Many Faces of Sandinista Democracy*. Athens: Ohio University Press, 1997.

_____. "Alemán Holds Press Conference in DC." *Nicaragua Monitor*, April 1996, 7.

_____. "Parties and Pacts in Contemporary Nicaragua." Paper presented at the 23rd meeting of the Latin American Studies Association, Washington, DC, September 2001.

Huerta, Juan Ramón. *El Silencio del Patriarcha*. Managua: Litografía El Renacimiento, 1998.

Huntington, Samuel. *The Third Wave: Democratization in the Late Twentieth Century*. Norman: University of Oklahoma Press, 1991.

IDA (International Development Association) and IMF (International Monetary Fund). "Nicaragua Poverty Reduction Strategy Paper." (August 2001). www.imf.org (August 15, 2001).

_____. "Preliminary Document on the Initiative for Heavily Indebted Poor Countries." (1999). www.worldbank.org (August 15, 2001).

IMF (International Monetary Fund). "Factsheet—Debt Relief under the Heavily Indebted Poor Countries (HIPC) Initiative 2002." www.imf.org/external/np/exr/facts/hipc (September 12, 2002).

_____. "Staff Report for the 2001 Article IV Consultation and the Staff-Monitored Program" August 2001. www.imf.org (September 2, 2002).

_____."Factsheet—The IMF's Poverty Reduction and Growth Facility". 2001. www.imf.org/external/np/exr/facts/prgf (September 12, 2002).

Imhof, Valeria. "Liberales forman ONG." *Confidencial*, no. 184 (March, 19-25, 2000) www.confidencial.com.ni (January 15, 2001).

Infopress Central America. *Central American Report*. Guatemala City: Guatemala (various). January 1999-May 2003.

INEC (Instituto Nacional de Estadísticas y Censos). "Datos Comparativos de Pobreza EMNV 93—EMNV 98." Managua: INEC, November 1999.

Interpón. *La realidad de la ayuda 1999/2000*. Barcelona: Intermón, 2000.

Isbester, Katherine. "Nicaragua 1996-2001: Sex, Corruption, and Other Natural Disasters." *International Journal* 56, no. 4 (Autumn 2001): 632-648.

ISSJ (International Social Science Journal). "Special issue on governance." *International Social Science Journal* 50, no. 155 (March 1998): 7-113.

Jarquín, Agustin. "Bipartidismo y Dictadura: Interview with Agustin Jarquin." *Confidencial*, no. 168 (November 14-20, 1999). www.confidencial.com.ni (August 21, 2002).

John Paul II. "Homilía en la Eucaristía Concelebrada en Managua." Documentos Conferencia Episcopal de Nicaragua, 1996. www.tmx.com.ni/~cen (August 27, 2002).

Jordan, Mary. "Nicaraguan Election Draws High Turnout Close Race Raises Concern in Washington," *Washington Post*, November 5, 2001, A17.

Jubilee 2000. *Deute extern, deute etern? Manual de campanya.* Barcelona: Justicia i Pau, 1998.

Kampwirth, Karen. "Confronting Adversity with Experience: The Emergence of Feminism in Nicaragua." *Social Politics* 3 (Summer-Fall 1996): 136-158.

Knight, Alan. "Populism and Neo-populism in Latin America, especially Mexico." *Journal of Latin American Studies* 30, no. 2 (May 1998): 223-248.

La Tribuna. "Legalizan dictatura." *La Tribuna* December 10, 1999. www.latribuna.com.ni (August 18, 2001).

Lynch, John. *Caudillos in Spanish America, 1880-1850.* New York: Oxford University Press, 1992.

Mailman, Toby. "Anti-Protest Bill Recalls Somoza's Regime." *Weekly News Update*, 7 June 1997. www.hartford-hwp.com/archives/47/277.html (July 9, 2001).

Mauceri, Philip. "Return of the caudillo: Autocratic Democracy in Peru." *Third World Quarterly* 18, no. 5 (December 1997): 899-912.

McFaul, Michael. "The Fourth Wave of Democracy and Dictatorship: Noncooperative Transitions in the Postcommunist World." *World Politics* 54, no. 2 (January 2002): 212-244.

Ministerio de Educación y Cultura. *Plan Nacional de Educación: 2000.* www.medc.gob.ni (February 13, 2002).

Ministerio de Hacienda y Crédito Público. *Informe de la Intendencia de la Propiedad.* www.hacienda.gob.ni (August 31, 2002).

Mittelman, James H. and Robert Johnston. "The Globalization of Organized Crime, the Courtesan State and the Corruption of Civil Society." *Global Governance* 5, no. 1 (Janurary-March 1999): 103-126.

Mohan, Giles and Kristian Stokke. "Participatory Development and Empowerment: The Dangers of Localism." *Third World Quarterly* 21, no. 2 (April 2000): 247-268.

Montenegro, Sofía. *Jovenes y Cultura Política en Nicaragua: la generación de los 90.* Managua: Hispamer, 2002.

_____. Interview by Karen Kampwirth, August 7, 2002.

_____, ed. *Movimiento de mujeres en Centroamerica.* Managua: Programa Regional La Corriente, 1997.

Montero, Alfred P. "Review Essay: Assessing the Third Wave Democracies." *Journal of Interamerican Studies and World Affairs* 40, no. 2 (Summer 1998): 117-134.

Montiel, E. and T. Sandino. "Agenda de Competitividad de Nicaragua para el Siglo XXI." Instituto Centroamericano de Administración de Empresas (INCAE). June 1999. www.agenda21.ni.com (June 17, 2001).

Morales, María Eugenia. Interview by Karen Kampwirth. Nandaime, Nicaragua, August 9, 2001.

Nicaragua Monitor. "Liberals Plan for Power Until 2016." (June-July 1997): 4.

Nicaragua Network. Hurricane Mitch Alert, #1. November 2, 1998. www.nicanet.org (June 16, 2001).

Nicaragua Network Midwest. Nicaragua Alert 16 (November 1998): 1-5.

_____. Nicaragua Alert. 19 (January 2001): 1-7.

Nicaragua News Service (April 26, 1998-April 23, 2001).

Niera Cuadra, Oscar and María Rosa Renzi. "The Economic Legacy of the Barrios de Chamorro Administration." *Revista Pensamiento Propio Managua*, no. 2 (September-December 1996): 7-11.

El Nuevo Diario. (April 1997-February 2002). www.elnuevodiario.com.ni/ (September 1, 1999-January 31, 2003).

Nuñez de Escorcia, Vilma. "The Deep Crisis of Sandinismo" *Against the Current* (July-August 2000): 26.

O'Donnell, Guillermo. "Illusions About Consolidation." *Journal of Democracy* 7, no. 2 (April 1996): 34-51.

_____. "Delegative Democracy." *Journal of Democracy* 5, no. 1 (January 1994): 55-69.

OECD (Organization for Economic Cooperation and Development). "Aid Recipients: 2000." www.oecd.org/dac/dac/images/AidRecipient/nic.gif (June 14, 2002).

_____. External Debt Statistics—Supplement 1985-1996. Washington: OCDE, 1997.

Oliveres, A. *Deute extern, deute etern?* Barcelona: Justícia i Pau, Col. Quaderns per a la Solidaritat, 1999.

Orozco, Manuel. "The Peril of Democracy in Nicaragua: Institutional Constraints to Political Competition and Citizenship Participation." *Working Paper*. Washington, DC: Inter-American Dialogue, August 2001.

Paris Club, 2002. *HIPC Initiative and Enhanced HIPC Initiative*. www.clubdeparis.org/en/presentation/presentation.php?BATCH=B04WP04 (August 2002).

Payne, Douglas W. "Nicaragua: Bottomed Out." *Dissent* 44 (Spring 1997): 39-42.

PNUD (Programa de les Nacions Unides per al Desenvolupament). *Informe sobre el Desenvolupament Humà 1999*. Barcelona: PNUD, 1999.

PNUD (Program de las Naciones Unidas para el Desarrollo)-Nicaragua. *El desarrollo humano en Nicaragua, 2000. Equidad para superar la vulnerabilidad*. Managua: PNUD, 2000.

Policía Nacional de Nicaragua. *Informe Annual 2000*. Managua: Policía Nacional, 2000.

La Prensa. Managua December 1999-September 2002 www.laprensa.com.ni/ (September 1, 2001- May 31, 2003).

Presidencia de la República. "Ley de Organización, Competencias y Procedimientos del Poder Ejecutivo." Draft Law, 1997. www.csd.gob.ni/ley_290.htm (October 30, 2003).

Quandt, Midge. *Nicaragua: The Promise of the New Politics and of Civil Society?* Interviews translated by Mark Lester. Washington, DC: Nicaragua Network, 2000.

Quant, Midge, *Voices of Sandinismo in Post Election Nicaragua.* Washington: Nicaragua Network Education Fund, 1997.

_____. *The Crisis in the FSLN and the Future of the Left in Nicaragua.* Washington: Nicaragua Network, 1998.

_____. *Nicaragua, The Promise of the New Politics and of Civil Society?* Washington: Nicaragua Network, 2000

Quirós, Ana. Interview by Karen Kampwirth. Managua, March 29, 2002 and August 6, 2002.

Reyes, Ovidio. "Reducción del Deslizamiento Cambiario. Una Propuesta para Disminuir la Inflación." Banco Central de Nicaragua. June 1999. www.bcn.gov.nic (June 2002).

Rivera, Manuel Espinoza. "Debate interno garantiza unidad: Una bancada sólida y comprometida." *Visión Sandinista* (November 1997): 2-3.

Rivera, Manuel Espinoza. "El congreso de mayo y sus expectativas: Oportunidad histórica para cambiar y vencer." *Visión Sandinista* (December 1997), 4.

Roberts, Kenneth. "Neoliberalism and the Transformation of Populism in Latin America: The Peruvian Case." *World Politics* 48, 1 (October 1995): 82-116.

Ruiz, Henry. "The FSLN Has Lost the Strong Ethical Basis that Motivated Us." *Envío* (May 2000). www.uca.edu.ni/publicaciones/envio/2000/eng/may (August 21, 2001).

Ryan, Phil. *The Fall and Rise of the Market in Sandinista Nicaragua.* Montreal: McGill & Queen's Universities Press, 1995.

Saldomando, Angel. *Violencia Social en Centroamérica: Ensayos Sobre Gobernabilidad y Seguridad Ciudadana.* Managua: CRIES, 1998.

_____. *Nicaragua: Con el Futuro en Juego.* Managua: CRIES, 1996.

Schmitter P. and T. L. Karl. "What Democracy is ... and Is Not." Pp. 49-62 in *The Global Resurgence of Democracy*, edited by L. Diamond and Marc Plattner. Baltimore: Johns Hopkins University Press, 1996.

Sebastián, Luis de. "Jubileo 2000, El perdón de la deuda externa." *Claves de la Razón Práctica*, no. 98 (December 1999): 31-38.

Secretaría Técnica de la Presidencia (SETEC). "República de Nicaragua, Estrategia reforzada de crecimiento económico y reducción de pobreza." July 2001. www.setec.gob.ni (November 19, 2002).

Soederberg, Susanne. "Grafting Stability onto Globalisation? Deconstructing the IMF's Recent Bid for Transparency." *Third World Quarterly* 22, no. 5 (October 2001): 849-864.

Soler, Miquel. *Huracanes sobre Centroamérica*. Barcelona: Casa de Nicaragua, 1999.

Talavera, P. "Crisis económica y condonación de la Deuda Externa en los países periféricos." Paper presentado en las Jornadas Internacionales sobre la Deuda Externa, Barcelona, 1999.

Tello, Mario D. and William Tyler. *La promoción de exportaciones en Nicaragua, 1997-2010: Experiencias y alternativas*. Managua: MEDE-MIFIN, 1997.

Theobald, Robin. "So What Really is the Problem with Corruption?" *Third World Quarterly* 20, no. 3 (June 1999): 491-502.

Transparency Internacional. *Corruption Perception Index, 2001*. www.transparency.org/ (October 30, 2003).

UNDP (United Nations Development Program). *Human Development Report, 2001*. New York: Oxford University Press.

UNDP (United Nations Development Program). *El desarrollo humano en Nicaragua 2000*. Managua: UNDP, 2000.

U.S. Department of State. *Nicaragua Country Report on Human Rights Practices for 1998*. www.state.gov/www/global/human_rights/1998_hrp_report/nicaragua.html (March 6, 2002).

Vaquero C. *La Deuda Externa del Tercer Mundo. Alternativas para su condonación*. Madrid: Editorial Talasa, 1999.

The Vatican. *Catechism of the Catholic Church, 2000*. www.vatican.va/archive/ccc/index.htm (October 30, 2003).

Vilas, Carlos. "Entre la Democracia y el Neoliberalismo: Los Caudillos Electorales de la Posmodernidad." *Socialismo y Participación* 69 (March 1995): 31-43.

Vivas Robelo, César Bosco. "La Iglesia y Alemán." *Confidencial*, no. 274 (January 20-26, 2002). www.confidencial.com.ni/2002-274 (October 30, 2003).

Vukelich, D. "La devastación de la deuda" *NACLA Report*. 1999. www.nacla.org/espanol/septoct99/deuda.html (August 2, 2001).

Walter, Knut. *The Regime of Anastasio Somoza: 1936-1956*. Chapel Hill: University of North Carolina Press, 1993.

World Bank. *Nicaragua Public Expenditure Review: Improving the Poverty Focus of Public Spending Report No. 23095-NI* (December 2001): 2-9. www.worldbank.org (May 15, 2002).

_____. *Republic of Nicaragua: Competitiveness Learning and Innovation Loan Report No. 21532-NI* (December, 2000). www.worldbank.org (May 15, 2002).

_____. *Nicaragua Poverty Assessment: Challenges and Opportunities for Poverty Reduction Report No. 20488-NI* (February 2001). www.worldbank.org (May 17, 2002).

Weyland, Kurt. "Neopopulism and Market Reform in Argentina, Brazil, Peru, and Venezuela." Paper presented at the 22nd Conference of the Latin American Studies Association, Miami FL, March 2000.

Winegardner, Jill. "Solidarity in Times of Internet." *Envío* 20, no. 237 (April 2001): 22-29.

World Bank Group *World Development Indicators Database 2002* wbIn0018.worldbank.org/.

XCADE. *La consulta social per l'abolició del deute extern a Catalunya.* Barcelona: Mediterrània, 2001.

Zimmerman, Lisa. "NLM Discusses Future Solidarity." *Nicaragua Monitor* (July 1999): 1, 10.

_____. "FSLN Congress Re-Elects Ortega." *Nicaragua Monitor* (June 1998): 1-2.

Index

About the Contributors

David Close is Professor of Political Science at the Memorial University of Newfoundland. He has published two books on Nicaragua, most recently *Nicaragua: The Chamorro Years* (1999).

Elvira Cuadra is a Nicaraguan sociologist, currently working as a researcher for the Center for the Study of Communication in Managua. She has studied problems of social and political violence in the 1990s, producing numerous articles, reports, and monographs.

Kalowatie Deonandan is Assistant Professor of Political Studies and former Director of the International Studies Program of the University of Saskatchewan, Saskatoon, SK. Her research focuses on liberation theology in Nicaragua and on international organizations.

David R. Dye holds degrees from Cornell and Stanford. He is a journalist who has lived and worked in Nicaragua for over twenty years, writing about politics, business, and economics.

Katherine Hoyt holds a Ph.D. from Rutgers University. She is presently the codirector of the Nicaraguan Network Education fund in Washington, D.C. Hoyt has extensive experience in Nicaragua, where she worked for the Sandinista government. She is author of *The Many Faces of Sandinista Democracy* (1997).

Karen Kampwirth is Associate Professor of Political Science at Knox College in Galesburg, Illinois. She is author of *Women and Guerrilla Movments: Nicaragua, El Salvador, Chiapas, Cuba* (2002).

Salvador Marti Puig teaches in the Department of Political Science and Public Law at the Universidad de Salamanca and is a Research Fellow in the Institute of Latin American Studies at the University of London. He has published several books on Nicaraguan politics, including *Rethinking the Sandinista Agrarian Policy and the Contra Rebellion, 1979-1987* (2001).

217

Andrés Pérez-Baltodano is Associate Professor of Political Science and Director of the Local Government Program at the University of Western Ontario. He is former Director of the Nicaraguan Institute of Public Administration. He writes frequently on the political role of the Church in the Nicaraguan newsweekly *Confidencial*.